MW01596236

YOUR
JOURNEY
WITH JESUS

ESSENTIAL STEPS TO BECOME HIS
DISCIPLE FOR LIFE

MANCIOS,
WE LOVE YOU ALL!

signature ¿ FAMILY

DR. GLENN PLASTINA

BOOKS BY THIS AUTHOR

REFOCUS: Your Self Coaching Guide to Reevaluate, Reset and Restart Your Life

ICHTHUS DRIVE: 21 Lessons I Learned in Driving and Moving Forward

JESUS: What a Wonderful Name Book 1

POWER MOVES: Face Your Giants, Solve Problems, and Win

THE ART OF MENTORING EMERGING LEADERS: An Ancient Model for Filipino Spiritual Leaders

THE BENEVOLENT RULE OF GOD: A Theology of Leadership

YOUR BEST YEAR WITH JESUS: A Daily Devotional on the 365 Names of Jesus in the Bible for Those Who Want to Know Him and Make Him Known

YOUR JOURNEY WITH JESUS: Essential Steps to Become His Disciple for Life

Published by

RADICLE BOOKS

Printed in the United States of America

DEDICATION

*To my wife and children
of whom I pray to walk in the pathway of Jesus*

*To all who answered the call to come and follow Jesus,
who keep pointing people to him,
and keep making disciples of all nations,
this book is for you.*

*To Him who is able to keep us all from falling
and present us faultless
To the only Wise God our Savior
Be glory and honor*

ACKNOWLEDGMENTS

When I became a husband and father, I embraced the thought that discipleship starts at home. I made a commitment to nurture my wife, Cay, and our three children, Johnne Elliott, Grenz Joshua, and Angel Kaye to love Jesus more than me as I love him more than my life and leadership. I would like to acknowledge their contribution in my journey as a follower of Jesus, as well as our family as followers of him who loved us and gave himself for us.

As I look back, I also acknowledge those individuals who discipled me as a young follower of Jesus. I'm forever grateful to Rev. Benny Rebaya who taught me how to share the gospel when I was an elementary student, Jun Sabas who discipled me when I was a high school student, and the late bishop Oscar Magallanes who mentored me when I was a pastor in Baguio City, Philippines. Of course, there were several seminary professors who molded me in my Christian life and spiritual leadership. Most significantly are Dr Manuel Badar, Dr. Jeremiah Lepasana, Dr. Tereso Casino, Dr. Engracio Samson, Dr. Nori dela Paz-Laquian, Dr. Anne Windus-Kelley, and Dr. Richard Wilson.

I'd also love to acknowledge our spiritual family at the ChristConnect Church (formerly Point Church Filipino) of North Carolina. As a new Jesus-centered, disciple-making church-plant transitioning to become a self-sustaining and self-replicating local fellowship at the heart of the Research Triangle, I'm honored to walk with you all in your spiritual journey. Thank you for your love, kindness, courage, and friendship, especially to Kris Tan, JB Soriano, and the whole families and friends.

To my mentors who walked with me in my leadership journey here in NC, my brothers-in-arms, Ralph Garay and Chris Hankins, both of you have been instrumental in my personal accountability and leadership growth as a spiritual leader. I'm also grateful for my fellow Asian-American pastors monthly fellowship for brotherhood, encouragement, and inspiration.

CONTENTS

INTRODUCTION: AN INVITATION TO FOLLOW JESUS

Blessed is the man
who walks not in the counsel of the wicked,
nor stands in the way of sinners,
nor sits in the seat of scoffers;
but his delight is in the law of the LORD,
and on his law he meditates day and night.
He is like a tree
planted by streams of water
that yields its fruit in its season,
and its leaf does not wither.
In all that he does, he prospers.
~ King David, Psalms 1:1-3

If every journey needs a reason to believe in before we move, this journey has three. Here are the 3 beliefs we must set: We believe...

1. We all need Jesus.

2. We all need to become his disciples.

3. We all need to be disciple-makers.

With all my heart and mind, I believe these core beliefs. Jesus is the only reason why I exist. He's the reason why I love, live, learn, and lead. I live to become like him in every way possible by his grace and for his glory.

Ralph Waldo Emerson famously said, "Life is a journey, not a destination." If life is a journey, then, *Christian life is a spiritual journey with Jesus to become like him.* It's the sacred adventure to become Christlike, a full and mature Jesus follower-and that's a wonderful "becoming"--you *becoming* like Jesus in the process.

Some of life's important questions boil down to what do you like *to become.* Do you want life to become better in every area of your life? Are you becoming who and what God wants you to be? Are you being conformed into the image of Jesus and becoming more mature in your faith? Do you want to become a better husband or wife and have a great marriage? Do you want to be a better person and employee in your workplace? Do you want to be a better leader, entrepreneur or investor? These are some of the essential questions in life relating to you becoming a better person as a whole. Whether you want to live wiser, happier, healthier, greater, and whatever noble things God placed in your heart's desires, it's about what you become.

However, there's a catch. *You become who you follow.* In a world where so many people and things want you to follow, the options are so many. If you follow the world, you become worldly. If you pursue material things, you become materialistic. If you follow Jesus, you become Christlike. That's just the way it is. When you follow the path of something good, you can expect that eventually you become good, better, and best. You grow into it. If anyone follows something bad, it's downright wrong, even stupid, to expect that something good will come out of it.

A Blessed Life

King David, who himself experienced and knew the outcome of his wrong choice and mistakes in life, knew the power of our choices. Two paths diverge, one good, one evil. You can choose what you will. But you must remember that for every choice, there's a corresponding consequence. If you want to be blessed, you have to follow a certain path. If you don't want to be blessed, then any path will do.

That's why, when David declared in Psalm 1, *"Blessed is the man,"* it carries with it a certain weight. To be "blessed" (*esher*) in Hebrew basically means a state of "happiness" or "blessedness." As an interjection or intensive exclamation, it can be translated as "Happy is he!" or "Blessed is he!" it is tantamount to saying "Blessed are you if you follow this path!" For King David, this spiritual path of blessedness can be taken like a two-lane street: *via negativa* (negative way) and *via positiva* (positive way). Let's take a look at these two:

Via Negativa - A blessed person lives *not* in a certain way. David emphasized what a blessed man does "not" do. If you take a close look at this text, there's at least three active descriptions. A blessed person does:

- **Not Walk** - A blessed person is known by what he does not do. He is not someone "*who **walks not in the counsel** of the wicked.*" He does not move or go in the advice, direction, and opinions of wicked people. It does not mean blessed people do not relate with non-believers. In fact, the opposite is true. Blessed people loved non-believers and sinners as God would love them. They just don't need to walk in their worldviews and ways.

- **Not Stand** - Another sign of a blessed person is that he or she does not stand "*in **the way** of sinners.*" This picture shows that a blessed person does not stand in agreement with non-believers who lived sinful lifestyles. Since a godly person knows that the path of sinners is unpleasant before God, he lived distinctly on different grounds. His spiritual journey or manner of life takes a godly course of direction, action or undertaking for God.

- **Not Sit** - There seems to be a gradual sequence in this picture. A person "*walks*" with others along the way, and then stops and "*stands*" somewhere, then "*sits*" together "*in **the seat** of scoffers.*" Here, the description mentioned, like "*the wicked,*" "*the sinners,*" and "*the scoffers,*" are likely the same group of people described in three ways. And sitting together with them symbolically means there is a common bond together as the word means "to sit," "to remain" or "to dwell." In other words, as a blessed person, you are known by who you walk not, what you stand against, and what you refrain from. So be careful who your friends are or the closest people you constantly live with because you become the average of them.

Via Positiva - A blessed person lives in a certain way. It's not only that there are certain paths a blessed person keeps himself away from and does not do. There are also decisions and actions that a blessed person pursues and does in a positive way. In verse 2, David identified the following:

- *A **blessed person delights in God's Word**.* David expresses this spiritual discipline or habit when he said, *"but his **delight** is in the law of the LORD."* The Bible is not a burden, but a blessing. Therefore, delighting in God's Word means you take pleasure in reading, knowing, and understanding the whole counsel of God's Word, not the counsel of the wicked. The word "delight" is closely connected with "blessed" because they both have the element of happiness, pleasure, and satisfaction. This is the *emotional* side of this spiritual habit. If you want to be blessed, you have to take pleasure in God's Word. Enjoy it, walk in it, and be blessed by it. As David prayed, *"Lead me in the path of your commandments, for **I delight in it**"* (Psalm 119:35).

- *A **blessed person meditates on God's Word**.* There seems to be a great connection in the spiritual growth of a person with the Word of God. Much research has been made on this link. As David continues to say, *"and on his law he meditates day and night."* The act of meditating (Hebrew *hagah* or "utter," "speak," "muse") on God's Word here has something to do with a focused thinking and deep reflection for a period of time. It is often made in a relaxed environment of silence and solitude for spiritual purposes. In Hebrew tradition, it also covers soliloquizing or speaking one's thoughts aloud when you're alone regardless of if someone is listening or not. This is the *mental* or *intellectual* side of this spiritual habit. If you want to live a truly blessed life, you must not only love God with all your mind, but should ponder upon his Word with all your reason or with faith seeking understanding. David exclaimed, *"Oh how I love your law! It is my meditation all the day"* (Psalm 119:97) because God's word makes him *wiser* and gives him *more understanding* in life (vv.98-99).

This overarching principle is exactly the main point why I wrote this spiritual development book. I have loved the Word of God since I was a child. It has been my source of spiritual insights, wisdom, and inspiration. I wrote this book with you in mind that as you go through the process of discipleship, you will only use this book as a supplement and not a replacement of the Scriptures. Get a good Old and New Testament Bible of your own (Currently, I'm using ESV–English Standard Version). I'm prayerfully asking you to always focus on God's

Word. Highlight your Bible or underline the verses you find here. It will help you remember these passages and get to know your Bible more. I won't mind if you skip the paragraphs of my explanations and illustrations as long as you will take note of the Scripture passages, meditate and reflect on them, and (please don't forget) apply it.

The Comparison

David, then, presented a vivid and wonderful imagery of spiritual growth that's deeply rooted, fruitful, lasting, and prosperous. In verse 3, he likened the blessed person into *"a tree planted by streams of water."* A tree is a living and growing plant that is heavily dependent upon the ground on which it is planted. But I don't want you to miss this important point. The word *"planted"* (*shathal*) actually came from the root-word "transplanted." In the context, it's likely that the "streams of water" (literally, "rivers") is a poetic simile of God's Word. Imagine your life planted in the world with all its worldviews, culture, systems, practices, lifestyles, and so on. From this godless environment God is uprooting you and transplanting you to another place of abundance and supply, as well as repositioning you in life for eternity and his glory.

As a result of God's spiritual transplanting work in your life, no matter how painful or challenging it may be, your life changed into something greater. You become a living, healthier, stronger tree, *"that yields its fruit in its season, and its leaf does not wither"* (Psalm 1:3). From a barren life, you become blessed. From futile, you become fruitful. You don't easily dry up because you feed and drink from the fresh and living water of God. *"In all that he does, he prospers."* While God did not promise that all who believe in him will become prosperous and profitable—and he also did not promise that we will not experience failures, pains, and frustrations—what the Psalmist is referring to is a prosperous journey. God will bring you to a successful spiritual journey in life, even a significant journey that makes a difference and matters to eternity. That evergreen life is yours to take.

God also reconfirmed this powerful truth through prophet Jeremiah. He echoes the same revelation to the people of Judah. Read what he proclaimed and absorb it,

> **Blessed** *is the man who trusts in the LORD,*

whose trust is the LORD.
*He is like a tree **planted** (shathal) by water,*
that sends out its roots by the stream,
and does not fear when heat comes,
for its leaves remain green,
and is not anxious in the year of drought,
for it does not cease to bear fruit. (Jeremiah 17:7-8)

The Contrast

As we return to David's Psalm, however, he boldly declared. *"The wicked are not so,"* meaning the sinner and scoffers will not "prosper" in God's way in the end. They will harvest the seeds of mockery, wickedness and sinful deeds that they have planted. They will enjoy their worldly pleasures briefly, *"but are like chaff that the wind drives away."* These are all vanities. As death knocks on the door, all the wealth will be gone, the powers removed, and pleasures ceased. Poetic justice will not remain elusive for the absolute and perfect justice of God will certainly come as the conclusion of everything: *"Therefore the wicked will not stand in the judgment, nor sinners in the congregation of the righteous; for the* LORD *knows **the way of the righteous**, but **the way of the wicked** will perish"* (Psalm 1:5-6).

Friend, God knows your way before you even started and he also knows how it ends. Take the path of God's righteousness or the way of the wickedness in this world. The choice is yours.

Beyond Blessed

Being blessed is not an accident. It is both a gift and a choice. God's blessings are gifts coming from his generous heart. Meanwhile, you've learned how to choose and be blessed by doing certain things in accordance with God's ways. It's like life. God has given you the ability to choose to be happy, but if you want something deeper than the pursuit of happiness, instead you go for God's gift of joy, then you aim to take the Blesser, not just the path of blessings in order to live a life that's *beyond blessed.*

When Jesus called his first followers, he said, *"**Follow** me, and I will make you fishers of men." Immediately they left their nets and **followed** him"* (Matthew 4:19-20).

6

Reading at face value, we'd be missing some precious truths here. The words "follow" have different nuances in the original language (All Greek or Hebrew meaning in this book is taken from *Strong's Exhaustive Concordance* or *Thayer's Greek Lexicon* which is also available online. For beginners, my favorite is Biblehub.org). The first word "***Follow me***" used the Greek "*deute*," which means "Come here!" or "Come after me!" Here, Jesus declared his intention for them that if they listen and accept his invitation, he intends to make these fishermen "fishers of men."

As people in the marketplace, turning their profession into a ministry is, indeed, a wonderful becoming. As such, they "***followed him***" (and Matthew used the word *akoloutheu*, meaning, "to accompany," "attend to" or "follow"). A lexicon highlights this word to mean "join one as a disciple" or "become his disciple" The biblical idea here is this: If you want to be a disciple of Jesus, you have "to cleave steadfastly" and "to conform wholly to his example, in living and if need be in dying also." Becoming a disciple of Jesus, therefore, is to make him your Lord and Master in every area of your life. He has complete reign in every aspect of your life and existence.

The truth is when Jesus invites people to "Come after me" or "follow me," it implies a journey. He leads, you follow. It's a journey *towards* Jesus and a journey *with* him all your life. When you embrace this ultimate invitation, you're on to the greatest adventure of your life, the sacred journey to eternity. It won't be easy, but with his grace and power, you can make it.

Of course, there had been lots of research work, studies, and materials made on life journeys. I myself benefited so much from the concept of "the hero's journey," ever since I was a young student studying theology and culture. Eventually, I also taught this subject briefly to some select students. In fact, there are many life stories in the Bible that resemble the hero's journey with the life of Jesus being a prime and perfect example. No wonder, through centuries, Christian life is often pictured as a journey with Jesus, when he said, "*I am the light of the world. Whoever **follows me** will not **walk** in darkness, but will have the light of life*" (John 8:12). In another circumstance, Jesus talked to the crowd and said to them:

*"The light is among you for a little while longer. **Walk** while you have the light, lest darkness overtake you. The one who walks in the darkness does not know where he is going. While you have the light, believe in the light, that you may become sons of light."* (John 12:35-36)

In all these passages of the Scriptures, Christian life is pictured as a spiritual walk. Jesus pointed out that everyone has a choice, to walk in darkness or walk in the light. The problem with people who are walking in the darkness is that they don't know where they are going and they don't even know they are in the darkness. But Jesus claimed to be, not just *"the light of the world,"* but the light that illuminates your spiritual journey. He will not only walk with you, but he will turn you into a child of light to lighten up the way for others to see Jesus. This amazing "becoming" is a gift. When Jesus transforms you and you become what he wants you to be, a mature and multiplying disciple, then you'll see his wonder working power to change your destiny.

When we say about Christian life as a life journey, we're not thinking about your recent trip to a vacation isle or pilgrimage tour (although some of these trips could mark your spiritual journey in many ways). Thinking of life as a journey or a spiritual "walk" is a metaphor, a figurative speech describing the Christian life, but not in a literal way. It's a symbolism, an explanation or comparison of an idea. For example, when someone sings, "Jesus, take the wheel," it doesn't mean that Jesus will literally appear, do the slick maneuvering, and avoid an accident. It means someone is desperate for help and is calling Jesus for help to take full control of the situation. As such, the idea of life as a journey is a comparison of it to an act of traveling, a walk of life.

The general idea of life as a journey means it is a forward moving process and progress. It covers the lifelong quest for self-discovery, personal development, and fulfillment of potential. As there's no one like you, there's also none like your journey in every way. One person's life journey is unique. Along the way of this journey is the presence of tests, problems, and challenges. But the idea is that through these difficulties comes development. But is this all there is to our life journey?

The truth is Christian life journey distinctly differentiates itself. It is not just a process; it is a Jesus-centered lifelong undertaking in everything. It's a different worldview and a different lifestyle. For Jesus, Christian life journey is about living and following him both as your Lord *and* Savior (and not either/or).

Jesus said, "**I am the way, and the truth, and the life.** *No one comes to the Father except through me*" (John 14:6). Have you noticed how Jesus emphasized that he is who he is the way-truth-life at the same time? He is not just a way, but not the truth and life; we cannot have him as truth, but not the way of life. In him, we have everything as he is our everything. Here, the way is not a paved road, but a living person. This verse emphasizes this unchanging truth: *The disciple's life journey is all about Jesus in every way*–and he is more than willing to walk with you all the way. Go and be blessed beyond measure.

I'm glad to journey with you and come alongside in this greatest adventure ever.

SECTION 1: THE JOURNEY

*"Walk in a manner worthy of the calling
to which you have been called"*

~ Apostle Paul (Ephesians 4:1b)

CHAPTER 1: WHERE AM I HEADING IN THIS JOURNEY?

For centuries, Jesus has been calling people to this greatest adventure ever: *to walk the Jesus way*. While billions of people professed identity with the *religion* of Christianity, how many were truly followers of *the person* named Jesus who is "the Way"? (Acts 19:23) While Christianity is growing and thriving in Africa, Asia, Latin America, Middle East, Russia, and other parts of the world, including those countries close and hostile to it, it is declining in the United States of America. Once it was considered a missionary sending nation, now, it is a mission field.

While the growing uptrend of Christianity around the world is very encouraging, the trend in the US is going the opposite way. According to a recent survey of Pew Research, American Christianity's trend is going down and projected to become a minority by 2050. Among the many reasons is the steady switching of many professing Christians to become unaffiliated "nones," even becoming agnostics or atheists. If this culture spreads globally (We can call this phenomenon "the great spiritual migration"), it could be a fulfillment of the great apostasy, desertion, and mass delusion that should happen before Jesus comes again (See 2 Thessalonians 2:1-12). As a matter of fact, major Christian denominations are losing millions of members every year. What went wrong?

The problem with professing Christianity but not following Jesus is that people embrace a form of "cultural Christianity," and not discipleship as Jesus intended it to be. It's a kind of cheap Christianity shaped by the current culture or dominant religion and not by the Lordship of Jesus nor Scripture. Some of the greatest challenges and problems of cultural Christianity, including those who profess devotion to a religion but not having a personal relationship with Jesus and living by it, are the following: *complacency, deficiency, and immaturity*. These three are the most common but high-risk levels of "faith" and I want you to consider walking the better direction. So let me explain this on a personal level.

Journey from Complacency to Commitment. This spiritual problem of complacency is a common point when a professing Christian becomes content with their present level of faith. There's no interest or effort to grow in their relationship with God and the Lord Jesus. Complacency is not interested in walking closer with Jesus, nor intentional in the spiritual rhythms of reading their Bible, prayer, serving God, or sharing the Gospel. It's spiritually stagnant, unmotivated, self-focused and self-absorbing. Why is this level of faith dangerous?

It's because *complacency leads to spiritual apathy.* When the person allows self-centeredness, slothfulness, and slackness to take a hold in their spiritual lives, that same person will not have spiritual desire or appetite to grow in his relationship with God and people. It's gloating and dying from within. But it should not be. If you humbly follow the path Jesus prepared for you, he will lead you with his steadfast love, like the one David talked about:

> **He leads** *the humble in what is right,*
> *and* **teaches the humble his way.**
> **All the paths of the LORD** *are steadfast love and faithfulness,*
> *for those who keep his covenant and his testimonies.* (Psalm 25:9-10)

I'm praying that you consider a better option: moving from complacency to a strong commitment in the path of following Jesus.

Journey from Deficiency to a Great Destiny. Spiritual malnutrition is a big spiritual problem. Think of walking through the hills and valleys of life and journeying without energy. Because of not walking with Jesus intimately, nor reading the Bible, they lack knowledge and deeper understanding of the truth and the teachings of Jesus. They're intellectually deficient or spiritually powerless and do not have a solid foundation in their Christian faith and living. When the culture dictates their minds, the weak and undiscerning ones easily follow (or swallow) false teachings, unbiblical beliefs and practices. They would easily flow with the culture and leave the faith, rather than stay with Christ faithfully.

Again, why is this faith level very dangerous? It's because *deficiency leads to lack of spiritual vitality and sense of eternal destiny with Jesus.* How dangerous would it be if you don't know if you're a healthy Christian or not? Or whether, you're saved or not? How do you really know what you truly believe is biblical and sound? And where does this kind of spirituality lead you? My prayer for you is the same with David as he asked God to search and lead him to the eternal path:

> **Search me, O God, and know my heart!**
> *Try me and* **know my thoughts!**
> *And see if there be any grievous way in me,*
> *and* **lead me in the way everlasting!** (Psalm 139:23-24)

Journey from Immaturity to Spiritually Healthy. As a result of complacency and deficiency, this faith-levels leads to spiritual immaturity. Immature Christians do not know the danger they are in. They do not know how to feed themselves spiritually and grow in their relationship with God. They are not equipped to live their faith in this world or incapable of equipping others to follow Jesus. Once a person is merely focused on *self* rather than *the Savior*, immaturity leads to unholy pride and other spiritual illnesses. So, why is this level of faith so super-dangerous?

Here it is: *Immaturity leads to uncertainty*. And that's not healthy spirituality. When Christians lack spiritual immaturity, they're easily offended and unreasonably childish. Just as few little struggles would make them leave their faith or abandon the teachings of Jesus for the sake of pleasing the world. They become easily frustrated, discouraged, and unmotivated to live for Jesus. As a result, they do not have discernment and wisdom to make the right decisions, take persistent actions, and commit to persevere in their faith. Such spiritual immaturity leads to future uncertainty. You have to move from immaturity to a healthy spirituality.

God's Word says, *"There is a way that seems right to a man, but its end is the way to death"* (Proverbs 14: 12). Unless a person will change the course of his "way" of life and leave behind these low and unstable levels of faith mentioned above, it's a life and death situation. I pray you chose life by following Jesus.

Reflection:

In your personal assessment, where are you in your present spiritual journey?

Would you consider yourself a new, growing, or a mature Christian? Rate yourself (1 being the lowest as new and 10 being the highest for mature).

1   2   3   4   5   6   7   8   9   10

Which verses mentioned above speak to you the most? Why?

CHAPTER 2: WHAT WILL YOU GAIN IN FOLLOWING JESUS?

L et's say for clarity's purposes that you want to know some of the important benefits for following Jesus. He himself promises to give your beneficial blessings and here's what it means for you.

You receive and experience eternal life in the here-and-now, not just in the life hereafter. In this journey, your starting point is a personal relationship with Jesus by faith. If you follow Jesus, your life journey crosses the path from death to life, both now and in the next life in eternity with God. Jesus promised, *"Truly, truly, I say to you, whoever hears my word and believes him who sent me has eternal life. He does not come into judgment, but has **passed from death to life**"* (John 5:23). Through faith in Jesus, he promised to give you a quality of life that lasts forever. You'll not only really live and eventually die or simply exist here on earth in the present, but you'll be with God forever. Jesus said in John 6:40, *"For this is the will of my Father, that everyone who looks on the Son and believes in him should **have eternal life**, and I will raise him up on the last day."*

You keep living an abundant life. In Peter's sermon at Pentecost, he quoted King David who put his trust in the coming Messiah saying, *"You have made known to me **the paths of life**; you will make me full of gladness with your presence"* (Acts 2:28). There are many "paths of life" in this world, but choosing the path of life is the way to go. You can choose the crooked ways or Christ the Way. Following Jesus means experiencing an abundant life. Jesus stated why he came for you. "The thief [Satan] comes only to steal and kill and destroy. I came that they may have life and have it abundantly" (John 10:10). Interestingly, Jesus used the word *"perissos,"* meaning "more," "greater," "excessive," "preeminence" or "advantage." But what amazes me about this quality of life is that Jesus is pointing out an all-around (*peri*) life or all encompassing. How do you like to live a life where all your bases are covered?

If the world thinks Satan has their best interests by following him and likes to give them success in exchange for their souls, even that success is meant to ruin their lives. But Jesus guaranteed you an "abundant" living and loving relationship with him. This abundant life is a kind of life that is eternal, meaningful, and totally enriching in every way. God has a purpose for your life and this life is completely great, truly rich, and overflowing in Jesus. In fact, what follows is all evidence of this all-encompassing quality of life.

You walk daily in the light of his will. Reflect on this. "*Again Jesus spoke to them, saying, 'I am the light of the world. Whoever **follows** me will not **walk** in darkness, but will have the light of life'*" (John 8:12). Imagine living in darkness, searching and struggling to survive, and not knowing where to go or what to do. That kind of life is not what Jesus has for you. He wants you to clearly see your life in the light, in view of his plan and purpose from the past, in the present, to the future, and for eternity . His light will be in you to illuminate your journey. He also gives you his Word, the Holy Scripture, as your light in your journey (Psalms 119:105).

You receive total forgiveness. At the core of the Christian message is this: "*Thus it is written, that the Christ should suffer and on the third day rise from the dead, and that repentance for **the forgiveness of sins** should be proclaimed in his name to all nations, beginning from Jerusalem*" (Luke 24:46-47). The greatest burden of humanity is sin. Jesus suffered and died on the cross to pay the penalty for our sins. When we follow him with a repentant heart, we can experience the forgiveness of our sins and be made clean before our holy God.

God's word promised, "*If we confess our sins, he is faithful and just to **forgive us** our sins and to cleanse us from all unrighteousness*" (1 John 1:9). If we have total forgiveness in Jesus, how well do you like living a guilt-free life on an everyday basis? How will it make a difference if God sets you free from any bondages, secret sins, shame, and self-condemnation? God forgives and he will lead you to the path of freedom.

You have power for living. Jesus promised those who believe and follow him to receive divine power which is the Holy Spirit (Acts 1:8). He is "the" Power of all powers. This truly unlimited power is for you and dwells within you. The Holy Spirit dwells *in you* (Romans 8:11). This life-giving power is always available for you to do God's will, live a Christ-like lifestyle, and have an empowered life journey. If you truly want to live a life-giving, prayer-filled, and Spirit-empowered kind of faith, then following Jesus is the best and most powerful and dynamic life you'll ever have. It is more powerful than any other self-help and self-development out there because you *walk by the Spirit* (Galatians 5:16; Romans 8:4). For who is greater than the One Lord who is living inside of your heart and walks with you?

You have peace and joy. We all know how stressful life can be, but Jesus promises his followers the experience of unconditional joy. In John 15:11, Jesus said to his followers, *"These things I have spoken to you, that my joy may be in you, and that your joy may be full."* That's also his desire for you in your life journey. If you are not experiencing perfect joy and heavenly delight in your life, what do you have to lose? Why hold on to your anxieties, worries and fears? Why not follow Jesus and receive his peace, assurance and faith that surpasses all understanding? Jesus said, *"Peace I leave with you; my peace I give to you"* (John 14:27a). If you follow him, that inner peace is yours to live out. But if not, he will not force his peace to dwell and cover you. It's a choice he wants you to make.

You have assurance forever. Did you know Jesus' warning in Matthew 7:21 saying *"Not everyone who says to me, 'Lord, Lord,' will enter the kingdom of heaven"*? Remember, Jesus spoke these words to those who seemingly know and follow him by doing great, mighty, and successful works. Yet, they were only assuming they are believers and followers of Jesus. It's not genuine faith. There's no need to put yourself in so much danger of presumption. If you follow Jesus, you will not assume in your life journey but be assured knowingly by the Word of God. John wrote, *"I write these things to you who believe in the name of the Son of God, that you may know that you have eternal life"* (1 John 5:13). Did he just say, "You may *know*" and not guess?

These promises among many, are the key benefits you have in Jesus when you follow him and make your life journey more meaningful and fully mature.

You might be asking, what does my life journey with Jesus look like? What makes your life's journey with Jesus so special or peculiar? Let me show you some of the uniqueness of your life journey in Jesus. This is just an overview of what life journey with Jesus is.

Life journey with Jesus is *the totality of your existence* here on earth from the beginning to eternity. It covers your whole life, even before your conversion to Jesus, not just the present and future. Long before you met Jesus, he's already given his invitation for the greatest adventure in the world: *you becoming Christlike.* How can this be? This life is made possible by the guidance of Jesus to those who believe in his name and keep following his teachings.

If you're familiar with "first things first," it is an assertion of setting our priorities right. If we apply it in Christian life, the same principle and practice apply. As Jesus leads, we follow. He comes first, and he's not the second priority. And that's not easy for all of us. But Jesus is unapologetic. If you completely trust him and his perfect plan, you'll understand the demand Jesus makes. "But seek first the kingdom of God and his righteousness, and all these things will be added to you" (Matthew 6:33).

Yes, in this quest for life, we know God has good and great plans for us. Jeremiah 29:11 clearly talked about it, *"For **I know the plans I have for you,** declares the LORD, plans for welfare and not for evil, to give you a future and a hope."* Indeed, God is thinking of you. The God who knows everything has a vision for your future. If we don't want to miss this great life and settle for less, we need to follow God's plan. But have we really understood what is required of it?

Life's journey with Jesus is a matter of faith and obedience to seek first things first. Jesus gave his commands. How obedient are we? Jesus also made promises. How trusting are we in his nature to accomplish what he said? God's promises are often predicated by our obedience. If we obey, he blesses; if we disobey, we hinder his full blessings to come.

What I love about Christian life journey is the opportunity of having our knowledge and understanding of God grow clearer, our faith going deeper, and our relationship with Jesus growing closer. As we seek to spend time in prayer and read his Word, we gain insights and power for living. We experience God's supernatural, life-transforming work in our lives as we equip ourselves to do his will and serve him in many ways. Our deeper understanding of God is essential for spiritual development in following Jesus.

So far, you might have realized that living for our own selves is somewhat empty or unfulfilling. Have you ever felt where you climbed the ladder of success and found out it's empty and lonely on top? Have you come to a point in your life where you're tired and said, "Is this all there is to life?" But Christian life journey is totally different. It's more than just an altruistic life shared with others. In Jesus, our life journey means loving and serving God and people.

Our love for God simply flows into loving our neighbors. When we follow Jesus, we live out our faith by demonstrating Jesus' compassion for the lost and lonely, the spiritually poor and needy. Through humility, Jesus' followers are forces of faith and blessings for others. They put their needs aside and do whatever it takes to meet the needs of others. That's the love of Jesus living in them and through them. While followers of Jesus walk through this life towards their eternal destiny, they think, love, and act like Jesus.

Reflection:

Among all the benefits mentioned above, which is more meaningful for you and why?

As you review and reflect on the verses pointed out above, which one made a deep impact in your heart right now?

CHAPTER 3: ARE YOU A FOLLOWER OF THE WAY?

The only reason why I wrote this book is to point people to Jesus in every way and help them become truly disciples in their spiritual journey. It means whatever we believe in and whatever we do, it's all connected and pointing to Jesus and following him. I pray you'll never lose sight of this sacred intention. While writing this book, I prayerfully consider these few groups of people.

A New Disciple. I'm writing this book for those who are starting out or recommitting their lives to follow Jesus. I was blessed to have leaders who helped and guided me to know and follow Jesus when I was a teenager. Even now, I still have mentors who helped me grow and become accountable for my life and leadership. Don't worry, I will not put everything I know here for that would take a long treatise. I won't bore you with that.

However, for your benefit, I only desire to bring the essentials to the table and let us feast upon God's truth. Allow me to be your coffee-drinking friend (with no sugar because I'm already over-sweet) and spiritual guide to help in little ways for your spiritual discovery, health, and growth as a disciple of Jesus.

A New Discipler. I always have great admiration for those who take seriously their faith and commitment to follow Jesus and serve others. They have the desire to disciple others, whether one on one, in a small group, or virtual. This book is for you too. Consider me as a mentor, catalyst, or coach if you will. You can use this book simultaneously. While you rediscover and learn God's Word and the teachings of Jesus here, you can use this book as a guide to help new followers of Jesus to grow in their faith.

This book is about our sacred adventure with Jesus the Lord and Savior. It's for our journey of becoming his disciple. I, too, am a fellow brother and follower of Jesus. I'm your co-journeyman in Jesus.

Biblical history pictures life with God as a spiritual journey. In fact, most of the Bible's content is narrative, meaning it's a collection of stories about life and faith in God described as a lifestyle walk. For example, *"Enoch walked with God"* (Genesis 5:22, 24). *"Noah walked with God"* (Genesis 6: 10). Abraham described his relationship with God as a "walk" of life, including Isaac (Genesis 24:40; 48:15). Some of the most meaningful life stories are the journeys of Abraham's unnamed servant, Jacob, Joseph, the Hebrew people, Moses, Joshua, David, and so on. Even the painful journey of the Israelites to exile is a powerful illustration of a spiritual journey gone wrong because of unbelief and disobedience.

How about in the New Testament? Well, the Gospel contains the sacred journeys of Mary and Joseph, Jesus and his disciples. Here, the ultimate subject of your life journey is presented and revealed: *Jesus Christ.* In the book of Acts, the sacred journeys of apostle Peter and Paul are evident, along with some of the churches and disciples. Again, you'll see how Jesus is the center of their life journey and quest for life.

However, the power of God's plan for the world and your life is that life has a definite destination. The book of Revelation shows the future and final destinations of God's people and those who are not. Friends, the great blessing about Christian life journey is not just about the path of the journey. Definitely, it is also about our destiny. It's all part of the journey. But the question remains: Are you a follower of the Way?

Did you know that today many people may profess as "Christians," but are not "disciples"? The root word and definition of a follower is "disciple" (Greek *matheteis*). A *"matheteis"* means "a learner," "pupil," or "disciple." It is closely related to *"manthano,"* meaning "to learn" or "be apprised" through increasing knowledge, practical experience, habit formation, and thoughtful reflection. Historically, in Jewish tradition, a disciple is someone who learns from a teacher and adheres to a certain belief and follows the teacher, thereby becoming like him as the student seeks to imitate his master's ways. For us to have common ground, when we use "follower," "disciple," or "learner" of Jesus, it's basically the same. We're referring to someone who believes in Jesus and follows his teachings and obeys his commands, thereby becoming like him in the process.

As such, when we use "disciple" or "Jesus follower," it doesn't mean someone who just follows some convenient teachings and does not necessarily believe in Jesus in everything. If I'll make an overview of the whole definition of a "follower" of Jesus, it goes this way:

- **Spiritually**, a true disciple and follower completely believes and trusts God for their salvation through faith in Jesus. By faith, a disciple lives to **"walk by the Spirit"** and **"keep in step with the Spirit"** in every way (Galatians 5:16, 25). He or she strives to be Christlike in character, attitude, passion for prayer, appetite for God's Word, living in the Spirit, and so on. This person is Christlike in every way. And this Jesus-likeness is demonstrated and fulfilled by being and becoming as a disciple-maker.

- **Emotionally**, a healthy and mature Jesus follower cultivates an intimate relationship with God through Jesus in the power of the Holy Spirit. Nothing is more important in between that relationship but faith, hope and love (1 Corinthians 13:13). A true disciple feels like Jesus and is filled with compassion, love, and care, especially for the lost (Matthew 9:36). In his book *Emotionally Healthy Spirituality: Unleash a Revolution in Your Life In Christ*, Peter Scazzero said, "emotional health and spiritual maturity are inseparable. It is not possible to be spiritually mature while remaining emotionally immature" disciple of Jesus.

- **Mentally**, a mature Jesus follower knows the truth and their spiritual state. A disciple keeps loving God with all his mind (Luke 10:27), learning and growing in the knowledge and understanding of God's grace and truth, especially revealed in the Bible (2 Peter 3:18). Being *"filled with **the knowledge of his will** in all spiritual wisdom and understanding"* is the cognitive or intellectual aspect of Christian life (Colossians 1:9b). However, information or stock knowledge is not enough. There's the enormous need for transformation in worldviews, mindset, understanding, and vision about God and his kingdom.

- **Physically**, a mature Jesus follower is committed to live out or act on his faith by being present in demonstrating and sharing the good news of salvation through Jesus with other people and discipling them *personally*.

While investing in the love of other people to follow Jesus and making disciples, a disciple serves with *hands* and feet, not just the *heart* and *head*. You live as a faithful steward of God's physical resources and "*glorify God in your body*" (1 Corinthians 6:20).

Each of these points and other aspects of your life will be amplified along the way in this discipleship journey so that each one will have a grasp what it truly means to be a disciple or follower of Jesus. I believe, to "*make disciples*" is so important for Jesus that he made it his final command for the church (Matthew 28:19). It is the God-given journey and process of living and growing in life as a follower of Jesus. The question is, will you follow Jesus now?

Several times, Jesus invited people to come and follow him, but the response is often personal. He said that if someone would *come* after him, that person should *deny himself, take up* Jesus' cross, and *follow him* so that he can transform them to become what he intended them to be: *becoming his true disciples* (Matthew 4:19; Mark 1:17; John 1:43). Most of these individuals were common persons working in the marketplace (Matthew 9:9). Meaning, Jesus' invitation has an intention and plan for transformation. That means becoming a disciple of Jesus is not an accident. It takes a conscious decision to respond to Jesus' call for discipleship.

Do you want to get closer to him and be with him forever? If so, his promise is for you to become like him and to be conformed into his purposes and plans. Surely, following Jesus means leaving behind something in our lives in order to pursue the most important things worthy for eternity. He is inviting you to leave your old life behind and become new to join him in his mission of proclaiming the good news of God's kingdom that could change people's lives, including yours.

What's next? Let me encourage you to make a step of faith—even if it's just baby steps. At least you're moving forward in your journey of faith.

Come to Jesus in humility. James said, "*Humble yourselves before the Lord, and he will exalt you*" (James 4:10). Put your trust in Jesus alone and become his faithful follower, living your life of humility according to his teachings. He's waiting for you. Think of him like knocking at your heart's door, waiting for you to open it, saying. *"Behold, I stand at the door and knock. If anyone hears my voice and opens the door, I will come in to him and eat with him, and he with me"* (Revelation 3:20). Will you open the door of your heart for Jesus to come in and have a personal relationship with you?

Commit to learn and follow Jesus by faith. Jesus is calling you. *"Learn from me,"* he invites (Matthew 11:29b. Here, Jesus used *"manthano,"* which is akin to *"matheteis"* or disciple). Start small. The early disciples learned about Jesus one day at a time. Sometimes, their knowledge and understanding are incomplete. But it's ok as long as you're learning and growing in your faith. After all, we cannot fully comprehend everything about God, Jesus, the Holy Spirit, or the mysteries he made in this world. Nonetheless, make a step of faith like them when they journeyed with Jesus one step at a time. Keep walking. By not giving up, you will grow in faith, understanding, and maturity.

Reflection:

How long have you been a Christian? Would you consider yourself a new disciple?

Do you want to live abundantly and please Jesus in every area of your life?

SECTION 2: A NEW BEGINNING WITH THE WAY

"I am the way, and the truth, and the life.
No one comes to the Father except through me.

~ Jesus (John 14:6)

CHAPTER 4: HOW CAN A MAN BE REBORN WHEN HE IS OLD?

In August of 2017, Pew Research Center surveyed Christians in the US about their beliefs on getting to heaven. They found out that only 46% of Protestants and 17% of Catholics believe that faith in God alone is needed to get to heaven, while a whopping majority of 52% of Protestants and 81% of Catholics say you both need good works and faith in God to get to heaven. It is evident that the majority of these Christians believe that heaven is something you need to work and earn, and that salvation is partly a human effort. How about you? Are you part of the status quo? What does Jesus our Savior have to say?

A famous catch-phrase from Stephen Covey says, "Begin with the end in mind." You might not agree with everything he says in his book *The 7 Habits of Highly Effective People*, but there's a nugget of spiritual truth in the saying also. Before you begin your spiritual journey, ask yourself: What do you see in the future: salvation in heaven or separation from God in hell? Where do you want to spend eternity? Where are you heading right now? Are you going in that direction or not?

My Sunday School teacher asked me when I was a 5th grade kid. "If Jesus returns today, would you go to heaven and be with him for eternity?" I was stunned because I wasn't sure. I know I've done wrong and there's no denying. I was lost. Then she dropped the next question: "If you were to die today and stand before God, and he asks, 'Why should I let you into my heaven?' What would you say?" I knew then I had to pay attention. That day was the turning point of my life, a new beginning that changed me forever–and you'll know why.

In our life journey, we face two separate ways ahead: the way of life or the way of death. Prophet Jeremiah mentioned it: *"And to this people you shall say: Thus says the LORD: Behold, I set before you **the way of life** and **the way of death**"* (Jeremiah 21:8). There's nothing in between. We have to choose and make a decision because there's no middle road. These two roads are the two divergent directions ahead of us and so we have to be careful with our choice because it determines our eternal destiny–*your* eternal destiny.

However, one of the biggest problems of life is when we're lost, we often don't know about it and how it will end. This ancient saying is true. *"**There is a way that seems right to a man, but its end is the way to death**"* (Proverbs 14:12). Not all people could understand this–not even one of the great religious teachers of Israel knew about it. Do you want proof? Read the story in John 3:1-18. It reveals the heart of the Gospel of Jesus and if there's one narrative in the Bible that you should know and understand, this is it.

> *Now there was a man of the Pharisees named Nicodemus, a ruler of the Jews. This man came to Jesus by night and said to him, "Rabbi, we know that you are a teacher come from God, for no one can do these signs that you do unless God is with him."*

> *Jesus answered him, "Truly, truly, I say to you, **unless one is born again he cannot see the kingdom of God.**"*

All his Jewish life, Nicodemus thought he was already good and religious enough to have God's approval, set himself to earn God's favor, and see his eternal kingdom, only to be confronted by Jesus that he needs to be *"born again"* or *reborn* in a spiritual sense. However, Nicodemus' knowledge and understanding (or lack of it) is still on a physical-material level, not understanding Jesus' point on how spiritual rebirth is needed for a person to be saved or having eternal life with God.

> *Nicodemus said to him, "How can a man be **born** when he is old? Can he enter a second time into his mother's womb and **be born**?"*

> *Jesus answered, "Truly, truly, I say to you, unless one is **born of water** and **the Spirit**, he cannot enter the kingdom of God. That which is born of the flesh is flesh, and that which is **born of the Spirit is spirit**. Do not marvel that I said*

*to you, 'You must be **born again.'** The wind blows where it wishes, and you hear its sound, but you do not know where it comes from or where it goes. So it is with everyone who is **born of the Spirit**."*

Here, Jesus is making a major spiritual emphasis by mentioning spiritual rebirth ("born") 5 times. As it takes a child to be *physically* born ("*born of the flesh*" that is called the first birth) and become a part of an earthly family, the same principle applies to God's family. A person must be *born again* in the *spiritual* sense (that's the second birth) to become a part of God's spiritual family. This spiritual reality is interchangeably used here "*born of water and of Spirit*" and "born of the Spirit." Both phrases are the same on a spiritual level. (I don't believe in the interpretation that the phrase "*born of water*" is referring to water baptism because historically and biblically, baptism cannot save.) This reference must have something to do with the prophecy of prophet Ezekiel way back 600 years before Jesus.

Prophet Ezekiel declared that God "*will sprinkle clean water*" upon his people. Such spiritual water will wash and clean his people from all their sinfulness and spiritual uncleanness due to idolatry. "*And I will give you a new heart, and **a new spirit** I will put within you. And I will remove the heart of stone from your flesh and give you a heart of flesh. And I will put **my Spirit within you**, and **cause you to walk in my statutes** and be careful to obey my rules*" (Ezekiel 36:25-27). This is a great promise that Jesus would fulfill.

In God's perfect time, Jesus our Savior came to earth as the perfect manifestation of "*the goodness and loving kindness of God.*" In the words the apostle Paul, "***he saved us**, not because of works done by us in righteousness, but according to his own mercy, by the **washing** of regeneration and renewal of **the Holy Spirit**, whom he poured out on us richly through Jesus Christ our Savior*" (Titus 3:4-6). Both in the Old and New Testament, the Spirit of God is closely connected with the idea of "water" and "washing" as a picture of regeneration, a sovereign work of God in giving a new life to a person who believes in Jesus as their Savior. But still Nicodemus struggled with the idea of "*that which is born of the Spirit is spirit*," meaning he must be "born again" in the spirit, not in the physical flesh.

*Nicodemus said to him, "**How can these things be?**"*

*Jesus answered him, "Are you **the teacher of Israel** and yet you do not understand these things? Truly, truly, I say to you, we speak of what we know, and bear witness to what we have seen, but you do not receive our testimony. If I have told you earthly things and you do not believe, how can you **believe** if I tell you **heavenly things?** No one has ascended into heaven except he who descended from heaven, the Son of Man. And as Moses lifted up the serpent in the wilderness, so must the Son of Man be lifted up, that **whoever believes in him may have eternal life.***

Notice how Jesus confronted Nicodemus' lack of spiritual insight on "*heavenly things,*" despite the fact that he is known with a highly-esteemed title as "*the teacher of Israel*" and not just any ordinary instructor of the Jewish faith. He should have known better, but he didn't. It's all because he "didn't receive" or "*believe*" Jesus' testimony by faith. There's still doubt and unbelief; he is still on the "earthly" level of thinking. He should have known the many prophecies in the Old Testament about the Messiah as symbolized in their history with Moses (Number 21:9) as well as "the Son of Man" in the book of Daniel. Nicodemus needs to believe in Jesus to have eternal life. As Jesus said, "*whoever believes in him may have eternal life.*" So, Jesus continued with the greatest news of all times:

"For God so loved the world, that he gave his only Son, that whoever believes in him should not perish but have eternal life.

This truth is the heart of the Gospel of Jesus. *God loves you.* Of course, the Father loved his Son, but he also loves you so much that it is more than enough for him to give and let go of his one and only Son to suffer and die for our sins. God knows that we as sinners cannot save ourselves on our own. We need a perfect Savior. While most people will not believe that only God can save them, thinking they have the human capacity to save their own selves, this truth will never change. Only those who believe will have eternal life and not perish. The good news is, believing in Jesus is open for *everyone*–as indicated in "***whoever believes***"--even if not everyone will believe it. Yes, Jesus came to this world that you might "*be saved through him*" and "*not perish*" in Hell due to the punishment of our sins. Jesus continued,

For God did not send his Son into the world to condemn the world, but in order that

29

*the world might be **saved through him**. Whoever **believes in him** is not condemned, but whoever does not **believe** is condemned already, because he has not **believed** in the name of the only Son of God.*

Indeed, God sent his Son for you. It is the total manifestation of his love for us all. If God wanted to condemn us, he could have just done it a long time ago. But out of his great mercy, *"God sent his only Son into the world, so that we might **live** through him"* (1 John 4:9). Jesus came to save you or that through him you might be saved and not be judged or condemned. How can this be?

Have you noticed how the word *"believe"* is repeated over and over again? While the word *"pisteuo"* for "believe" is often used in the New Testament with several meanings, like trusting someone or some things (e.g. God's revelation, truth, promises, etc.,), in this context, faith for our salvation is given to Jesus alone. Here, "to believe" means to "entrust one's spiritual being" to Jesus. You completely trust him for your salvation. You can only be born again and have eternal life if you *believe* in Jesus. This is what being "born again" means. It is not a denomination, a church, or a religion. It is a new life of being saved from death to life through faith in Jesus.

Is salvation really by faith alone? The truth is, in the Old Testament, prophet Habakkuk clearly stated that *"**the righteous** shall **live by** his **faith**"* (Habakkuk 2:4b). Since we do not have a righteousness of our own because we are all sinners, indeed, we can only live by faith, completely trusting in God's righteousness to be given to us. Even the apostle Paul is consistent with this biblical truth that the Gospel of Jesus is God's power *"for salvation to everyone who **believes**, to the Jew first and also to the Greek. For in it the **righteousness** of God is revealed from **faith** for **faith**, as it is written, '**The righteous shall live by faith**'"* (Romans 1:16-17).

Paul also argued that *"one is justified by faith apart from works of the law"* (Romans 3:28). As such he spent the whole chapters of Romans 4-6 explaining how Abraham, who lived long before the law of Moses was given, was justified by faith and not by good works. He also presented that we can be reconciled and have peace with God not because of our own good works but by virtue of faith (For more about the biblical idea of you having God's righteousness and salvation by faith, see also Galatians 2:15-3:14)

If Jesus said that you must believe in him that you might be saved and have eternal life, would you trust him completely? Would you put your faith in him alone for your salvation? The truth is God loves you. He wants you to choose the path of a new life, the eternal and meaningful life in the kingdom of God, not death and condemnation from God. But you have to be spiritually "reborn." How? By *believing* in Jesus with your heart and soul.

In the next chapter, let me show you how your life journey can move to a new level: *to choose the path of life.* We will set our journey from lostness and having no relationship with God to being saved and having a personal, healthy, and growing relationship with God through Jesus Christ by faith.

Reflection:

What have you learned in the words of Jesus about believing in him, the only Son of God? And what are the eternal consequences if you do not believe in him?

Have you been born again? When did you receive Jesus as your personal Lord and Savior? _____

What is your level of certainty whether you are saved or not? (1 being lowest and 10 being the highest)

   1   2   3   4   5   6   7   8   9   10

CHAPTER 5: WHAT WENT WRONG AND HOW TO GET OUT OF IT?

W̲e all live in a lost broken world. Just take a look at all the broken relationships that broke a lot of people's hearts. How many promises were broken? In many ways we have broken lives. We are all broken people who lost our spiritual way. But it was not like this from the start.

"In the beginning," the Bible reveals that *"God created"* everything in heaven and earth–and *"God saw that it was **good**"* (Genesis 1). When God created the first humans, he had a perfect relationship with Adam and Eve whom he created in *"his image."* As humans, we are created in the image of God. Genesis 1:27 says,

> *So God created man in his own image,*
> *in the image of God he created him;*
> *male and female he created them.*

What does the image of God mean? For some, this "likeness" is about the soul and spirit, or free-will or ability to reason or be creative, and other spiritual traits. In my dissertation, this image has something to do with God's rulership where he created humans to be his royal representatives and have dominion over all creation. Regardless of what you think about yourself, whether good or bad, high or low, you are an image-bearer and a blessed one. Genesis continues to narrate this reality: *"And God **blessed** them. And God said to them, "Be fruitful and multiply and fill the earth and **subdue** it, and have **dominion**"* (v.28). God's plan was to have perfect harmony and relationship with his precious creation, that they might freely walk in his ways and enjoy their lives abundantly.

However, something unexpected happened. Adam and Eve fell into sin when they disobeyed and rebelled against God and rejected his will. It's what we call "spiritual lostness" that results in all kinds of brokenness. It's a terrible mistake they made because there are some devastating results of their sin and spiritual lostness, even for us.

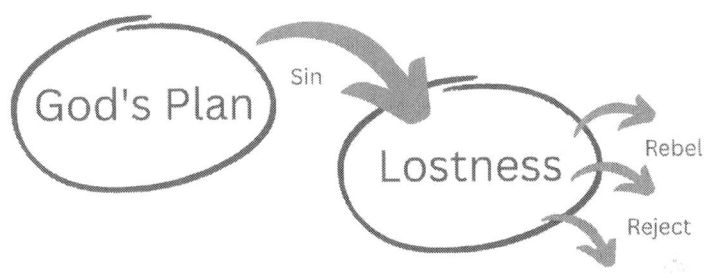

Disconnection From God. Evidently, when the first humans who were our first parents lost their way, their relationship with God was severely broken. As a result, we were lost in sin too, meaning, we are spiritually "separated" and *disconnected* from God because we also inherited and shared the same human and sinful nature with them (Ephesians 2:11). As Paul says, *"None is righteous, no, not one; no one understands; no one seeks for God"* (Romans 3:10-11). Because our sinful nature rejects God in every way, we do not have true righteousness on our own, only self-righteousness and sin.

- ***Death spread to everyone.*** Because of Adam's sin and rebellion, sin opened and paved the way for evil to come into this world and it resulted in death (both physical and spiritual) for everyone. Theologians call this "imputed" sin and unrighteousness as Adam represents all of us. Paul said in the book of Romans 5:12, *"Therefore, just as sin came into the world **through one man,"***—that's Adam—*"and death through sin, and so **death spread to all men** because **all** [not few or some, but all have] **sinned.**"* This spiritual reality means the disobedience of Adam brought us sin and death. His sin extended upon us. That's why we're sinners, you and I.

- **Desperately not enough.** In another chapter, Paul already said, *"For all have sinned and **fall short** of the glory of God"* (Roman 3:23). Again, not few, not most, but we are "all" sinners. No human is exempted (except Jesus in human form). Because God is holy and we are not, we fail to meet his absolute and perfect standard. The more we stay in that pathway of denial and life of sin, we move further away from God. Why? The answer is this: *"If we say we have not sinned, we make* [God] *a liar, and his word is not in us"* (1 John 1:10). If we do not agree that we are sinners who need to repent or ask forgiveness of our sins, we accuse God of lying and assume for ourselves that we are telling the truth. That's why the sad thing about being a sinner is not realizing we are sinners.

- **Deserving death and punishment.** Sin separated us from our holy God, and without a Savior, we would remain in a state of brokenness, lostness, condemnation, and death. We need healing; we need direction, forgiveness and hope; and we need a new life. That's why Paul emphasized this truth: *"For **the wages of sin is death,** but the free gift of God is eternal life in Christ Jesus our Lord"* (Romans 6:23). Because we are sinners, we will pay the penalty for our sins. We only deserve death (both physical and eternal) in return for our sins. If the penalty of sin is death, then, our only hope is receiving God's "gift" of life, which is found in Jesus. The only question is will you *receive* the gift or *reject* it?

What's your way out from the power of sin and death? Friend, search for Jesus the Savior to help you out of this terrible situation. Did you know that the way of death is wide open and big, while the way of life is narrow and small? Let's be careful and think seriously about this question: What is my way out of this spiritual lostness, shackles of sin, and severe condemnation?

- **Enter the narrow gate.** Jesus said, *"Enter by **the narrow gate**. For the gate is wide and the way is easy that leads to destruction, and those who enter by it are many"* (Matthew 7:13). That "narrow gate" symbolizes Jesus. The people of this world walk to the highway of death without realizing it is leading them to hell and eternal destruction. But Jesus is offering you an exit route. He is your way to salvation and eternal life. But you must decide whether or not to enter the door.

- ***Know the Way to heaven.*** Many religions teach and people believe that there are many ways to heaven. It sounds good, but Jesus claimed the opposite. He is the only way. So either these people were right and Jesus was lying, or Jesus spoke the truth and these people saying otherwise are wrong. Both can't be right. In John 14:1-4, Jesus said to his disciples. "*Let not your hearts be troubled.* **Believe in God; believe also in me.**" That means believing in God is the same as believing in Jesus and vice versa. Jesus, then made a promise, "*In my Father's house are many rooms. If it were not so, would I have told you that I go to prepare a place for you? And if I go and prepare a place for you, I will come again and will take you to myself, that where I am you may be also. And* **you know the way to where I am going.**"

Did they hear it right: "*You know the way to where I'm going?*" Almost all assume they did. Among the disciples, however, someone was honest enough to seek the right answer and the way of this ultimate journey. It came from the unlikely candidate, Thomas, aka "the Doubter." "*Thomas said to him, '***Lord, we do not know** *where you are going.* **How can we know the way?**'" (John 14:5).

Yes, at first, the disciples did not perfectly know where they were heading. In fact, at the beginning, they didn't know everything about Jesus. It was a gradual journey of discovery as Jesus walked with them and drew them close to him. At first, they didn't know that God "*foreknew*" and "*predestined*" them "*to be conformed to* **the image** *of* [God's] *Son*" (Romans 8:29). They are getting to know the great mystery of the Son. "*He is* **the image of the invisible God**" (Colossians 1:15a). In this sacred journey, you are being transformed into the true image of God, into the likeness of Jesus.

Thank God. Thomas was not a presumptuous know-it-all. He courageously asked one of the greatest questions of eternal importance: *How can we know the way?* This question is still timeless and needed for us today. Your response matters: Either you will just *assume* or you will *ask* the question about the true way.

Reflection:

In whose image are we made of? What does it mean for you?

What have you learned about our fallen human nature? What are the consequences of our sins and sinful nature?

CHAPTER 6: HOW CAN WE KNOW THE WAY AND WHAT TO DO ABOUT IT?

This matter is the ultimate quest of our life journey. This issue is one of the most important questions we must deal with and know the answer to with certainty. After all, it's best to know where the bus is going before taking a long trip, right? We can never take this spiritual reality for granted because it is a matter of eternal life or eternal death, salvation or condemnation. Here is the essential truth you must know: *God made a way for you and me. Jesus is the Way.*

The main reason why Jesus came to this world was because of God's initiative to make a way for us because he knew how lost we are. God gave us his perfect demonstration of love through Jesus at the cross, even though we were completely lost and living in sin. *"But God shows his love for us in that **while we were still sinners, Christ died for us**."* (Romans 5:8). For whom did Jesus die? For you; for me; for all. If Jesus is the perfect embodiment of God's love for you, do you think we deserve him? He is God's love *in person* to send you the message of hope even though you and I don't deserve it. But he wants us to find our way back to God.

Jesus told us that he is the Way—the Only Way. Thanks to Thomas's honesty in asking, *"How can we know the way?"* In response, Jesus revealed himself clearly. *"Jesus said to him, 'I am the way, and the truth, and the life. No one comes to the Father except through me'"* (John 14:6). That's an exclusive and absolute claim by Jesus. He is the only way to eternal life. It's not good works, church, religion, or any other saints; it's not even by yourself, no matter how good you think you are. There is no other Savior besides Jesus, pure and simple.

The truth is Jesus is the only one who can save us from our sins and he offers us a way out of condemnation and eternal death. Is this claim true? The

Scripture says, *"And there is **salvation in no one else,** for there is no other name under heaven given among men **by which we must be saved"** (Acts 4:12). That has always been the core and eternal message of true and biblical Christianity. Since we have sinned and are separated from the holy God, we have nothing in common with his holy nature; our relationship with him is severed and estranged. But because of our heavenly Father's love, he gave us Jesus the Savior as our only way to him and be reconciled.

Believing in Jesus is the Way to eternity. Do you still remember the personal encounter of Jesus and Nicodemus? Jesus says in John 3:16, *"For God so loved the world, that he gave his only Son, that **whoever believes in him** should not perish but **have eternal life."*** The message is very clear that God loves you and me unconditionally and sacrificially. It's the very reason why our heavenly Father gave Jesus to be our Savior in whom we can live forever if we fully believe in him for our salvation and not depend on our own strength and ability. Salvation is completely a gift of God. You don't work for it, for if you work for your salvation, it ceases to be a gift. You must trust Jesus completely to be saved.

Repent and change your course from sin to God. Repentance is essential in Jesus' message. It's a sign of genuine faith. He said, *"The time is fulfilled, and the kingdom of God is at hand; **repent and believe in the gospel"** (Mark 1:15). What does it mean to repent? To "repent" (Greek *metanoia*) means "a change of mind," referring to the inner change of a person. Repeatedly, Jesus emphasized repentance from sin and turning to God. One great proof that a person genuinely believes in Jesus is repentance of sins, resulting in God's forgiveness and freedom.

The Gospel is about Jesus who suffered and died *for our sins*–sins that must be forgiven. According to the Scriptures, he rose again from the dead on the third day to prove to you that he is our source of eternal life. That's the good news of Jesus.

Since God did not take sin lightly, why should we? It would be unthinkable for a professing disciple to be an "unrepentant believer." That's an oxymoron, a deceptive and progressive lie of Satan. An unrepentant person is not a believer and a believer cannot ever be unrepentant. That's why in the Gospels, Jesus repeatedly called people to repent many times. Repentance is a state of mind and a posture of the heart to seek and ask God's forgiveness for all our sins and to agree that we are sinners, unable to save ourselves. Not only that, to repent means to change our minds and hearts by turning away from our sinful ways and following the Way, which is Jesus.

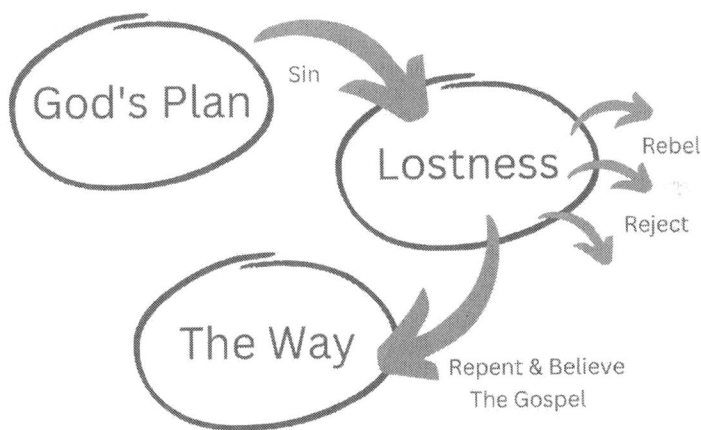

The truth is repentance is for you and I, for everyone, including Christians. The moment we have done something wrong or lost our way, we can return and come home to God and ask forgiveness. But above all, anyone who does not have a personal relationship with Jesus must come to a point in his or her life to turn their backs from their sins and turn their way towards God.

Friend, will you make the greatest decision ever? Take a moment and pause. Don't let this opportunity pass you by. Sit down and reflect prayerfully. This opportunity could be the greatest decision you can ever make in life before it's too late.

Accept the truth about Jesus as revealed in the Holy Scriptures. Accepting (or rejecting) our Lord and Savior Jesus is the greatest decision a person can make in this life. You must be fully convinced and persuaded by God's truth about who Jesus is. As mentioned already, we are all sinners. There's no way we can save ourselves based on our own abilities or achievements. But God loves you so much that he gave Jesus to be your Savior. But do you accept this truth as revealed in the Holy Scriptures?

It says in John 1:12, *"But to all who did **receive** him, who **believed** in his name, he gave the right to become children of God."* Here, to "receive" means to "actively lay hold" or consciously take Jesus into your heart by faith and full trust. It involves your volition or assertiveness as a receiver. To receive Jesus is also the same as to "believe in his name" that he alone is your Lord and Savior. As God's sufficient gift, accepting or receiving Jesus into your heart as your Savior means you totally believe in Jesus and completely trust him for your salvation. As a result, that makes you a rightful part of God's family. You become God's child and God becomes your Father, not Satan. This way, you live within God's plan as you believe and follow Jesus.

Believe in Jesus. To "believe" means to accept something as true or existing. But the Bible teaches that believing in Jesus is more than just accepting a fact. It requires faith. Accepting Jesus as our personal Lord and Savior is *an individual decision* that each of us must make *by faith*. It's the greatest decision of having confidence in Jesus for your salvation from sin and eternal destination with God.

For example, a Roman jailer once asked the apostle Paul and Silas, *"Sirs, **what must I do to be saved?**"* And they said, *"**Believe in the Lord Jesus**, and you will be saved, you and your household"* (Acts 16:30-31). Here, believing in Jesus as your Savior means you fully trust him that he alone saves you from your sin and its consequences. Everything in you (your heart, mind, and spirit) must be fully convinced and persuaded that Jesus alone is your Savior and Lord.

Confess "Jesus is Lord." If you acknowledge in prayer to ask God's forgiveness for your sins, he will forgive you. If you confess Jesus as your Lord and Savior, God will grant you the salvation you need. The Bible says, *"If you **confess** with your mouth that **Jesus is Lord** and **believe in your heart** that God raised him from the dead, you will **be saved**"* (Romans 10:9). Jesus' death on the cross and resurrection from the grave (as a whole story) is the center of the Gospel message. To "confess" (*homologeo*) means to "agree" or "speak the same," meaning, you speak with your mouth and declare in agreement that Jesus is, indeed, Lord. This verbal confession must come from your heart, not just an empty lip service.

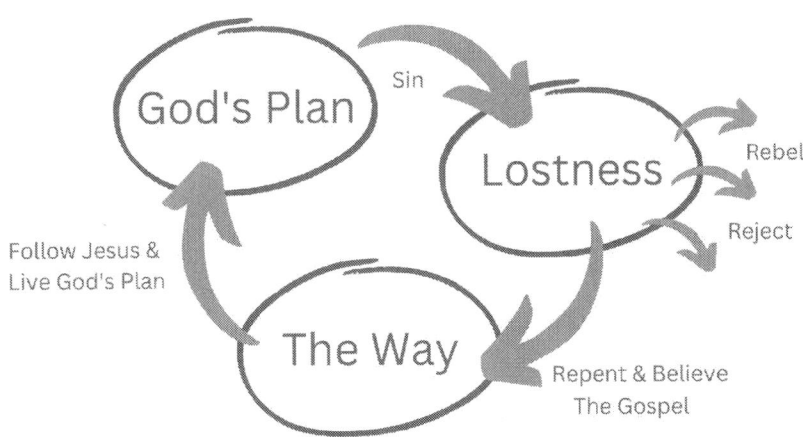

As Paul says, *"For 'everyone who **calls** on the name of the Lord **will be saved**'"* (Romans 8:13). He emphasized calling upon God in prayer. Jesus is the only one who can save us from the penalty of our sins and he offers us a way out of our brokenness and sin. He can save us from ourselves and heal us, making us whole as a human being. The only way for us to follow Jesus and live God's plan for an abundant life and have eternal life is through Jesus alone.

Thus, the most important questions remain: *Have you made that decision and fully trusted Jesus as your personal Lord and Savior?* If not, will you open your heart and accept him as your Lord and Savior, truly believing that he alone can save and forgive your sins?

Friends, I encourage you. Call upon the name of Jesus. Accept him as your personal Lord and Savior. Open up your heart for him and believe with all your heart that he alone saves. Trust him with all your heart. Then, you can begin your journey of faith in him, through him, and for him.

Remember my encounter with my Sunday School teacher in the beginning of this chapter? I made the greatest decision to start my faith journey with Jesus as my Lord and Savior. It's been my greatest adventure ever. I pray that you'll also do the same. From the beginning to the end, Jesus is your life. Your life is Christ. We have eternal life because of Jesus. And that eternal journey starts now.

If you want to start a new relationship with God through Jesus Christ, you can call on him directly in a personal way through prayer. You can thank him for his love and ask for forgiveness for all the sins you've done against him. Confess that Jesus is Lord and tell him that you completely believe in him as your Lord and Savior. Ask him to change you and indwell you heart that you might be with him forever. You can also pray a prayer like the one below, but please remember that this prayer will not save you. It is your faith in believing in Jesus that saves.

If you decide now to trust Jesus as your Lord and Savior, pray something like this:

> Our Father in heaven, you are holy and true. I'm so grateful for your love and sacrifice. I have sinned against you but because of your mercy and grace, you sent your one and only Son Jesus Christ to suffer at the cross for my sins and die as the penalty of our sins. He was buried and on the third day he resurrected from the dead and is seated at the right hand of the Father. Indeed, I confess, Jesus is Lord. Please forgive me for all my sins and save me from eternal condemnation. Change my heart, O God and mold me to be like your Son Jesus. In you I trust alone. In Jesus' name, Amen.

Signed: _____   Date: _____

Reflection:

Have you made the decision and fully trusted Jesus as your personal Lord and Savior?

If you wholeheartedly prayed the prayer of acceptance by faith and with all your heart, congratulations! Welcome to the family of God. Heaven is rejoicing in heaven right now. Jesus said, *"Just so, I tell you, there will be more joy in heaven over one sinner who repents than over ninety-nine righteous persons who need no repentance"* (Luke 15:7). Remember this day as your spiritual birthday, your spiritual rebirth.

SECTION 3: ASSURED TOWARDS THE DESTINY

"And this is the testimony,
that God gave us eternal life,
and this life is in his Son.
Whoever has the Son has life;
whoever does not have the Son of God does not have life."

~ John the Beloved (1 John 5:11-12)

CHAPTER 7: WHY DO WE NEED TO HAVE AN ASSURANCE OF SALVATION?

One Sunday afternoon, a young lady in the church called my attention and had me sit comfortably. After a short conversation starter, she asked me this question: "Glenn, do you know for sure if you're going to heaven someday?" I noticed she emphasized "for sure" in that question. As a sixth Grade kid, I was hesitant and unsure to answer it. But, perhaps I just wanted to save my face, I half-heartedly said, "I will!" hoping if i fake it, i'll make it.

She then gently dropped the next question: "So, if you're going to die today and stand before God, and he would ask you, "Why should I let you enter my heaven?' what would you say?" I replied, "I don't know." I thought to myself, nobody told me about that question before. But one thing I know, when I look at myself, I've done lots of bad things a kid normally does. I disobeyed my parents; I stole toys from a store or a kid; I fought with kids in the neighborhood; I lied many times that I lost count of it, and so on. As a kid, I didn't think I'm going to make it to heaven someday. (Just a friendly note: If you feel the same, I'd highly advise you to go through chapter 1 and fully understand it before you proceed).

Shortly, the young lady started sharing to me how God loved me. Even though I'm a sinner, God gave his Son Jesus to die for my sins. This news was very familiar to me because I've heard it before. So, when she asked me to make a decision to accept Jesus into my heart, I refused to do so. She asked why. I told her. "It's because I've already done it. I trusted Jesus and accepted him as my Lord and Savior on April 22, 1987, 2PM!" That's just a few months ago when that conversation happened. I already have that personal relationship with God through Jesus in my heart.

The problem I got when I was a kid (and very young in my faith) was this: Nobody told and taught me about my assurance of salvation in Jesus. My previous Sunday school teacher introduced me to Jesus and gave me that opportunity to give my life to him as my Lord and Savior, and repented for my sins. I was seemingly "spiritually abandoned" for a moment. I was not discipled right after I gave my life to Jesus.

Of course, I don't like that to happen to you. I don't want to give you false hope either. If you have not trusted Jesus as your Lord and Savior, you have to settle that in your heart and make the decision for yourself. (Before you proceed on this section, make sure you took the previous section for your sake and understanding of this topic.)

When you travel, at least it's great to know it's safe to take the road and reach your destiny. That's why some of us would check the weather forecast and assess whether our journey is safe or not. As humans, we have an inherent desire for certainty. But when it comes to "eternal security" we want to know why we need it. Does the Bible even teach "the assurance of salvation"?

In this world, there are two types of Christians: First, there are genuine believers in Jesus who are "***saved but not sure***" whether they have assurance of salvation. It means they know that they have accepted Jesus as their Lord and Savior and have repented of their sins. However, when you ask them if they are certain that if they die anytime, they're not sure if they will enter heaven or not. Second, there are true believers in Jesus who are "***saved but secure***" about their eternal salvation. It means they repented of their sins and accepted Jesus as their Lord and Savior. They are confident based on God's Word that they are assured of their eternal destiny to be with God forever. My goal in this section is if you belong to the first side of Christians (saved/unsure), I pray that you'll be able to move to the next side (saved/secure). As a follower of Jesus, being saved and knowing you have eternal security means a lot in your spiritual journey.

Of course there are various people who are also like the ones I identified in the two lower quadrants. First are the "***unsaved and unsecured.***" These are self-professing "Christians" but are actually not in a personal relationship with God nor completely trusted him for their salvation. They do not believe and are unsure they're going to heaven through Jesus Christ alone when they die. They just attend church, do good, or assume they are Christians because they do not belong to any non-Christian religions.

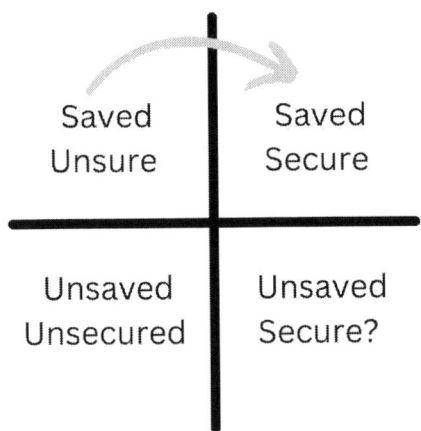

Secondly, there are also those who are "unsaved and secured," at least in their assumptions. These are self-professed to be "Christians" but do not have a genuine relationship with God nor completely trust him for their salvation, but still think they're going to personally earn and enter heaven someday by their own effort, traditions, religiousness, or rituals. Both of these groups below are considered "cultural Christians." Just because they were not born Muslims, Buddhists, Hindus, or anything else, they assume they were "born Christians," so to speak.

The truth is we will all stand before God and regardless of how you feel or think, this truth will stand and will never change: *Some will enter heaven and some will not.* Read and reflect on what Jesus said in Matthew 7:21-23.

> **Not everyone who says to me, "Lord, Lord," will enter the kingdom of heaven,** *but the one who* **does the will of my Father** *who is in heaven. On that day many will say to me, 'Lord, Lord, did we not prophesy in your name, and cast out demons in your name, and do many mighty works in your name?' And then will I declare to them, "I never knew you; depart from me, you workers of*

lawlessness."

Even if someone calls on Jesus' name, like "Lord, Lord" (or sometimes swears on the name of the Lord), Jesus refuses to acknowledge their calls. Here, it appears that these people even served, told people about God, exorcize demons, and even performed miracles. But Jesus, who is all-knowing God, denied that he intimately knew them. Calling by lip service that Jesus is your Lord and working in his ministries will not save you. Only your faith in the suffering and death of Jesus for your sins at the cross and his resurrection—or the Gospel of Jesus—can pay for your eternal destiny and save you.

What do these words of Jesus mean to you? What does doing the heavenly Father's will mean? Definitely, it's not by good works. These people who did good works were still denied by Jesus. *"For this is **the will of my Father**,"* Jesus said, *"that **everyone** who looks on **the Son** and **believes in him should have eternal life**, and I will raise him up on the last day"* (John 6:40).

Yes, indeed, it is God's will that you receive eternal life and defeat death. However , this life is more than just immortality. It is a quality of life in the here and now, not just in the afterlife. Over and over again, Jesus emphasized that if you want to be saved, you've got to believe in him. Salvation is by faith alone and it is for "everyone." There's no other Savior and Lord but Jesus who died on the cross for our sins and rose from the grave.

If salvation is by works, then Jesus' sacrifice is insufficient and incomplete. But, no. Since the beginning, salvation is through faith and not by works. After all, it wasn't you who died on the cross and surely you have no power to rise from the grave on your own if you die. If you can't take that wholeheartedly, are you willing to take the risk of standing before God and learn it's too late?

When you die and you'll stand before God, there's no turning back. The decision you made here on earth, whether you *received* or *rejected* Jesus, will no longer change in heaven. So if you make a decision for Jesus, it must be done here while you're still alive. But some people would delay their decision until it's too late. It baffles me. Why would anyone do that?

If there are some reasons why we need assurance of salvation, these are very important ones:

- Assurance of salvation is taught in the Scriptures. Either we receive this truth or reject it. But we cannot have both. That's why we all need to study the Scripture to know the truth and be confident in God's unfailing promises.

- Assurance of salvation builds your faith on a strong foundation. It keeps you away from believing that you yourself contributed to your salvation. Your assurance must be grounded upon the Word of God, not your personal opinion but on God's revelation.

- Assurance of salvation gives a healthy level of confidence in your journey that God, as well as Jesus Christ, is able to keep you till the end. John F. MacArthur Jr., in his book *Saved Without A Doubt: Being Sure of Your Salvation,* emphasized this. "Being assured of our salvation is no arrogant stoutness. It is faith. It is not presumption [sic]. Rather it is confidence in God's promise."

Reflection:

In your own words, why do you need an assurance of salvation and why does it matter for you?

Is calling "Lord, Lord" or doing good works enough for you to earn salvation? Why or why not?

CHAPTER 8: WHAT DOES "ASSURANCE OF SALVATION" MEAN?

There are many definitions and nuances when it comes to the definition of "assurance of salvation." For new followers of Jesus, this definition is a great summary. "Assurance of Salvation" can be defined as *the believer's complete and unwavering confidence in God for the hope of eternal salvation.* It's a result of your genuine faith in Jesus as your Lord and Savior, as evidenced in your willingness to repent for the forgiveness of your sins and be redeemed from its eternal consequences (which include death and eternal separation from God). Because it is the total belief and inner confidence in Jesus, you have joy and peace in your heart that you are completely safe and secure in God no matter what. As such, assurance of salvation is the same with your "eternal security in Jesus."

Here are the preconditions: *You must be a genuine believer in Jesus Christ to have a genuine assurance of salvation.* In your life journey, there must be a point or day in your life you were "born again" spiritually. You had made a conscious decision that you've completely trusted Jesus as your Lord and Savior. After you've expressed your need for a Savior and asked for total forgiveness of your sins, you can also see the continuing transformation and change in your life and character of becoming like Jesus.

You don't have to be perfect. You just have to be a new creation where God is changing your life to be more like his Son Jesus. If there's no change in one's life, it is very difficult to confirm that a person is truly saved, because transformation is the strongest proof that someone is spiritually reborn in Jesus.

Let me point this out ahead. The phrase "assurance of salvation" is not found in the holy Scriptures, just like the words "Bible," "Trinity," and others. But it doesn't mean it does not exist or is not being taught in God's Word. This argument is also the same about the word "disciple" when it did not appear in the Epistles of Paul.

Firstly, assurance of salvation is not a feeling of arrogance or superiority. Foremost, God's gift of salvation is free and by his grace alone. You can only brag about the Giver, but you cannot brag about yourself. The reason is clear. According to apostle Paul, *"For **by grace** you have been saved **through faith**. And this is not your own doing; it is **the gift of God**, not a result of works, so that no one may boast"* (Ephesians 2:8-9). The truth is our salvation is an undeserved favor from God. It's all by his immeasurable grace. We benefit from it because he has given us the faith to believe in Jesus who suffered and died at the cross for our sins. We must remember that we're sinners, so no matter how hard we work, we're still short. We will never earn our salvation through personal effort or good works. So, if God gave us this precious gift of salvation, definitely, his purpose is true: Don't brag, but be humble and grateful.

Salvation

Not...		Is...
Own Doing		By Grace
Result of Works		Through Faith
Boast		Gift of God

Secondly, assurance of salvation is not a license to live in sin or practice disobedience. It's true. As long as we're in this world, we still commit sin. It does not cancel or revoke God's gift of salvation for you, but you cannot abuse his grace by practicing sin in your life. It's bothersome to hear someone say, "Once saved, always saved. Therefore, I'm free to sin." The truth is no genuine believer in Jesus can say, "Oh, since I became a Christian already and I'm saved forever, now I can do whatever sins I like doing and even more!" That's a delusion of the Devil. In John's words, *"Let no one deceive you"* (1 John 3:7)

In 1 John 3:4-6, John the Beloved was dealing with this misconception and false belief that crept in inside some churches. He said, *"Everyone who makes **a practice of sinning** also practices lawlessness; sin is lawlessness."* Here, John wrote to the believers that if someone keeps living in sin, it's tantamount to living in lawlessness. It is a common understanding for true believers when he said, *"You know that he [Jesus] appeared in order to take away sins, and in him there is no sin. **No one** who abides in him **keeps on sinning**; no one who **keeps on sinning** has either seen him or known him."* It means if you're a true believer in Jesus, you neither commit and enjoy habitual sins nor intentionally keep on disobeying God and not suffer the consequences. It's because Jesus came to destroy and none should enjoy sin.

John also further said, *"No one born of God makes a **practice of sinning**, for God's seed abides in him; and he **cannot keep on sinning, because he has been born of God**"* (1 John 3:9). This means if a person is truly born again, he will never deliberately live in sin. It does not mean a true believer cannot commit mistakes or sin. Have you noticed John's repeated phrase *"a practice of sinning"*? Why would Jesus suffer and die for our sins if he just wants us to do more of it? Assurance of salvation is not a free pass for doing what Jesus came to die for and paid the price.

So, why do some Christians still struggle with assurance of salvation? Most of the time, we do not know about assurance of salvation because no one taught about it or explained it to us. That's why discipleship is very important. However, even though we went through discipleship, from time to time, we have "self-doubts" about our salvation. Actually, it is normal in our spiritual journey to experience doubt temporarily. It is also normal to have questions in your faith for a moment. But you must also have the desire to find the answers to your questions. The big problem is when doubt stays longer in your heart and mind and is bothering you for a long time. Why do Christians doubt their salvation? What's the root cause for lack of eternal security?

If there's one big threat to your assurance of salvation, you'll likely find it here in apostle John's words: "*We know that everyone who has been born of God does not keep on sinning*" (1 John 5:18). It's known by experience that a true believer in Jesus does not continue to live a disobedient life and enjoy a sinful lifestyle. In the same way, *a believer who returns to a lifestyle of sin will certainly experience doubt* because sin has a deceptive power to weaken and break down anyone's faith.

Ask yourself. Why would anyone be confident about their eternal destiny if they know they are breaking God's heart? If you truly love God, why would you be self-assured if you left him as "your first love"? When a believer lives in sin, as well as willfully, decisively disobeys God, doubt will creep inside his or her heart and mind. Of course, how can you become confident in God's presence and say you have eternal security if you're acting like a disobedient child of God?

Recently, there is a trending movement going on in many progressive Christian circles. They call it "The Current Deconstruction of Christian Faith." It looks very philosophical and respectable because it seems to be working for some. The goal for them is to confront hard questions about your faith. Some have said they benefited from it. But some totally left their faith. It's like dismantling an engine, removing its parts, and when you begin to reconstruct it, you don't know how to do it. How much more if you try to operate a sick dog, sliced it open in your effort to save it, and when you try to close the wound, you know nothing about surgical operation?

Doubt drives deconstruction of faith. That phenomenon called "deconverted from Christianity" is very subtle but it's not new. There were, are, and will be professing Christians who left, are leaving, and will leave. Take a look at 1 John 2:19. "*They went out from us* [meaning they left the faith or the church]*, but they were not of us; for if they had been of us, they would have continued with us. But they went out, that it might become plain that they all are not of us.*" It's sad when someone you know has attended church, served in the ministry, led others to Christ, or preached but fell out of faith. True, some genuine believers may backslide, but if they have not returned to the fold until their death, apostle John is saying they are actually "*not of us*" in the first place, meaning these are not true or genuine believers in the first place. Just like Judas, he died in his unbelief even though he followed Jesus closely, but his faith was far from him.

You have two choices. If you struggle in your faith, you can use it to strive more, ascertain, embrace it, and become mature. Or if you struggle, you can run away and escape the test. But you may not know if you'll be able to get back on your faith until it's too late. In the first place, it's your responsibility to know if you actually do have it. Doubt will drive you closer to God or drive you away from him. Have faith and move from uncertainty to certainty.

Reflection:

What is your level of confidence in having an assurance of salvation right now? (1 being lowest and 10 being the highest)

    1   2   3   4   5   6   7   8   9   10

Is your assurance of salvation a license to sin? Why or why not? Explain it from the Word of God.

CHAPTER 9: HOW CAN YOU HAVE THE ASSURANCE OF SALVATION?

In answering the question above, we will also answer these questions: What are the Bible passages that teach about eternal security? And what are the benefits of having an assurance of salvation in your faith journey? Here are the things you must *know and apply* in your faith journey in order to have assurance of salvation as a new believer in Jesus. Or as a mature follower of Jesus, these action steps will strengthen your conviction about your eternal security.

First, have total faith in Jesus and his promised words. God's word is very clear. *"Now **faith is the assurance** of things hoped for, **the conviction** of things not seen"* (Hebrews 11:1). Without faith, it is impossible to have assurance of your total security in God. You must have faith that the eternal hope you're longing for in your heart, the total forgiveness of your sin and eternal life are yours forever when you trusted Jesus as your Lord and Savior. Do you remember the story of Jesus and Lazarus who died?

> *Jesus said to her* [Martha, Lazarus' sister], *"I am the resurrection and the life. Whoever believes in me, though he die, yet shall he live, and everyone who lives and believes in me shall never die. **Do you believe this?**" She said to him, "**Yes, Lord; I believe** that you are the Christ, the Son of God, who is coming into the world.""* (John 11:25-27)

Here, faith or belief in God through Jesus is the key to eternal life. It's not your personal ability because you do not have power to stop death, how much more give eternal life to yourself. You are not God. Without Jesus, there's no salvation and eternal security. Jesus twice said to Martha about whoever *"believes in me."* That's total faith in Jesus. You must believe in him for your salvation, and not to believe in yourself to attain it. Trust his *powerful words*, not your personal works.

Second, base your knowledge about eternal security on God's Word, not on your personal speculation or feelings. The truth is there's no such thing as your truth, only God's truth. John the Beloved wrote to Christian believers that their faith in Jesus is not a secret knowledge of truth but rather God's truth that they can personally know. He stated his purpose of writing his letter, "*I write these things to you who believe in the name of the Son of God, that you may know that you have eternal life*" (1 John 5:13). John used the word "know" to emphasize that eternal life is something we can know and perceive based on God's revelation and personal experience. It's not just solid information but it is biblical knowledge based on God's revelation, experience with God, and his ability to speak truth.

Biblically, assurance of salvation is not an emotional appeal and is not dependent on how you feel. Regardless of what people feel, God's truth stands on its own. That's why eternal security is *not a speculative theory but spiritual truth.* It's not an assumption or guessing game for you to play. Regardless of your opinion, God's truth is unchanging. What you don't know, you don't know. But what you already know, you should know more from the Scripture for God revealed it already. That's why everyone should read and study their Bible to know the essential teachings of assurance of salvation.

Third, remember that assurance of salvation is totally dependent upon having Jesus in your heart as a believer, and no one or nothing else. Many Christians are not sure about their eternal destination because they "add more things" to Jesus, instead of having Jesus alone for their salvation. It's Jesus +. The moment you entertain the idea that you can add and do something to gain more to what Jesus has done at the cross for your sins or believe in some creeds, sacraments, unbiblical traditions, etc., you will never have eternal security.

Some Christians grew up in some faith traditions that taught them to observe rituals and practices without asking serious questions whether these "rights of passages" are really means of salvation. Some workers are also negligent. They don't want to teach the assurance of salvation because they're afraid that believers will grow cold in their faith. So, for them, it's ok to teach nothing about eternal security because if the people think they can lose their salvation, then they'll be forced to work and be faithful, or perhaps give more financially.

56

There are sincere practices (some are true and some are sincerely wrong) but God's Word is true. The Bible said,

> *And this is the testimony, that **God gave us eternal life**, and **this life is in his Son**. **Whoever has the Son has life**; whoever does not have the Son of God does not have life.* (1 John 5:11-12)

There's only two sides here and nothing in between. Either you have Jesus or not. If you have Jesus, you have eternal life. If you don't have Jesus, you do not have eternal life. That's it. There's no middle ground. Your eternal destiny is all about Jesus. It depends on him alone. The only thing that matters now is: *Do you have him in your heart or not?*

If you have not trusted Jesus for your total salvation and repented of your sins, there's no assurance of salvation. But we must also understand that we have brothers and sisters in Christ who truly believe in Jesus as their Lord and Savior but do not adhere to the teaching of the Bible about eternal security. Does it make them "less Christian"? I would say, No. We still love them. You must love them, too, as your brothers and sisters in Jesus.

I would even dare to say that *your faith in the doctrine of eternal security does not determine your future salvation.* Not embracing the teaching of eternal security won't send you to hell. Why? If you truly believed in Jesus as your Lord and Savior and repented of your sins, that alone saves you from eternal death and the consequences of your sins, including your future sins. However, it makes a huge difference in your spiritual journey if you know and believe the holy Scripture that you are secure in Jesus. You will live more with joy and peace of mind knowing that you'll be with Jesus for eternity no matter what.

Fourth, be confident upon the abilities of both the Father and the Son to keep you as a believer secure forever. The teaching about assurance of salvation is based on the guarantee that both the Father *and* the Son are able to keep the believer forever. That's why assurance of salvation is not about your act of maintaining your salvation. It is an indication of your spiritual discernment to hear what Jesus said.

> *"My sheep hear my voice, and I know them, and they follow me. I give them eternal*

*life, and they will never perish, and **no one will snatch them out of my hand.** My Father, who has given them to me, is greater than all, and **no one is able to snatch them out of the Father's hand.**" (John 10:27-29)*

Jesus clearly stated that he gives eternal life to those who believe and truly follow him. He also assured that his true followers will not perish (see also John 3:16). Both he and the Father are holding the believers in their divine hands. Jesus is holding you when he said *"my hand."* But not only that, God the Father is also holding the believers in his hands. Jesus also emphasized twice that *"no one"* will be able to *"snatch them out."* That's his absolute declaration. Are we listening and believing in what Jesus is saying here?

Some Christians would even say, "Yeah, both the Father and Jesus are holding the believer, but *what if he or she will jump out* of God's hands and Jesus' hands?" Is this question silly? You might ask, why would someone do that, especially if you're a genuine believer? But remember that God has given human beings "the freedom of will," right? We're not a pre-programmed robot. We have the choice to obey or disobey or leave the faith. So, my question is *what made you think that God will let go of you if you do so?* If he said he won't let go, why would you think otherwise?

Fifth, understand that assurance of salvation is a supernatural and continuing work of God in you as a believer until it's complete. Most, if not all, believers started in their Christian journey not knowing about assurance of salvation. Does it mean eternal security does not exist? Of course, not! Whether we know it or not, it's still the truth. Obviously, those who shared the Gospel of Jesus were not able to teach the assurance of salvation immediately for some reasons. Most believers have just started their journey with the fact of being born again, having accepted Jesus and being saved. But in most cases, assurance of salvation comes next through Bible study, discipleship, and spiritual reflections. Understand what Paul said here. *"And I am sure of this, that **he who began a good work in you** will **bring it to completion** at the day of Jesus Christ"* (Philippians 1:16).

When Paul said, *"I am sure,"* that's talking about faith, a healthy confidence, assurance and certainty in God. Think of your spiritual journey. *Even before you met Jesus, God was already at work in your life.* He led you to him and gave you faith to believe in Jesus. You *may not know everything* about Christian faith but you are still saved when you believe and repent and ask for the forgiveness of your sins. The Bible teaches that God *"will"* (not maybe) *"bring to completion."* He is going to finish what he started doing inside of you. Now, do you believe that he is able to do this in your life? Paul's conviction is clear: *"I'm sure of this."* For him, there's no place for doubt. It's assurance, not arrogance.

Sixth, be convinced of the certainty of God's inseparable love for his children. The beauty of the biblical Christian faith is that it is humble enough to admit that we have nothing to brag about before God, but it is also confident that there are principles in this universe that stick to the end. Here's a divine revelation that will never change even if you like it or not. *"For I am sure that* **neither** *death nor life, nor angels nor rulers, nor things present nor things to come, nor powers, nor height nor depth, nor anything else in all creation,* **will be able to separate us from the love of God in Christ Jesus our Lord"** (Romans 8:38-39). Nothing in this world can separate you from God's love. And Paul once again affirmed, *"I am sure."*

We all know that life is full of uncertainties. But Paul also tells the early church, including us, that our faith is full of certainties. It's not because of our belief in faith itself, but because of God's promise and ability to stand on his word. Whatever possible reasons or assumptions anyone has in mind that is thought to separate God's children away from him, that reason does not exist. The truth is we are inseparable from God forever. If you have Jesus in your life, nothing in this world can separate you from his love—not now, not ever, not forever.

Seventh, keep in mind: Jesus promised to never cast away those whom God has given him. Many Christians struggle with the idea of eternal security because it's often difficult to separate their feelings and other emotional conditions from God's faithful and true promises. If you're in a relationship with another human being, it's really uncertain whether the person you're in love with will change or not in the future. That makes you vulnerable. But it is different with God. His character and nature are totally different.

Yes, he knows our unstable emotions but it doesn't change the absolute truth.

His words are rooted upon his perfect and powerful nature. So when he promises something, he will do everything to accomplish it. Reflect on these promises of Jesus to his disciples and the crowd of people who listened to him.

> *"**All that the Father gives me will come** to me, and whoever comes to me **I will never cast out.** For I have come down from heaven, not to do my own will but the will of him who sent me. And this is the will of him who sent me, that **I should lose nothing of all that he has given me,** but raise it up on the last day. For this is the will of my Father, that everyone who looks on the Son and believes in him should have eternal life, and I will raise him up on the last day."* (John 6:37-40)

In other words, Jesus welcomes all of those who believe and come to him. And for those who come and believe in the Son, they will have life everlasting. Even if they die, they will rise again on the resurrection day. But did you know that those who heard these words from Jesus had mixed responses? Some believed, some doubted, and some rejected it. As for you, however, your choice of response matters. If you are wondering whether Jesus will turn his back from you if you go to him, think again. *He said he will never ever cast anyone who comes to him in faith.* If you sense that God is leading you to Jesus, follow him.

Once you are in Jesus you also have to keep in mind that *he is not willing to lose a single person whom God has given him.* Even if we die (and someday we will and it's just a matter of time) Jesus will raise us up on the last day. Since we do not have personal power to raise ourselves from the grave, our eternal security rests upon Jesus. If Jesus promised this, is your faith increased enough to trust him to give you eternal life no matter what?

In all these reflections we've made from the Word of God, here are the important takeaways you must apply in your spiritual journey.

- *Affirm Jesus' certain promises of eternal life for you as a believer.* As you walk through this life towards your eternal destiny, stand on Jesus' promises, not on your personal feelings and opinions.

- *Build your full assurance in God through his Word.* The conviction on eternal security is taught in the Bible. Read, reflect, and remain in it at all cost. It will make a difference in your spiritual journey.

- *Come to Jesus if you have not really trusted him fully for your personal salvation.* If your doubt is lingering and getting longer, is it possible that you have not truly and fully trusted him as your Lord and Savior? There's nothing wrong with being sure.

- *Do not delay.* The longer you procrastinate, the more you will give the devil a foothold in your heart to plant seeds of doubt and destruction. The reason why a generation in Israel was cut off in their journey and not able to enter the Promised land was because of unbelief. Don't repeat the same mistake.

Let these words of Jesus sink in your heart and mind. *"Truly, truly, I say to you,* **whoever hears** *my word and* **believes** *him who sent me* **has eternal life.** *He does not come into judgment, but has passed from death to life"* (John 5:24). The overall purpose of assurance of salvation is to make our faith firm in Jesus for the glory of God. It's not to create a spiritual superiority complex. That should teach us humility. It is a testimony of God's faithfulness and credibility. Let your life journey and eternal destiny be a testament of God's glory.

Reflection:

Review the major verses on assurance of salvation. Memorize, especially, 1 John 5:11-12. How will you know if you have assurance of salvation?

In whose ability this assurance of salvation depends upon? In yours or in God and Jesus? Explain.

SECTION 4: READING YOUR MAP

*"Your word is a lamp to my feet
and a light to my path."*

~ King David (Psalm 119:105)

CHAPTER 10: THE WAY OF TRUTH OR TRADITIONS?

A story has been told many times about a little girl who asked her mother, "Mommy, why do you cut the ends off the meat before you cook it?" The girl's mother told her that she thought it added to the flavor by allowing the meat to better absorb the spices, but perhaps she should ask her grandmother since she always did it that way.

So the little girl finds her grandmother and asks, "Grandma, why do you and Mommy cut the ends of the meat off before you cook it?" Her grandmother thought for a moment and answered, "I think it allows the meat to stay tender because it soaks up the juices better, but why don't you ask your Nana, after all, I learned from her and she always did it that way."

The little girl is getting a little frustrated, but climbs up in her great-grandmother's lap and asks, "Nana, why do you cut the ends off the meat before you cook it?" Nana answered, "I don't know why these women do it, I did it because my pot wasn't big enough."

We all know that we have our own beliefs, customs, and practices inherited from one generation to another, as well as through our overall environment. Families have their little traditions to celebrate, like birthdays, anniversaries, Thanksgiving, Christmas, etc. Even schools have their own institutional traditions handed down to their students, like JS Prom, singing their school anthem, etc. Churches passed down beliefs and practices to their parishioners or congregants. Because of these long-held beliefs and practices, most people feel secure, peaceful, and content. As humans, it gives them a sense of being established, predictable, and confident because nothing would come as a surprise, threat, or disorderly. Not only that, they have a sense of long connection with the past.

While most, if not all, of us want to know "the truth" when we go to our teachers, doctors, lawyers, CPAs, and the like, ironically, many don't want to know the truth when it comes to their long-held beliefs and traditions. Most don't bother whether a tradition that's handed down to them by their religious leaders comes from Jesus and the holy Scriptures or not. It's ironic that when people hear things from their leaders, they do not ask questions about the truthfulness of their teachings and traditions. They are far more concerned about their temporal relief and customs through their traditions rather than their clear belief in the truth that would impact their souls and spirits, even eternal destiny.

Truth matters. Every true follower of Jesus should seek the truth, no matter what the cost. It's because in truth there is freedom. Jesus claimed that he is *"the Way, the Truth, and the Life"* (John 14:6). In our spiritual journey, Jesus is the pathway to salvation and freedom, the absolute truth we seek, and the abundant life we live. You may ask, *what is Jesus' view about the truth of the holy Scriptures and how did Jesus react to religious traditions?*

Whatever Jesus says and teaches about them is the truth. We should care more for our relationship with Jesus in spirit and in truth. As such, if our traditions are in conflict with the truth, what should we do? What would you do if you found out that your church tradition is inconsistent with or contradicting the Word of God? How would you respond if these traditions were "added" to the teachings of Jesus and proclaimed as coming from God but are actually not?

The Relationship Between the Truth and Tradition

In the long history of people's spiritual journey, even in Christian churches in its broadest sense, there are several views about the relationship between the truth and tradition. Here are the following:

- *Tradition is "Equal" to the Holy Scriptures.* Generally, many Christians believe that their church tradition is equal with the Word of God. Their church led them to assume and adhere that their "tradition" is tantamount to God's revelation and is on the same level as the holy Scriptures. Even if these traditions are not written or found in the Bible, these once added and institutionalized traditions are considered "divine" and equivalent to God's truth in the Scriptures and have to disregard their conscience. The adherents are not encouraged to question it. What's worse is that some of these traditions are even taught to save those who keep them and Jesus' completed work at the cross is not enough. This is an unbiblical view.

- *Tradition is "Above" the Holy Scriptures.* Some Christians believe that their tradition is above and beyond the holy Scriptures. This usually comes with an authoritative founder, leader, or angel with new revelations, secret teachings, and strange interpretations that are over-the-top of the Bible. More often than not, the followers of this view claim to believe in the Bible but are actually denying its truth. They claim that the Scripture was corrupted but will not tell you who, what, when, where, and how. If you ask them this question, "Let's say, if the Bible contradicts your religious textbook, which one will you believe and follow?" you'll hear that they will believe their "sacred" text rather than God's Word as an authority for faith and practice. Cults often do this by subjecting the Bible under their man-made beliefs and traditions. Again, this is another unbiblical view.

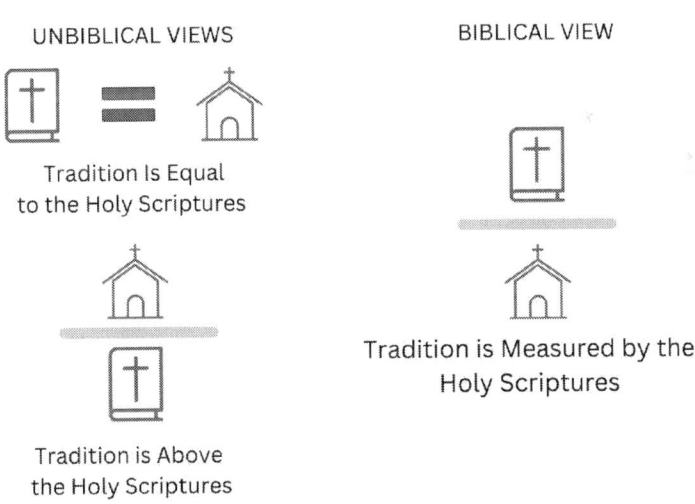

UNBIBLICAL VIEWS

Tradition Is Equal
to the Holy Scriptures

Tradition is Above
the Holy Scriptures

BIBLICAL VIEW

Tradition is Measured by the
Holy Scriptures

- *Tradition is "Measured" by the Holy Scriptures.* Some Christians believe that the Bible is the sole foundation for faith and practice. They hold that traditions must be measured by God's Word and Jesus, the Living Word.

There are traditions that are helpful in keeping you healthy spiritually, emotionally, physically, etc. Some of the examples are having regular family devotions on certain days of the week, prayer before meals, staying longer on Christmas day, spending Thanksgiving together, fasting regularly, among the few. However, no tradition or sacraments supersede or is equal to the Holy Scriptures. In fact, every tradition is re-evaluated whether it is consistent with God's Word or not. Whatever is wrong must be corrected, even stopped if it is unbiblical. Jesus wants his followers to be on this side when it comes to God's truth in relation to traditions.

During the time of Jesus, people practiced traditions and they did not know whether it was consistent with the truth and of God's commands or not. But as followers of Jesus, we must live in the truth. We cannot live to simply assume that everything we received and practiced is right and true from a biblical perspective, because it could hinder us in growing spiritually healthy. There's also a reason why tradition is called "tradition," because it has a tendency to stifle our relationship with God and, in the end, betray him (the Old French *tradicion* came from the Latin *traditio(n)*. Interestingly, this Latin root-word *tradere* does not only mean "to deliver" or "surrender." It also means "to betray"). Come to think of it. If the truth sets us free, it also means that anything that is not true, even if it's a long-held tradition, leads to bondages, especially if one holds these traditions as more important and superior than the Word of God. Tradition can be treacherous. We all must be discerning.

The Problem of Tradition

The truth is the most difficult people that Jesus had to deal with during his time here on earth were the hyper-religious and tradition-hardened leaders and people. A classic example in the Scriptures is found in Mark 7:1-13. It shows the key dynamics between the truth of God and traditions of men. Let's read it.

> *Now when the Pharisees gathered to him* [Jesus], *with some of the scribes who had come from Jerusalem, they saw that some of his disciples ate with hands that were defiled, that is, unwashed. (For the Pharisees and all the Jews do not eat unless they wash their hands properly,* **holding to the tradition of the elders,** *and when they come from the marketplace, they do not eat unless they wash. And* **there are**

many other traditions that they observe, such as the washing of cups and pots and copper vessels and dining couches.) And the Pharisees and the scribes asked him, "Why do your disciples not walk according to the tradition of the elders, but eat with defiled hands?"

The Gospel of Mark narrates that some Pharisees and scribes, who were religious leaders in Jesus' time, observed that his disciples were not observing an old-age tradition. Here, traditions are supposedly believed as some teachings and practices of their elders handed over with an unbroken chain of progression. It is quite interesting that Jesus' disciples were actually Jews themselves, and yet they seemed to have neglected washing their hands before they ate. Perhaps they did wash their hands but not in "the proper way" that religious Jews require in their ceremonies. But these religious leaders thought they were special and superior. They thought Jesus' disciples were not religiously educated enough or mature spiritually to have missed this particular hand-washing ritual. They must have considered them religiously unclean and unfit to serve in any path of sacred works for God. Jesus must have seen their disdain for his disciples and for him as their teacher. Jesus' words were revealing.

*And he [Jesus] said to them, "Well did Isaiah prophesy of you **hypocrites**, as it is written,*
*"This people honors me with **their lips**,*
*but their **heart is far** from me;*
*in vain do they **worship** me,*
*teaching as **doctrines** the commandments of men.'*

You might think Jesus was pretty tough and not compassionate here. But tough circumstances call for tough confrontations. Jesus quoted Isaiah 29:13 to point out the problems with traditions and rituals.

Firstly, traditions can lead people to hypocrisy. Many times, super-spiritual and ultra-conservative people easily hide in rituals with their lives left unchanged by the Gospel of Jesus. They think by doing the external actions and customary practices in performing their beliefs and traditions is enough to cover up their inner problems. But Jesus is more concerned about the change of heart rather than the conformity to man-made traditions.

Secondly, traditions can harden the heart, for over familiarity with it breeds contempt before God. Due to repetitions of rituals, prayers easily become lip-service devoid of meaning and sincerity. The longer the tradition has been held, it becomes superficially routine and ritualistic and not a heartfelt relationship with God.

Thirdly, traditions, when left unchecked, can lead to false worship. Oftentimes, traditions started as a meaningful attempt to make sense of the sacred or establish some regularity and security in people's spiritual walk. But many times, it deviates a little and the longer it goes and farther it moves, it often ends in idolatry. The ritual becomes the rule and God's Word becomes secondary. That's why traditions become vanity and idolatry as it becomes the divine authority.

Fourthly, traditions can be a form of legalism and a direct violation of God's commandments. For Jesus, when traditions become doctrines, it replaces the truth of God with the opinions of men. Some religious leaders would disregard God's laws with other "man-made" laws and traditions. Following a tradition that violates God's clear commands is an act of disobedience. The worst thing for a church to do is to remove God's commands and replace it with their traditions that overstep it. That is a form of apostasy, a renunciation of belief in God's truth. Jesus spoke of this departure from the truth due to tradition. Read carefully what Jesus revealed here.

> *You **leave** the commandment of God and **hold** to the **tradition** of men."*

> *And he said to them, "You have a fine way of **rejecting** the commandment of God in order to **establish** your **tradition**! For Moses said, 'Honor your father and your mother'; and, 'Whoever reviles father or mother must surely die.' But you say, 'If a man tells his father or his mother, "Whatever you would have gained from me is Corban"' (that is, given to God)—then you no longer permit him to do anything for his father or mother, thus **making void the word of God** by your **tradition that you have handed down**. And many such things you do."*

The Three Stages of Tradition Moving Away from the Truth

Here, apostasy–or the departure from God's truth–happens gradually. Jesus clearly pointed out the progressive departure in three stages in his following answer.

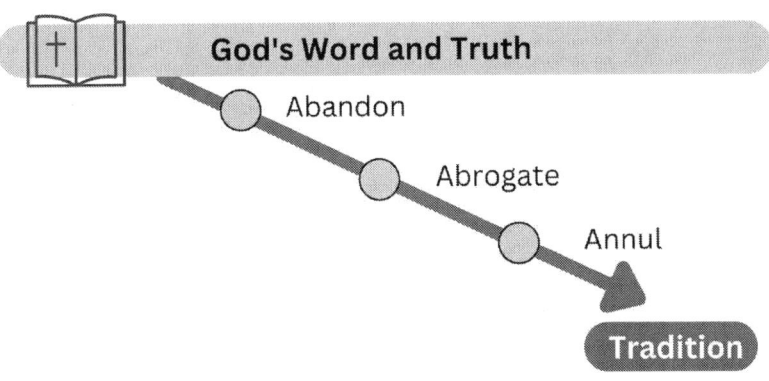

The first stage is to "Abandon" God's Truth for tradition. Jesus highlighted that these religious leaders and their people "left" God's commandment to follow and hold traditions not made by God. They even believe that God made these traditions, but they're not. The word *"leave"* (Greek *aphentes*) in verse 8 means to "abandon," "send away," or "leave alone." Because of their tradition, they let go of God's truth, disregarded his clear commands, and departed from his teachings. This word even meant they did not discuss these things with their people, instead they imposed them without any thought of the truth.

Not only that, these religious leaders "hold" or "cling" to man-made traditions. But we must take note that the word "hold" used here is very strong. It means "rule" or "master" (from *krateu*). They keep holding on to their traditions adamantly as if it is their master and ruler, instead of God as their final authority and Lord. That's already a sign of bondage that a person could not easily get out of.

The second stage is to "Abrogate" God's Truth for tradition. Jesus highlights the next stage when these religious leaders *"rejected"*–actually in original language "keep rejecting"–God's commandments which have been laid down in his

Word. The word *"atheteite"* in verse 9 means "to do away" or "set aside." There's a stage where they still believe that God's Word exists, but as they elevate their traditions, they set God's Word aside as if it is inferior to their man-made tradition.

In other words, God's authority was "made of no effect," and they "broke faith" with God's teachings and rule. In today's idea, it is tantamount to "cancel" God's truth in favor of "establishing" or "keeping" *(teresete)* human traditions. Jesus emphasizes here how these religious leaders "keep guard" or "watch over" their traditions to be unquestionably strictly observed by their followers. What happens next is tragic and is a point of no return.

The final stage is to "Annul" God's Truth at all. When Jesus confronted these religious leaders, he used the strongest word possible to describe their devotion to tradition rather than to God and his truth. In verse 13, Jesus pointed out how these religious leaders were finally *"making void the Word of God."* The Greek *akyrountes* or "making void," also means to "invalidate" and "revoke." In essence, these religious leaders and their followers considered God's Word as if it does not exist. Their tradition has become their ultimate authority and they revoked God's Word like it is a law of man that they have just invalidated as nothing.

The worst part of this stage is when those who have known the holy Scriptures would start berating and mocking it by making up stories that the Bible is full of error, contradictions, and falsehood. They will call the good God "a monstrous evil," "tyrant lawgiver" and so on. They would delude themselves into "proving" that God's Word is merely a human fabrication without divine authority. You should not wonder why there are those who were former or professing "Christians" who never experienced God's transforming power through His Word and they became adamant atheists, skeptics, and "deconversionsists."

For Jesus, however, traditions are NEVER "equal" to holy Scriptures, because the Scripture and its truth is far more superior.

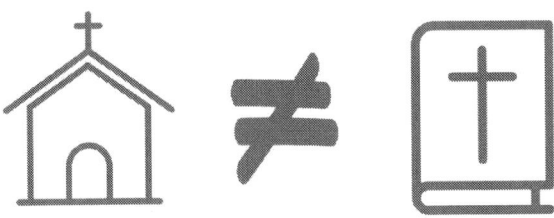

Traditions are NEVER Equal to the Holy Scriptures

Just imagine how religion or rituals can annul a relationship with God. In a deeper sense, Jesus emphasizes the sad reality of how these religious people made God's Word of "no authority" or "binding power" over their traditions. Instead, they made the holy Scripture as invalid and turned their traditions as divine authorities. This stage is where the Scripture is just a footnote to their doctrines and traditions. It's the ultimate cancel culture where what matters is long-held tradition without the love of truth, or worse, rituals apart from a personal relationship with God.

If this misuse and abuse of tradition and the annulment of God's Word has happened in Jesus' time, what makes us sure that it will not happen in the church? Is Jesus showing us here how his church will also experience spiritual departures in some ways where evil men, like wolves masquerading as harmless sheep, would mislead God's people by establishing traditions that blatantly disregards or twists the Scripture into their own beliefs and practices?

Listen to what Jesus said, *"Beware of **false prophets**, who come to you in sheep's clothing but inwardly are **ravenous wolves**"* (Matthew 7:15). These are the ones whom Jesus referred to as "workers of lawlessness" who annulled God's laws and made their own laws and traditions (see verse 23). The same is true for the apostle Paul. After his missionary journeys, he bade farewell to the elders of the churches in Ephesus city. He echoed what Jesus warned. *"**I know** that after my* *departure fierce wolves will come in among you, not sparing the flock; and from among your own selves will arise men speaking twisted things, to draw away the disciples after them"* (Acts 20:29-30). The goal of false teachers is always to deceive true disciples of Jesus and impose unbiblical teachings.

If you're not convinced that these things could happen in the church, you can also read what Peter himself wrote, just a few years after Jesus ascended to heaven. Here's what he wrote probably 67-68 AD in 2 Peter 2:1-3.

> *But false prophets also **arose among the people**, just as there will be **false teachers** among you, who will **secretly bring in destructive heresies**, even **denying the Master** who bought them, bringing upon themselves swift destruction. And many will follow their sensuality, and because of them **the way of truth will be blasphemed**. And in their **greed** they will exploit you with **false words**. Their condemnation from long ago is not idle, and their destruction is not asleep.*

Yes, we all have our own traditions and rituals or have been exposed to them through our families, religion, or culture. But these traditions, be it customs and teachings that have been handed down from generation to generation must be reviewed from the holy Word of God. Based on the apostle Peter's statement above, we can ask the following questions about the traditions we have.

- Who made or developed this certain tradition and when did such tradition start? Is this tradition made to cater to the greed of its makers by using deceitful words and practices or it advances God's kingdom agenda?

- Is this tradition claiming to be the "truth" replacing the Bible or does it subverts the Scriptures and denies Jesus' authority?

- What are the effects of this tradition? Is it to build spiritual growth or break the lives and faith of disciples of Jesus by subjecting it to old traditions? Does it enslave people to follow the rules and legalism but not develop intimacy of relationship with God?

The question, does history repeat itself? If so, what do you need to do? It seems inevitable that traditions will happen. In fact, there will always be traditions that can and will be made.

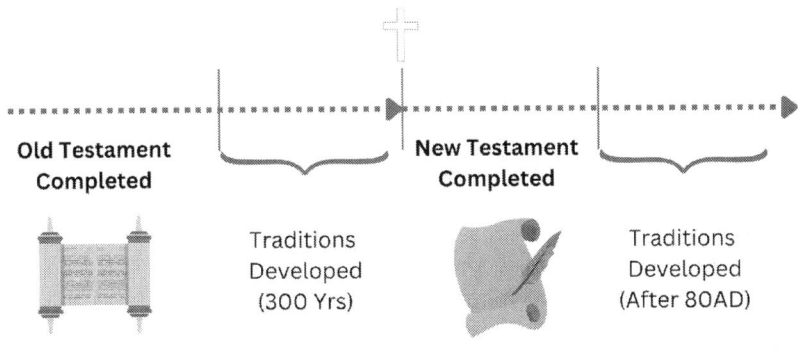

When the Old Testament books (e.g. books of Laws, Prophets, and Writings) were completed, religious traditions developed after it. That's approximately within the 300 years in between the book of Malachi, the last book of the Old Testament, and Jesus' time. Before Jesus ascended to heaven, roughly 33 AD, he verbally taught his disciples and these eyewitnesses began telling and spreading the good news through word-of-mouth for years. So, yes, traditions do exist. There was a point in time of Christianity that it went through the "oral traditions" because the New Testament was not yet written and completed. It means Jesus verbally passed his message and teachings to his apostles who were first-hand witnesses, and they also did the same process of verbally transmitting the gospel to the first generation Christians.

In one of the early letters of Paul, he mentioned this unwritten process when he said, "*To this he* [God] *called you through our gospel, so that you may obtain the glory of our Lord Jesus Christ. So then, brothers, stand firm and hold to **the traditions** that you were **taught by us**, either by our **spoken word** or by our letter*" (2 Thessalonians 2:14-15). As one of the eyewitnesses of Jesus, Paul encouraged the believers to stand and hold their grounds spiritually upon the true teachings that had been handed to them by Jesus who ascended to heaven and entrusted the gospel to them. He even said to these believers of Jesus, "*Now we command you, brothers, in the name of our Lord Jesus Christ, that you keep away from any brother who is walking in* *idleness and not in **accord with the tradition that you received from us***" (2 Thessalonians 3:6).

However, when the first generation eyewitnesses of apostles and disciples were growing old and dying, and some strange words, teachings, and stories began to proliferate among churches, there was an urgent need to write and preserve everything they know that's true and correct the false teachings and doctrines that penetrated the church. The apostle Peter and Paul led the way. As such, by the power of the Holy Spirit, the New Testament books were written, fully completed, and compiled not later than 80 AD, with few years of "oral history" and "tradition" before it. By then, it was easy to correct the false teachings because the eyewitnesses were still alive until the New Testament was completed. But when the Bible was completed, it concluded that there was no need for more "revelations." The apostle John warned us not to "add" or "take away" anything from it (Revelation 22:18-19).

Practical Action Steps: The biggest challenge is after 80 AD, history repeats itself. Will you stand and hold your ground like Jesus did? Or will you find yourself being confronted by Jesus and his Word? Nonetheless, here are some action steps you can take.

Read your Bible and be open to receive and reexamine what was taught for you to believe. We all have our own set of beliefs and practices. That's a given. Do not assume that everything you got is simply ok. Even in this study itself, you must examine it and read the Scripture if what is being said here is consistent with God's Word. When the disciples of Jesus in Berea heard the apostle Paul, "*they **received the word** with all eagerness*," but it didn't stop there.

According to Luke, the writer of Acts, they were also, "***examining the Scriptures daily to see if these things were so***" (Acts 17:11). It doesn't matter if it was Paul or not, they check everything with the Scripture. Be like them. Do your homework. Study the Scripture and not just rely on your received teachings and traditions. Christianity is more than just a religion of rituals. It is a transformative relationship with Jesus.

Be diligent in studying God's Word and truth, because it sets you free and sets you apart for God's purposes. Traditions can be tricky. Many times people equate them with the truth. But if you want to know and build your life on the truth, build it on God's Word. The apostle Paul encouraged his protege, Timothy, with these words, *"**Do your best to present yourself to God** as one approved, a worker who has no need to be ashamed, rightly handling **the word of truth**"* (2 Timothy 2:15). The King James Version translates this as *"Study to shew thyself approved unto God."* Indeed, when you study God's Word, you must be focused, you pay attention, and be diligent in doing it. Let God's Word be God's Word– and let it speak to you.

Be discerning in identifying any false teachings and traditions that keep people in spiritual bondages. The apostle Paul warned believers that human tradition can lead you away from the truth and enslave people to set them in bondage if they are not careful. He exhorted the believers in the city of Colossae. *"See to it that **no one takes you captive** by philosophy and empty deceit, according to **human tradition**, according to the elemental spirits of the world, and not according to Christ"* (Colossians 2:8). The picture here is like a group of people who have fallen victim and chained as spoils of war. There is a spiritual warfare here.

Traditions have spiritual powers; they could enslave you if you keep doing them in violation of God's commands. The worst thing that could happen is when those who believe in Jesus will embrace a different gospel that is unChristlike, unChristian and unbiblical. Instead of God dispensing his grace to his people, many would create and cling to traditions as means of God's grace. That could be considered "another gospel" or a false gospel like the one that Paul firmly opposed when he said,

> *I am astonished that you are so quickly deserting him [God] who called you in **the grace of Christ** and are **turning to a different gospel**—not that there is another one, but there are some who trouble you and want to **distort the gospel of Christ**. But even if we or an angel from heaven should preach to you a gospel contrary to the one we preached to you, **let him be accursed**. As we have said before, so now I say again: If anyone is preaching to you a gospel contrary to the one you received, **let him be accursed**.* (Galatians 1:6-9)

Have you noticed how serious Paul was when it comes to keeping you on track in your spiritual journey and not be diverted to another way? Why is Paul so emphatic in declaring to the false teachers to let them "*be accursed*" (meaning, you don't need to curse them because they already are)? Is it because some would claim to be "messiah" who demands following or even an angel who appeared and preached another gospel, teachings, and revelations in order to form new groups and traditions? Some would also self-appoint themselves as new apostles of Jesus and proliferate strange doctrines and practices. You have to watch out.

Be careful if any tradition becomes your identity because if it is, it indeed becomes your idol. If you're a Christian, you are who you are because of Christ, not because of your religion, church, tradition, work, habits, or what have you. Any teachings and traditions that deviate and contradict the Word of God and tend to replace God in your heart, they must be cross examined and corrected. Whatever Jesus is silent about, it is something non-essential and inconsequential, meaning these are not very important.

Lots of people put value to their traditions. These things must be compared, critiqued, and measured based on Jesus' explicit statements and teachings. For every disciple of Jesus, every tradition, belief, and practices must be seen through the Holy Word of God and must be measured by it. You don't turn them into your idols.

Don't build your own tradition at the detriment of your personal spiritual growth. Establishing a spiritual habit, like reading the Bible, prayer, evangelism, etc., no matter how good it is, it does not have to become a mindless ritual, heartless routine, or personal tradition that would enslave you. You can avoid starting "*in the spirit*" and ending "*in the flesh*" by keeping your spiritual rhythms in check (Galatians 3:3). That's why it's necessary to have spiritual evaluations regularly in order to see if you're turning any tradition as your own truth. Then, you can correct if you're moving away from your relationship with God and make a u-turn while you can.

Friend, whatever has been transmitted to you, whether these are something like passed-on costumes and beliefs handed from generation to generation, these traditions have a "theology" behind it. These are not harmless ones. A tradition turned into a doctrine is believed to have divine authority even though these are not established in holy Scripture nor explicitly taught by Jesus. Oftentimes, these traditions are based on obscure passages that can easily be twisted. You must understand that traditions are not always true. They may have begun with "a spark of truth" but along the way of passing it from one generation to another, lies and falsehood crept in and those who were naive or gullible will just assume that it's still the same truth in the beginning.

Jesus knew how deeply rooted the Jewish people were. If you believe you're traditional enough, think again. The problem of holding on to human traditions without knowing the truth can be resolved. As Jesus spoke to the Jewish believers, "*If you abide in my word, you are truly my disciples, and you will know the truth, and the truth will set you free*" (John 8:31-32). If you want to remain in God's truth, abide in God's Word. That's the only way for you to become a faithful, free, and fruitful follower of Jesus.

Reflection:

Why should every disciple measure their received traditions based on the truthfulness of God's Word?

What was the attitude of Jesus in dealing with traditions that do not stand and follow God's Word? And how does that impact you?

CHAPTER 11: WHY DO YOU NEED TO READ THE BIBLE?

Have you ever been to vacation spots or other countries that's totally unfamiliar to you? How about when you moved yourself or your family into this country? For me, I love traveling. I left my family and hometown when I was 16 and traveled to Manila for three days and nights. I remember that day, when I packed my only military bag with a few clothes, a Bible, and no ticket to go home. Since then, I've been to places I never thought I'd go, like the island paradise of Palawan, Batanes, Maui, and so on; or flew to foreign countries like Hong Kong, Hawaii, Macau, China, Malaysia, Korea, Israel, Jordan, Egypt, or North America.

I know many of us were not born on this side of the world or place. But even when we talk about local trips, we move from familiar to unfamiliar places. What do we usually do, especially in those rest areas along the highways? We get our travel guides or check our GPS to get information about this new place we're entering. I like this quote from George Guthrie in his article "How to Read and Study the Bible,"

> "Think for a moment about a trip you have taken. You left home, traveled to your destination, and had various memorable experiences. Perhaps you experienced a culture different from your own and found that the greater the cultural differences between home and destination, the greater the effort needed to communicate and to learn in your new environment. Yet you persevered, experienced new people and places, and were enriched by it all."

In our spiritual journey, our travel guide is the Word of God, which is also called the "Holy Scriptures" or "the Holy Bible." We know that we live in this darkened world. We cannot afford to walk through this life without a spiritual light. King David realized this a long time ago when he said, "***Your word*** *is a lamp to my feet and* ***a light to my path***" (Psalm 119:105). Indeed, God's Word is your eternal street light. You won't walk in the dark for his supernatural light is with you wherever you go.

Without the Word of God, we have a very difficult journey ahead. We risk getting lost or, worse, we would find ourselves walking in a midnight road without light and no direction. Just imagine what would happen to you if you walked on a mountain trail in the darkest night without a flashlight or any form of light. Pray that you have a night-vision goggle or you'll simply stumble and fall.

The problem that we have today is: we've been bombarded by so much to watch, read, and hear that our minds have become numb to the overload of information. That's the biggest problem of the Information Age. Our brains could no longer process anything because it falsely appears we know everything. And we wonder, are we just some mindless consumers of every bit of information we see on this small screen on our phones? Or why should I add the Bible to this endless stream of data? Honestly, you may ask, *what will I benefit from reading the Bible?*

Reading the Bible is important for the following reasons:

First, the Bible is the most important and powerful book to read in this world. The Bible is God's book. He speaks through it. In the past, God's people, including lots of theologians today, believe that the origin of the Bible is God. This conclusion is not just a speculation by some men who conspired to elevate the Scripture but the Bible itself testifies that the Holy Spirit played an important role in its writing process. There is an inherent divine power in it in revealing God and the things of God in order to transform lives. The apostle Peter pointed it out. *"For no prophecy was ever produced by the will of man, but **men spoke from God as they were carried along by the Holy Spirit**"* (2 Peter 1:21).

The Bible was written for more or less 1500 years by 40 human authors with different professions with one singular theme, which is the continuing, redemptive story of God from the beginning (in Genesis) to eternity (in Revelation). And the single thread that binds it together is Jesus Christ, the Son of the Living God and Savior of the World.

The Bible is so important that it's translated into more than 1,500 languages and studied by more scholars than any books in this world. But it is more than just a literary genius or classic literature. To great lengths, the Bible is the most impactful book in the world as a whole. You can visit the Museum of the Bible in Washington DC and realize that the Bible is "the" foundation of civilization. It highly influenced governments, laws, arts, media, economics, leaders in history, and so on. Did you know that many Ivy League universities started as "Bible schools" because of their religious roots? Harvard, Yale, Princeton, Brown, Dartmouth, and University of Pennsylvania, were all founded as religious schools, but eventually became secular and lost their mission. Nonetheless, despite all these unfortunate departures, it tells the Bible is, indeed, powerful and influential in influencing the world.

THE HOLY SCRIPTURES

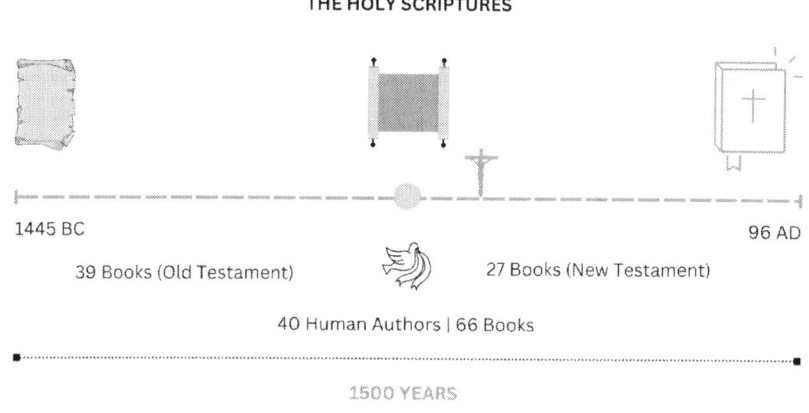

1445 BC

39 Books (Old Testament)   27 Books (New Testament)

40 Human Authors | 66 Books

96 AD

1500 YEARS

The Bible is also the most read book and written about. That's why it's called "The Book of all books," because countless books, journals, and other documents have been written about it, like classics, commentaries, inspirational novels, cultural critiques, and so on, not to mention all the preachings and Bible studies around the world every moment. There is no other book more important, more influential, more transformational, and more powerful than the Bible. If you're not reading it, you're missing an important part of history. Literally, you're missing a lot in your life if you're not reading and meditating on it. But the Bible is more than just a piece of history. It is one of the greatest gifts of God to humanity and for you as an individual. Don't take it for granted. Cherish and treasure it by reading and applying it for yourself.

Second, the Bible stood the test of time because it is eternal and true. The French philosopher, Voltaire (1694-1778), allegedly predicted, "One hundred years from my day, there will not be a Bible on earth except one that is looked upon by an antiquarian curiosity-seeker." While the exact quotation couldn't be found in his voluminous writings, similar claims or variations of indictments from him did exist. Fifty years later, after his death, his very house where he wrote most of his blasphemous writings against the Bible and Christianity became the Evangelical Society of Geneva's storehouse for Bibles. The Scriptures shouldn't be scoffed.

Jesus said, *"Heaven and earth will pass away, but **my words will not pass away"*** (Matthew 24:35). It means God's Word is everlasting. It will last far longer than this universe. Even if the world as we know will cease to exist, God's Word continues to exist. Whatever promises it gave, it will be accomplished; whatever prophecies it revealed, it will come to pass. Theologians and scholars agree that the Bible is eternal because it is the Word of God. Its origin is God, not merely human wisdom. That is why it is timeless. So many attempted to abolish, burn, and destroy the Bible, but it remains indestructible. It stands the test of time.

Think about today. Will the politically correct culture be able to cancel or censor the Bible? Is "cancel culture" forever, or is it just a culture that changes, just like the Enlightenment era that Voltaire enjoyed in mocking the Bible? Did you know that there were already a lot of attempts in history to ban and burn the Bible, but they all failed. Why? It's because the Bible is the eternal, timeless, and indestructible Word of God. Civilizations come and go, but the Word will stand. Cultures change but God's message through the Bible remains constant. Here's what Gordon Fee and Douglas Stuart said in *How to Read the Bible for All Its Worth*,

> Because the Bible is God's message, it has eternal relevance; it speaks to all humankind, in every age and in every culture. Because it is the word of God, we must listen — and obey. But because God chose to speak

his word through human words in history, every book in the Bible also has historical particularity; each document is conditioned by the language, time, and culture in which it was originally written (and in some cases also by the oral history it had before it was written down). Interpretation of the Bible is demanded by the "tension" that exists between its eternal relevance and its historical particularity.

Third, the Bible shows you how God revealed himself for us because the 66 books in the Bible are equally inspired by God or "God-breathed." What does *"inspired by God"* mean? Is the Bible like those inspirational and motivational books? The answer is "no." The idea of the Bible as *"inspired by God"* is found in the Bible itself. *"All Scripture is breathed out by God"* (2 Timothy 3:16). The King James Version translates *"All scripture is given by* **inspiration of God.**" In Greek, "inspiration" means the Bible is *"God-breathed"* (*"theopneustos"* = *"theo"* or God + *pneustos* or "breath," "wind," "spirit," and this later word is the root word of *pneumatics*). This expression reveals the divine origin and nature of the Scriptures. Of course, during the time of the apostle Paul, the "all scriptures" here refer to the Old Testament.

The first generation Christians were very much familiar with the stories and teachings of Jesus and were retelling these stories to others. The need to write these stories and teachings emerged as many of them were dying. Later, Jesus' disciples would write the Gospels, Acts, the general Letters, and Revelation for the churches and leaders. Before the end of 90 AD, all these books were already written and were used in most Christian churches.

The early church, through the guidance of the Holy Spirit, recognized these books that became the collection of the New Testament. But as the years went by and the church grew fast in all known world at that time, some forgeries and false writings came out and crept into some churches. So the early Christians responded and reacted to it. They have to identify which books are truly "inspired" and coming from God and keep them, and take out those that are not and discard them. This long process went on for two centuries until there's great need to fully recognize which books are part of the inspired canon or list of sacred Scriptures, along with the Old Testament.

In the Council of Hippo (Africa, AD 393) Christian church leaders identified, recognized and affirmed the 66 books (39 books in the Old Testament and 27 books in the New Testament) as the whole collection of the holy Scriptures. One hundred years later, that decision was reaffirmed in the Council of Carthage (AD 397). How did they do it? By identifying every book's inherent power as "God-breathed." Yes, they identified the truthfulness of its content, the credibility of each book's authorship, and its continuing use in Christian churches since the earliest period, but they also identified its transforming power coming from God.

Fourth, the Bible tells you what you need to know and believe about God, the world, humanity, and Jesus. As we continue to read 2 Timothy 3:16-17, it says, "*All Scripture is breathed out by God and **profitable for teaching**, for **reproof**, for **correction**, and for **training** in righteousness, that the man of God may be complete, equipped for every good work*" (2 Timothy 3:16-17). In other words, the Bible helps us to know about what to believe, and what not to believe. We measure every teaching and tradition by the standard of the Scripture. That's why *the Bible is the sole authority for our faith and practice.* Whatever the Bible teaches, we teach; whatever it reveals, we believe; whatever it commands, we do.

When the Bible is said to be "profitable," it's not about financial gains. It is about its *usefulness* and *advantages*. Some of the great uses and benefits in reading, knowing, understanding, and applying the Bible are the following:

- **Teaching** - It means "instruction" or applied teaching *didaskalia*, see also 1 Timothy 1:10; 4:6,13; 5:17; 6:1,3). It is referring to Christian doctrine. The Bible teaches us the truth and helps us in discerning false teachings about God, Jesus, humanity, salvation, and so on. Because the Bible is the Word of Truth, we can discern, identify, and refute what are considered false teachings, false Gospels, unbiblical traditions, including demonic teachings (1 Timothy 4:1). Above all, everything we essentially believe in must be taught from the Bible.

- **Reproof** - This word means the Scripture is useful for "inner conviction." The Bible makes an objective basis for "persuasion" or what to approve and disapprove in our culture. For example, we must know the difference between loving people and reproving behaviors that are not consistent with the will of God. Loving people in the truth does not mean we affirm everything. A parent loves their child but it doesn't mean he approves of the wrongs they did.

- **Correction -** *Epanorthosis* literally means "setting straight (right) again," or "reformation." Through the Scriptures, we can do course correction in our journey if we lose our way. We also correct our wrong notions and ideas based on the Word of God objectively. Even in the church, we must be willing to be corrected. Again, the reason why parents correct their children is not because they hate them but because it is wrong. To some extent, this word also covers the restoration, even improvement of life and character.

- **Training -** This versatile word originally means "the rearing of a child" (*paideia*), "discipline," or "training." Sometimes, it refers to "chastisement" or "discipline" (Hebrews 12:5-11). However, when properly used in Christian life, it is about the entire training and education for the cultivation of the soul and core values. Hence, the Bible is our training manual for living, leadership, and everything in life's growth and spiritual health. That's why those who want to become leaders must become trained learners. They have to be developed and equipped to do the task.

These are just some of the key benefits we gain if we make the Holy Scripture as the map of our life journey and the sole foundation of our faith and practice. If you want to know the essentials of our faith in God, the Bible should be our source. Whatever teachings you know, it must be measured by the Word of God.

The ultimate purpose, however, is not to get more information, but for the transformation of the person. Here, Paul clearly emphasized the purpose: *"that the man of God may be complete, equipped for every good work"* (v.17). We must be ready to be equipped for the work of the Lord and the Scripture plays a vital role in every way or process, no matter what.

Fifth, the Bible teaches you how to live and grow mature as a follower of Jesus. In his book, *Final Word: Why We Need the Bible*, pastor-author John

MacArthur highlights the role of the Bible as "the catalyst of spiritual growth." If you're a follower of Jesus, you cannot separate the Scripture from your spiritual walk. It is your guidebook on how to have a personal relationship with God through Jesus. It shows us the story of God who loves people, not just how to get to heaven and be with him as our final destination. The Bible is our constant guide. As Paul said to Timothy,

> *But as for you, continue in what you have learned and have firmly believed, knowing from whom you learned it and how from childhood you have been **acquainted with the sacred writings**, which are **able to make you wise for salvation through faith in Christ Jesus**.* (2 Timothy 3:15)

This truth is the major reason why we use the Bible as the main source of our learning in spiritual habits, rhythms, and disciplines. If you want to learn more on how to pray, worship, evangelize, forgive, and so on, you need to go back to the Bible for a strong foundation. Even if we want to keep knowing God, the Gospel and how to communicate it, or trusting God and living in obedience and purity, all of these, and more, are in the Scriptures. It shows you the will of God so that you grow and become mature in your faith-walk. On top of these things, the Scripture will keep you from sinning. Read and reflect on what King David said.

> *How can a young man keep his way pure?*
> *By guarding it according to **your word**.*
> ***I have stored up your word in my heart,***
> ***that I might not sin against you.*** *(Psalm 119:9, 11)*

You cannot live a holy life without the Holy Bible. One of the major reasons why atheists don't like the idea of God is because they know that if there's God who revealed himself through his Word, they will be held accountable for their lifestyles. But as Christians, we're not making God in our own imaginations. We allow the Scripture to shape our beliefs and behaviors. We believe and follow Jesus to be like him. It's us becoming Christlike and we can only achieve that through the power of God's Word. As such, we need to learn how to make the Word of God an essential part of our lifestyle as Jesus followers.

Take this prayer of Jesus for you and meditate on it. "*Sanctify them in the truth;*

your word is truth" (John 17:17). Jesus set you apart to follow and serve him. If you want to serve God, you must be sanctified in the truth. This truth is the Word of God. Read it.

Reflection:

What is your level of knowledge and understanding about the Bible right now? (1 being lowest and 10 being the highest)

1   2   3   4   5   6   7   8   9   10

From what you have learned so far about the importance of the Holy Scriptures, what is God teaching you about it? And how are you going to apply it in your life?

CHAPTER 12: HOW WILL I READ THE BIBLE REGULARLY?

In January 2019, Lifeway Research did an online survey of 2,500 Protestant and non-denominational church goers about their consistency in reading the Bible. It is part of the Discipleship Pathway Assessment study where Bible reading is one of the most predictive aspects for spiritual maturity. They found out that consistent reading of the Bible helps a person become more Christlike in their lives.

This instructive part is a simple overview only. Definitely, if anyone wants to know how to read and study the Bible, that would require extensive training. I highly recommend Gordon Fee and Douglas Stuart's other book *How to Read the Bible Book by Book: A Guided Tour.* But this part should be a good start for you to start feeding yourself with the Word of God, grow spiritually healthy, and become a mature believer and follower of Jesus.

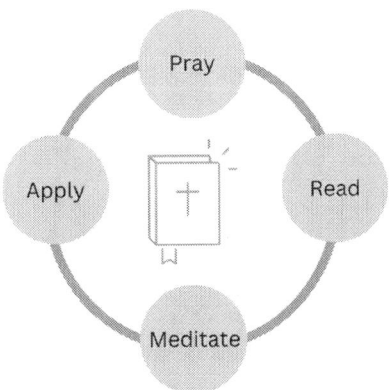

First, pray for your spiritual appetite. A Christian who lives without regularly feeding their soul and spirit with the Word of God becomes spiritually sluggish and stagnant in their life journey. Their journey is compared to walking on a treadmill. They plod for long and become tired in the end, but they are still on the same spot. Spiritually speaking, without spiritual food, we walk with an empty stomach and could become malnourished in the long run. We know travelers collapse because they lack sustenance. That should not happen to you spiritually speaking.

The Word of God said, "*Man does not live by bread alone, man* **lives** *by* **every word that comes from the mouth of the LORD**" (Deuteronomy 8:3b). Even Jesus quoted and reaffirmed this principle in Matthew 4:4. "*It is written, 'Man shall not live by bread alone, but by every word that comes from the mouth of God.'*" Both in the Old and New Testament, the Word of God is the food for your soul. Prophet Jeremiah spoke about this when he said, "**Your words** *were found, and* **I ate them**, *and your words became to me a joy and the delight of my heart*" (Jeremiah 16:16). It's not that he ate the scroll or that you'll eat the pages of your Bible, but it means you feed your soul and spirit like you cannot live without it. If you try to live apart from God's Word, you're only doing yourself total harm spiritually. Why won't we pray for spiritual appetite? As King David once said,

> *Blessed is the man*
> *who walks not in the counsel of the wicked,*
> *nor stands in the way of sinners,*
> *nor sits in the seat of scoffers;*
> *but his delight is in the law of the LORD,*
> *and on his law he* **meditates** *day and night.* (Psalm 1:1-2)

This passage means taking pleasure in meditating upon the Word of God. However, have you ever noticed how you suddenly feel tired, sleepy, or sluggish when you're attempting to read the Bible? If the Word of God is a spiritual food, do you think the Devil will just sit down and do nothing to stop you from reading and meditating on it? He would rather feed people with junk food than the real food from God. So always remember. If you want to read the Bible regularly like you feed yourself regularly, prepare your heart and mind before reading the Bible. How?

- Pray a simple prayer to make your heart and mind open to what God is telling or teaching you today.

- Ask the Holy Spirit to give you wisdom and discernment in knowing and understanding the holy Scriptures. He is the ultimate author of it.

- Let that prayerful attitude remain in you as you read God's Word with humility and thanksgiving.

Second, set a quiet time alone with God to read the Bible. Meditating upon the Word of God is an ancient practice. It's not new. Godly men and women in the past and present disciplined themselves   in intently reading the Bible. Read Joshua 1:8.

> *"This Book of the Law* shall not depart from your mouth, but you shall *meditate on it day and night,* so that you may be careful to do according to all that is written in it. For then you will make your way prosperous, and then you will have good success."

In reading the Bible, there are simple matters to consider. Here are the following:

- *Time* - If there's one person who knows what's the best time for you to read your Bible regularly, it's YOU. For some, the time is in the morning, for others, it's evening, but for some, it's in between breaks to connect with God. You decide what's the best time for you. The most important thing is that you can do it consistently.

- *Place* - Look for a quiet place where you can be alone with God. However, if you're comfortable in a cafe, it's ok as long as you can have time with God and focus. It may be your room, kitchen, garden, a park, and any other place that may serve your purpose. For many of us who have kids, families, and friends, or co-employees in the workplace, finding a good spot for quiet and reflection may be challenging. But you can be creative in choosing your venue for devotion.

- *Tools* - It is valuable if you have a journal notebook and pen or electronic notepad to write your thoughts and reflections. Take notes or pictures through your phones. The same thing to do in preaching in order to remember what you've learned. If you have a 1-Year Bible reading plan, choose the passage, chapter or paragraph and read between 4-5 minutes. It's also ok to have a devotional book, but it is only a supplement. Go directly to the Bible and don't replace it. The most important thing is to monitor your schedule and be consistent.

- **Bible -** One of the best ways of doing your Bible reading is to choose a single book, like John, Mark, Proverbs, etc. But if you want to start small, then begin with 1 John, Romans, Galatians, Philippians, and the like. Once you're set, pray before you read your Bible. Be still and ask the Holy Spirit to enlighten you as you read the Bible. Regarding which version or translation, use what's good for you and easy to read. I used to read the Bible in the King James Version during elementary and high school years. Then I used the New International Version. Currently, I'm using the ESV-English Standard Version. If you like to do some variety, like I do, you can use a vernacular Bible.

Third, meditate. If we continue reading Joshua 1:8, take note of the emphasis: *"This Book of the Law shall not depart from your mouth, but you shall **meditate on it day and night"*** (v.8a). To "meditate" (from Hebrew *hagah*) means to "moan" or "growl" (like expressing inarticulate words) or "ponder," which is a careful thinking process before you make a decision or reach a conclusion (Psalm 1:2). In its old form, it means "to muse" (or be absorbed in thought) "to speak," "to utter" (Psalm 37:30), "to declare" (Psalm 35:28) or even "to devise" a plan. When you meditate upon God's Word, you think deeply and focus your mind for a certain period of time. The purpose of meditation is often spiritual; that's why we don't take it lightly.

When you meditate upon the Word of God, you read slowly and not in a hurry. Observe the basic reading and meaning of the text of who, what, when, where, and how. However, as a beginner, don't be bogged down by the details. You can summarize the whole passage in your own words. Then, move deeper to connect the Word with your heart and spirit.

- Ask questions like *who is God here?* Or *who is Jesus in this passage?*

- *Is there something that the Holy Spirit is showing or teaching me here? What is it?*

- Prayerfully think and ask, *is there something here that God wants me to know, learn, and be grateful for? Is God speaking to me through this passage?*

Trust the process of meditating upon the Scripture. Why? It's because the Word of God powerfully works in itself, even without our intervention. It speaks to our innermost being when we are open and receptive to it. That's why we can rely on the Bible. Read this verse, for example.

> For **the word of God is living and active**, *sharper than any two-edged sword, piercing to the division of soul and of spirit, of joints and of marrow, and* **discerning the thoughts and intentions of the heart**. (Hebrews 4:12)

Fourth, apply it. Don't read the Bible just for the sake of reading it. That's like reading the driver's manual and not following what it says. It's not a matter whether you will have a crash or not, it's just a matter of time. It's a disaster waiting to happen. But don't fall into that deception. Reading the Bible requires action as your application, especially those that God commands us to obey.

If we continue reading Joshua 1:8, it says, *"Meditate on it, so that you may* **be careful to do according to all that is written in it**" (v.8b). As such, when you read the Bible, ask questions like these:

- *Is there a command or instruction I need to obey? What do I need to do?*

- *Is there a sin I need to confess to God? Is there a habit I need to correct?*

- Bottom line question: *How can I apply this passage in my spiritual walk with God and become a faithful follower of Jesus?*

The purpose of these questions is to get you to respond to the Word of God and to take action. In fact, this truth is at the center of the Great Commission when Jesus said,

> *"Go therefore and make disciples of all nations, baptizing them in the name of the Father and of the Son and of the Holy Spirit, teaching them* **to observe all that I have commanded you**. *And behold, I am with you always, to the end of the age."* (Matthew 28:19-20)

Based on the Great Commission, the greatest mark of a mature disciple is not the stock knowledge about the Bible or about God. It is *to do* or obey his commands. This call for observance or action is also evident in other parts of the Bible. For example, listen or read what James said.

> *But **be doers of the word**, and not hearers only, deceiving yourselves. For if anyone is a hearer of the word and not a doer, he is like a man who looks intently at his natural face in a mirror. For he looks at himself and goes away and at once forgets what he was like. But the one who looks into the perfect law, the law of liberty, and perseveres, being no hearer who forgets but **a doer who acts**, he will be **blessed in his doing**.* (James 1:22-24)

Once again, it is not those who hear only, but those who apply the Word of God. It's still in line with what Jesus said for those who call him, "Lord, Lord." What matters most is those who do the will of God (Matthew 7:21; Luke 6:46).

Protect your spiritual journey. Be prayerful when you read the Bible. Did you know we are in a spiritual battle? Did you know who is *"the prince of the power of the air"* (Ephesians 2:2) who is in control of the evil systems of this world? You must not wonder why someone wants to keep anyone from the Word of God. That's why Paul commanded the believers to do the following: *"Take the helmet of salvation, and the sword of the Spirit, which is the word of God"* (Ephesians 6:17).

The truth is you are a spiritual warrior. Your weapon is the Word of God. You have spiritual enemies in spiritual realms. But if you're not reading and using your Bible, you are vulnerable against the enemies. You must protect yourself. So, in this spiritual journey, if you look at the whole idea of this spiritual discipline in Bible reading or "reading your travel guide," the basic task is to follow the MAP, which stands for:

- **M** - Meditation

- **A** - Application

- **P** - Prayer

What's our main take away here? *Build your life on the Word of God.* Can you afford to build your life and in the end, everything you worked for will just crumble?

*"Everyone then who **hears** these words of mine and **does** them will be like a wise man who **built** his **house on the rock**. And the rain fell, and the floods came, and the winds blew and beat on that house, but it did not fall, because it had been **founded on the rock**. And everyone who hears these words of mine and does not do them will be like a foolish man who built his house on the sand. And the rain fell, and the floods came, and the winds blew and beat against that house, and it fell, and great was the fall of it."* (Matthew 7:24-27)

Don't waste your life and years building for nothing. Whether you're building your life, your marriage, your family, your success, and anything else, build it on a strong foundation, which is the Word of God. Read it. Live it.

Reflection:

Before you read the Bible, what should be the posture of your heart?

Is it enough to simply hear or reflect on the Word of God and not apply it in your life? Explain your answer.

SECTION 5: CELEBRATE THE JOURNEY TOGETHER

"But this I confess to you,
that according to the Way,
which they call a sect,
I worship the God of our fathers,
believing everything laid down by the Law
and written in the Prophets,
having a hope in God."

~ Apostle Paul (Acts 24:14-15a)

CHAPTER 13: WHAT IS WORSHIP?

W orship is a journey of getting closer to God's presence. Have you ever tried to walk with friends on a hiking trail, like a state or national park and when you reached the top or the destination, you're all amazed by the great wonders of God's creation and simply experience the Lord in all his beauty and splendor? How did you feel?

How about visiting the Holy Land? I remember visiting Israel, Jordan and Egypt with friends and the power of worshiping together in the land where Jesus walked. One late afternoon, our group boarded a "worship boat" in the Sea of Galilee. The boat took us to the middle of the sea, we just worshiped together with songs played in the air. It was an ethereal or otherworldly experience realizing this was the same sea where Jesus "walked" on the surface of the water (Matthew 14:26; Mark 6:49). It's a moment of celebration knowing this is where heaven and earth met and these hills and valleys were witnesses to their Creator who came down from heaven and lived among humans. No wonder, there were so many places of worship that were made to commemorate events and persons related to Jesus' journey.

The point is this. In many instances of our journeys, there are moments for personal or joint reflections of deep gratitude, honoring God, and getting closer with him. These are times of celebration where you stop, stand, sit and rest in the presence of God. This supreme principle is the highest in every area of our lives: *A disciple of Jesus is foremost a worshiper. You were made for worshiping God.*

"Worship" comes from the old English word "*weorthscipe,*" meaning "to ascribe worth to someone or something." A dictionary broadly defines "worship" as "the feeling or expression of reverence and adoration for a deity." It also adds, "the acts or rites that make up a formal expression of reverence for a deity." These definitions are too general. We need to go deeper because there is more to worship that meets the eye. There are deeper truths we need to know and see from a biblical point of view.

For me, I define worship as *our utmost response of reverence and awe in wonder to the glory of God*. It happens when there's a God-encounter and all that we are–our inmost thoughts and being–worships God. It means when I'm aware and conscious of God's glorious presence, holiness and love, then my body, soul, and spirit cannot help but be moved in worship. Everything that I am and everything I do must be an act of worship, nothing else matters. This definition begs the question: *Who do we worship?*

We worship God alone and it is exclusively for him. We do not worship angels, saints, or anything in creation. In Exodus 34:11-17, Moses clearly forbade God's people to worship any other gods, graven images, and idols because "*the LORD, whose name is Jealous, is a Jealous God*" (v.14). From Exodus, Leviticus, Deuteronomy, and other books of the Bible, we can learn so much about the history of worship in Israel and how it is designed for worshiping God alone..

In the New Testament, the conversation between Jesus and the Samaritan woman in John 4:1-45 is revealing about the ultimate design for worship. But let's focus on how Jesus viewed worship in his answer to the woman.

The woman said to him, "Sir, I perceive that you are a prophet. Our fathers worshiped on this mountain, but you say that in Jerusalem is the place where people ought to worship."

> *Jesus said to her, "Woman, believe me, the hour is coming when neither on this mountain nor in Jerusalem will you worship the Father. You worship what you do not know; we worship what we know, for salvation is from the Jews. But the hour is coming, and is now here, when* **the true worshipers will worship the Father in spirit and truth, for the Father is seeking such people to worship him***. God is spirit, and those who worship him must worship in spirit and truth." (John 4:20-24)*

The Samaritan woman assumed that worship is about the *place*, but for Jesus it's about the *people* of God worshiping in a certain way. There are several principles of worship that we can learn from this encounter of Jesus with the Samaritan woman.

First, worship is at the core of human nature. When the Samaritan woman mentions that their *"fathers worshiped"* somewhere in the high place of Samaria, she's simply stating a general fact rooted in human consciousness that God wired people like us to worship him and experience his divine presence. Since ancient times, worship comes naturally to all people, not just Jews, but because of our sinful nature, worship is distorted in many ways.

If you read Romans 1:18-25, Paul said that *"what can be known about God is plain to [humanity], because God has shown it to them"* (v.19). Since the creation of the world, God's *"invisible attributes"* have been revealed but people exchanged God's truth for a lie and his glory for his creation. *"They worshiped and served the creature rather than the Creator"* (v.25). Idolatry has always been the problem of worship because it is intended for God alone, not for anything or anyone else. As disciples, we need to give worship only to God and nothing beside him.

Second, worship is central to the journey of God's people. In the Bible, Israel's ancient fathers worshiped God. It is an essential, collective consciousness and experience of God's people where they revere the holiness and majesty of God. They usually have a designated "place" of worship like the city of Jerusalem or a mountain in Samaria, etc. It's where they can gather to demonstrate their devotion, magnify God's greatness, express their gratitude, and honor him with their prayers.

In the Old Testament, God's people publicly worship in many ways:

- Gathering in a place of worship (like a tabernacle, temple or synagogue)
- Making music, singing, playing instruments, etc. (Psalm 150)
- Reading, listening, and studying God's Words (Nehemiah 8:1-12)
- Giving of gifts to God or offering sacrifices (mostly in Leviticus)
- Serving in the ministry (like those Levites, singers, servers, etc.)

Third, worship is commanded in the Scripture. When Jesus mentioned about the *"worship the Father,"* he is emphasizing the utmost importance of worship in their spiritual life. Worship is intended and meant for God alone and no one else beside him. That's why in the 10 Commandments, God's people knew that they were forbidden to have other gods, or "bow down" to carved images and serve them. It does not matter if one will whitewash bowing to images as a form of veneration, the act of bowing down in reverence before a graven image is forbidden in the Word of God. God even commanded Israel to observe a day of rest and worship (Read Exodus 20:1-11).

Did you know what that one thing God and Satan have in common? Worship. Both of them wanted to be worshiped. If you remember the time Satan tempted Jesus, he said, *"All these I will give you, if you will **fall down** and **worship me**"* (Matthew 4:9). Jesus' reply was hard-hitting truth. *"Be gone, Satan! For it is written, '"You shall **worship the Lord your God and him only shall you serve**"'* (v.10). Jesus is quoting from Deuteronomy 6:16. Indeed, worship is intended only for God alone.

Have you realized now how Satan wants to offer you anything just to keep your worship away from God? What would you do if Satan would sell his proposition to you: *"If you, then, will worship me, it will all be yours"*? (Luke 4:7). Will you bow down to him and accept whatever your heart desires, like money, fame, and glory among many? If Satan wants something, he will lie to his teeth to the end. He will promise you everything just to keep you from worshiping our Savior and King. Satan will even keep saying to anyone that it is harmless to bow down to graven images, even though God commanded against it.

Fourth, worship is conducted in spirit and truth. With all the styles and popular trends of worship around the world, it can be chaotic and confusing. But Jesus is stating an unchanging principle in worship. *"True worshipers will worship the Father in **spirit and truth**"* (v.23). He re-emphasized it again, meaning, you cannot take this for granted. *"God is spirit, and those who worship him must worship in **spirit and truth**"* (v.24). This non-negotiable revelation is so important that Jesus repeated these two elements.

The first *element in worship is* **the Spirit.** The word "spirit" (Gk *pneuma*) can be generally interpreted as "spirit" or "wind," "breath," but in proper form (based on the context) it can mean "Spirit," which is referring to God's Spirit or the Holy Spirit. Generally, every disciple of Jesus must consider worship as a *spiritual act*, experience, and reality. It is where the worshiper meets God, encounters him, and has that feeling of reverence to the holy. On a deeper level, since worship is spiritual, worship is an inner working of the Holy Spirit in us.

We know "God is spirit" (*pneuma*). So when we worship him, our spirit and soul draw closer into his presence, reconnect with our Father, and commune with him. We worship in the power of the Holy Spirit, not in our own ability.

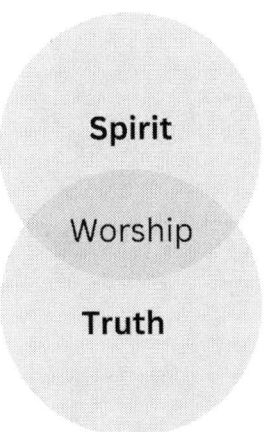

The *second element in worship*, although not second in importance, is **the Truth**. It means truth makes true worshipers and true worshipers are guided by the truth. That's why worship and discipleship go together. It's both important for every worshiper, especially worship team members to be a disciple-learner of truth and a devoted worshiper. When Jesus said *"we worship what we know,"* he was not exaggerating. Jewish people worship God with the truth of the Scripture as their foundation. Worship is not merely a subjective, emotional reverence, response, or experience. It definitely has an emotional aspect, but this emotion is guided by knowledge of the truth, which is the Word of God. Every true worshiper, whether attender or minister, must know their Bible to become better.

A true disciple worships both in "spirit *and* truth," not either/or. These two elements cannot be separated. What happens when you separate them? If you only have the spirit without the truth, worship easily leads to *emotionalism* and *false worship*. False worship happens when it is not based on God's truth. Of course, this does not mean true worship does not involve emotion. True worship involves the whole person, including emotion and passion. On the other hand, if you remove the truth from the spirit, worship will not have a foundation. It becomes *dry* and *lifeless*.

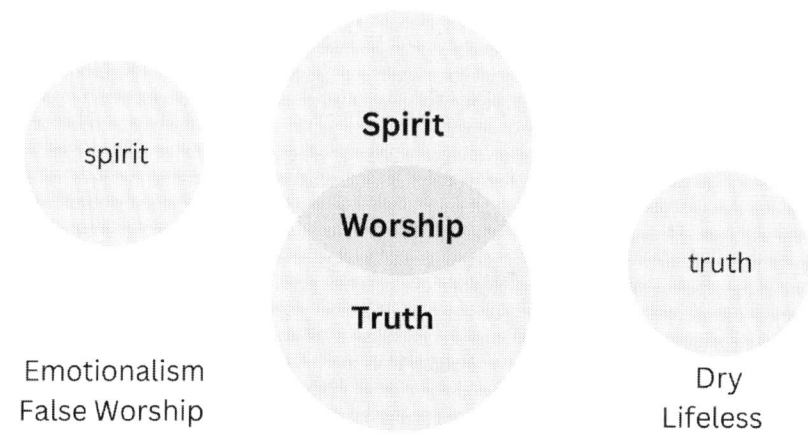

Emotionalism
False Worship

Dry
Lifeless

It's easy for a "worshiper" to claim his or her own truth and not God's truth. It would easily lead to assumptions and idolatry. *The spirit provides life to worship and truth provides foundation.* Jesus warned us about the danger of false worship when he criticized the hypocrisy of the Pharisees,

> *This people honors me with their lips,*
> *but their heart is far from me;*
> **in vain do they worship me,**
> *teaching as doctrines the commandments of men.'* (Mark 7:6-7)

For many years, religious leaders in Israel, especially the Pharisees, were very orderly and legalistic. However, this does not mean that being orderly is always an acceptable worship before God. The Pharisees were so organized, but in the assessment of Jesus, their worship is distant and unacceptable to God. They created doctrines and traditions on worship that are not based on God's Words and they want people to observe it to the letter. Their words and actions seemed to worship God but their hearts were distant from God. It's vanity.

Truly, God is looking for true worshipers. Jesus said, *"**The Father is seeking** *such people to* **worship** *him"* (v.23). He is not looking for the most gifted, talented, popular, or intelligent. He simply said that one must worship what you know and not *"what you do not know"* (v.22). If you want to worship God, you must know him and grow in your knowledge and faith.

Reflection:

What is your level of understanding about worshiping God right now? (1 being lowest and 10 being the highest)

1   2   3   4   5   6   7   8   9   10

What is worship for you and how do you define it? Cite a verse to support your definition.

CHAPTER 14: WHY DO WE WORSHIP?

For me, true worship means *giving God his true worth*. Anything less than what's worthy for God is not worship. It's cheap. If you don't like people who treat you as cheap and worthy of something less, just imagine if we do the same attitude in approaching God. One might ask, is God really that desperate that people should worship him? Is he some kind of a narcissistic and egotistical personality in heaven that he should get adoration and admiration from his people? Let me help enlighten you about worshiping God through the following reasons.

First, we worship God because of who God is and what he has done. Although we must not separate the two (his nature and his actions) but if needed, we must worship God for his nature and character, not just for what he has done.

> *"Worthy are you, our Lord and God,*
> *to receive glory and honor and power,*
> *for you created all things,*
> *and by your will **they existed** and **were created**."* (Revelation 4:11)

In his nature and character, God is God and is worthy of worship. In his being God alone, that should compel everyone of us to worship because God is absolutely worthy. So, not giving him the worship he deserves is nothing but short, ungrateful, and cheap worship. It is a manifestation of our sinful nature against a holy and pure God. As disciples, knowing who God is and deserving all worth, we must worship him for he alone is worthy. In his action, God created all things. Apart from him, we are nothing. We don't exist. As Creator of everything, and we as his creatures whom he loved, blessed, cared, and redeemed, God deserved to be worshiped. In fact, you *"were created"* to worship God. Since we were made to worship, as God's children, we must worship the Father in spirit and truth, as well as with all what he's worth.

Second, we worship God because of who we are. Do not misunderstand this statement. It does not mean we worship ourselves but that we, as a church, are a people of worshipers. That's our reason for existence: to proclaim the excellencies of God before the whole world. The Psalmist proclaimed a great invitation for all God's people,

> *Oh come, let us **worship** and **bow down**;*
> *let us **kneel** before the LORD, our Maker!*
> *For he is our God,*
> *and we are the people of his pasture,*
> *and the sheep of his hand.* (Psalm 95:6-7)

In the same spirit, the apostle Peter also expressed clearly to the early church:

> *But you are a chosen race, a royal priesthood, a holy nation, a people for his own possession, that you may **proclaim the excellencies of him** who called you out of darkness into his marvelous light.* (1 Peter 2:9)

If you only know who you really are in Jesus and who is this God who made you, you cannot help but worship him and be totally grateful. As part of the church of Jesus, you were made to *"proclaim the excellencies,"* glory and honor of God.

Third, we worship because it is the highest purpose of our existence here on earth and it will last to eternity. Do you know what is that one thing God's people do here on earth that we will keep on doing in heaven? You're right, worship. God created you and everyone else to worship him. See this vision of eternity from John the Revelator.

> *After this I looked, and behold, **a great multitude** that no one could number, from every nation, from all tribes and peoples and languages, standing before the throne and before the Lamb, clothed in white robes, with palm branches in their hands, and crying out with a loud voice, "Salvation belongs to our God who sits on the throne, and to the Lamb!" And all the angels were standing around the throne and around the elders and the four living creatures, and **they fell on their faces** before the throne and **worshiped God**, saying, "Amen! Blessing and glory and wisdom and thanksgiving and honor and power and might be to our God forever*

and ever! Amen." (Revelation 7:9-12)

This heavenly vision of great celebration would be the perfect and purest event and form of worship because sin no longer exists in heaven. Up there, we no longer have Bible studies for we will all know and understand everything; no more evangelism for the lost ones will be separated from those who believe in the Gospel of Christ. Everything will be *worship* where we adore him for who he is, praise him for his greatness, and enjoy God's holy and loving presence forever. The only question is *will you be there.*

While we are still here on earth, let's practice worship. Every worship opportunity is our rehearsal and every rehearsal is an act of worship.

Reflection:

Think and reflect about God's character and nature (e.g. holy, love, just, etc.) or what he has done (salvation, protection, guidance, etc.). Praise him for these things.

Read Revelation 4:11. What is your response to the truth that you were made to worship?

CHAPTER 15: HOW SHOULD WE WORSHIP?

I f you carefully study the history of worship from Genesis to Revelation, there are at least three major sides: personal, family, and public. Currently, digital worship is happening around the world.

Family Worship   **Personal Worship**   **Public Worship**

Digital Worship

- *Personal Worship*. Personal is private and in solitude. When you worship in your personal devotion and having your time alone with God, that's personal worship. Every believer in the Bible is a worshiper in their personal life. This side is the most important aspect in our life as a worshiper. It is the center of our spirituality as a disciple of Jesus.

- *Family Worship*. There's also another side of worship that we see in the Bible and that's family worship. It usually happens at home where parents, children and relatives worship together. When you do a family devotion whether at home or somewhere else as a family, that's family worship.

- *Public Worship*. This is where you attend and join other believers to worship God and celebrate regularly. Public worship happens when a body of believers gather together to worship God in a church, worship center or designated place, just like the Israelites at the tabernacle, temple or synagogue. You must not take this regular act of worship lightly.

- How about *digital worship*? Today, the digital and online church is a new development in the history and ministry of the church. Anyone can worship both on a personal level (sometimes using an avatar) and public level (with multiple online worshipers) without any local or national border. Who would have thought that churches could worship together online and not just in person? Whatever can be said about digital worship, there is no doubt that God is using technology for his glory. In fact, Point Church Online has inspired "microsites" to thrive during the Covid19 pandemic. Other churches were also planted and the Gospel has penetrated and is heard in closed countries.

Since worship in various ways is a lifetime journey, here's what you can do if you want to be a better worshiper and give honor to God according to the Scripture. These are general principles for every true worshiper.

First, commit to worship together whenever possible. Worshiping together requires an extra level of commitment. Some Christians go to church if they only feel good or have other benefits. However, when there is some discomfort, worship becomes a secondary priority. But the early disciples are different. Most Bible scholars believe that the church of Jesus Christ started during the celebration of the Day of Pentecost when the believers were gathered "*all together in one place*" (Acts 2:1). The Holy Spirit came and filled the assembled believers, the Gospel was preached, and people got saved (Read Acts 2:14-41). This is how Luke captured the big picture of what the church looked like then.

> *And they **devoted** themselves to the apostles' teaching and the **fellowship**, to the breaking of bread and the prayers….And **day by day**, attending the temple together and breaking bread in their homes…praising God and having favor with all the people.* (Acts 2:42-47)

Yes, the early church gathered on a *daily* basis, not just once a week. They meet everyday in the temple (big assembly) or homes (small groups), depending on

106

the locations. In their daily gatherings, they have the teaching of God's Word, breaking of bread, prayers, worship, giving, and so on. This practice went on through history. The author of Hebrews even mentioned it in his encouragement.

> *And let us consider how to **stir up one another to love and good works**, not **neglecting to meet together**, as is **the habit** of some, but encouraging one another, and all the more as you see the Day drawing near.* (Hebrews 10:24-25)

Meeting together is a major part of their church's rhythm of life or habit. The word "habit" here is ethos, meaning a "custom" as prescribed by their habit, characterizing the early church's spirit and culture as a whole. If you are tempted to just put worship services in the comfort zones, especially on Sunday's only and not commitment, think again.

Second, praise and worship God with a right heart and spirit. When you come (or go anywhere) to worship God, focus on him, not much on people. He is *the audience of One.* Remember, you have come for God, not for a celebrity speaker, a show of performance, or even to impress people with your presence or stage production. We come to God and offer him a worship sacrifice that is acceptable and fitting for the King of kings and Lord of Lords. And that worship must come from the heart that recognizes the holiness and glory of God.

> *Therefore let us be grateful for receiving a kingdom that cannot be shaken, and thus **let us offer to God acceptable worship, with reverence and awe,** for our God is a consuming fire.* (Hebrews 12:28-29)

In approaching God through worship, we must recognize his holiness. We should draw closer to God and be consumed by his holy, consuming fire. We must not offer him some strange "fires" of sacrifices or offerings that he does not agree with (Leviticus 10:1-3). Instead, we must come before him with deep respect and humility, confess our sins, and offer only what is acceptable.

Third, worship in an orderly manner. Since the Bible times, true worship has mostly been well-ordered, but not always (like in the case of David who worshiped spontaneously in 2 Samuel 6:2–22). If you carefully study the history of worship in the Old Testament, you will notice the way God's people did worship in an orderly manner. It's like everything has a prescription in public worship, from the requirements for the priests and Levites, to the major steps of doing the services and sacrifices, and so on. There it seems God was in the details, but in the New Testament, the church has a simple flow of community worship.

Today, it is a struggle of some churches who have different backgrounds and religious upbringing. With all the diversities and varieties of worship style, the general guideline for public worship is to worship God in an orderly manner. This main principle or directive is taken from the messy worship services of the Corinthian believers. Paul asked them, "*What then, brothers? When you come together, each one has a hymn, a lesson, a revelation, a tongue, or an interpretation. **Let all things be done for building up**"* (1 Corinthians 14:26).

Since many of them want to do their own thing in their worship gathering, they have the tendency to be disorderly, chaotic, or disorganized. As a result, they confused their attendees. For Paul, our worship services should have a simple and efficient order that people can easily follow. The reason being is this: "*For God is not a God of confusion but of peace*" (1 Corinthians 14:33). Since many believers have their own preferences, if you follow everyone, where will the church be led? Does it mean it can be pulled in all directions or contain all the programs that everybody wants? Since every church has its own personality, its flow of worship should be guided by this major directive: "*But **all things should be done decently** and **in order**"* (1 Corinthians 14:40). Every church leadership must determine their way of public worship that builds up God's people and blesses those who come to seek God.

The biggest challenge in the Bible is this: There is *no specific flow of worship* in the Bible. If there is, then it could have been done today by all churches in specific sequence. We only have some insights on what were included in their worship gathering. Some of them are found here:

> *Let the word of Christ dwell in you richly, **teaching** and **admonishing** one another in all wisdom, **singing** psalms and hymns and spiritual songs, with thankfulness in your hearts to God. And whatever you do, in word or deed, do*

everything in the name of the Lord Jesus, giving thanks to God the Father through him. (Colossians 3:16-17)

Addressing one another in psalms and hymns and spiritual songs, singing and making melody to the Lord with your heart, giving thanks always and for everything to God the Father in the name of our Lord Jesus Christ. (Ephesians 5:19-20)

We can only have a flow of worship but every church has their own choice and culture of worship. Whether liturgical, traditional, contemporary, emerging, and whatever style, these are the major elements of worship:

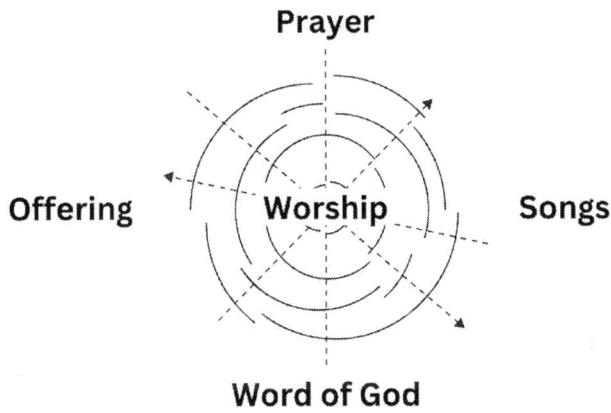

- *Prayers* - This form of worship is expressed in many ways, like opening prayer, prayers during singing, before preaching, for offering, closing prayer and benedictions.

- *Songs* - This form of worship is expressed through *"singing psalms, and hymns and spiritual songs"* or *"making melody"* (like composing new songs). Today, we often call it "praise and worship."

- *Word of God* - The ministry of *"the word of Christ"* is expressed in preaching the Gospel, "teaching and admonishing," reading and listening, evangelizing and so on. These are all forms of worship through the Word of God.

- *Offering* - Since the earliest history of worship, expressing *"thankfulness"* in heart is through generosity, offering a sacrifice, giving of offering, or money for the work of the ministry.

Fourth, worship God with every part of your whole being to live a lifestyle of worship in the power of the Holy Spirit. Living a life of worship cannot be attained by our own ability. It's because worship goes against our sinful and weak human nature. We need to be filled with the Holy Spirit. That's why Paul said that as Christians, we *"who **worship by the Spirit of God** and glory in Christ Jesus and put no confidence in the flesh"* (Philippians 3:3). So how can this life of worship be possible if our sinful flesh keeps struggling with our spirit?

If you want to make worship as your lifestyle, this is one thing you should do. Mark your Bible and make sure that this Word of God will also mark your life. Highlight it but don't forget to heed this instruction from the apostle Paul.

> *I appeal to you therefore, brothers, by the mercies of God, to **present your bodies** as a **living sacrifice**, holy and **acceptable** to God, which is **your spiritual worship**. Do not be conformed to this world, but be transformed by the renewal of your mind, that by testing you may discern what is the will of God, what is good and **acceptable** and perfect.* (Romans 12:1-2)

Paul is exhorting, even to the point of begging, all disciples of Jesus to *"present"* or offer themselves to God in a form of a *"living sacrifice."* This could be interpreted as offering yourself as an individual and/or yourselves as a whole church. In the Bible, an offering is something devoted and committed exclusively for God. Every sacrifice must be in their best qualities in order to be *"holy and acceptable to God"* because it is being offered for his excellencies. In this case, Paul is imploring the believers to give and devote themselves acceptably to God.

Here, having a lifestyle of worship requires a different mindset–a spiritually transformed and renewed mindset. Paul is not talking about your brain inside your skull. He is talking about your way of thought, your state of mind and consciousness that is God-centered. This spiritual lifestyle is far superior than any self-help out there because this lifestyle is empowered by God's Spirit and grounded on God's Truth. This lifestyle is where every aspect of your life is centered upon worship for the glory of God.

Worship

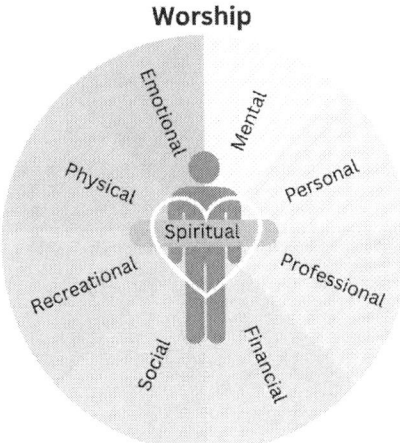

Here's how a worship-centered life of a disciple looks like:

- **Spiritual** - As a disciple, at the core is your spiritual life, the center of your worship lifestyle. This is where your spiritual center is. Your spiritual rhythms and habits, your goals and actions are all designed for God's glory.

- **Mental** - As a disciple, we keep on learning about God as we listen to him speak to us through his Word, read godly books, learn the things of God, and so on. As we meditate and experience God's grace everyday, we come to know him more and make him known to others.

- **Emotional** - As a disciple, you glorify God by living an emotionally healthy, Spirit-filled temperament, and godly personality. You love God intimately, passionately, and with deep gratitude. You love your family and also have compassion for the lost and your community.

- **Physical** - As a disciple, you take care of your physical health, you feed it well, and do everything to glorify God with it. Whatever you do with your body, you always think if these things glorify God or not.

- *Personal* - As a disciple, will you align your ambition with God's vision? How about your personal goals with the Great Commission? Or your business with God's business? A true disciple who lives for the glory of the King has his own personal life ordered under the priority and pursuit of worship.

- *Professional* - For students who follow Jesus, your ultimate aim is to be educated to pursue a God-pleasing career, and if you want the best, follow your calling or vocation. Whether God is shaping you to become a professional, employee, entrepreneur, investor, and so on, his desire is for you to manifest his glory in the marketplace. You are or will be his ambassador in this world.

- *Financial* - You know how mammon wants to be worshiped. But as a disciple, your devotion to God comes first. Money is neutral but it can magnify who you really are, whether you serve God or allow yourself to be monopolized, living a lifestyle of worship means making God the master of your money.

- *Social* - Today, "social" life has radically changed. In fact, we've just seen the massive power of social media to control even well-meaning Christians. Are you conscious of how to glorify God with your social media and your whole social life? Living a lifestyle of worship means allowing God to use your social life as his platform. So when you post anything on your social media, ask: How is God glorified in this post?

- *Recreational* - One of the great areas of worship, and yet remains less explored, is worship through relaxation because people tend to get busy and are addicted to hustle. Learning how to eliminate hustle ruthlessly seems far remote for many. But living a lifestyle of worship means your leisure, relaxation, entertainment, hobbies, interests and so on are God-pleasing. Even when you're alone, you are conscious that God is with you.

These are the embodiments of a life of worship. If you develop these qualities in every aspect of your life, then both your private and public life of worship show no difference. You are who you are when you're alone or when you're worshiping together with fellow believers. As Paul said, "*So, whether you eat or* *drink, or whatever you do, **do all to the glory of God***' (1 Corinthians 10:31). Yes, you heard it right–do *all*, not few or more, but all for the glory of God.

Reflection:

What is the most important lesson you learned in this chapter about worship? Explain it in your own words.

Memorize Romans 12:1-2. Reflect and internalize the whole idea revealed in these two verses.

SECTION 6: TAKING THE PLUNGE DOWN THE RIVER

"We were buried therefore with him
by baptism into death,
in order that, just as Christ was raised from the dead
by the glory of the Father,
we too might walk in newness of life."

~ Apostle Paul (Romans 6:4)

CHAPTER 16: WHAT IS BAPTISM? AND WHAT IS IT NOT?

What's your story about baptism? Did it ever clarify your faith in Jesus or it only made more confusion because you just jumped in with the band? When I was an infant, my grandma (on my mother's side of the family) "borrowed" me from my parents and had me baptized without their knowledge. Maybe because I was born in a mixed-faith family. At that time, my dad was a backsliding Christian and my mother was a nominal Christian also. Both of them never got to church regularly when I was born. So, my parents and siblings were not a church-going family.

One vacation at my grandma's town, I was a 4th or 5th grader then, she brought me to a park and she asked, "Did you know you were baptized *as an infant* in that big church?" while pointing to an old grand cathedral. "Really?" I replied and wondered what she meant. That experience had me thinking. At that time, I wanted to know more about baptism by reading the Bible.

During my 5th Grade, I already started my faith journey when I accepted Jesus as my Lord and Savior. I began reading the Bible from Genesis to Revelation, but I could not find a single baby who was baptized. Instead, I read about Jesus being baptized and many others who are old enough to understand what it is. That fascinated me. When my youth pastor encouraged me to be baptized, all the more I wanted to understand and take baptism seriously. So, I made a decision that if ever I want to be baptized the way Jesus did, I must understand and get it right first from the Bible before I do it. I clearly remember the day I consciously decided to follow Jesus and be baptized *as a believer* and follower.

In the next step of our life journey with Jesus, my goal here is for you to discover (or rediscover) and understand the biblical teachings of baptism. What you'll know and understand here should be enough for you to comprehend what a biblical baptism is. Then, if you have not done it as a believer, you'll decide what to do about it. And if you've already made it, you'll fully appreciate what you've done and recommit yourself to the Lord.

What comes to your mind when you think of baptism? Here are some of the key teachings in the Bible about Christian baptism that could help you in following Jesus..

First, baptism in the Bible is your first step of obedience to Jesus Christ. Here's a sound definition of baptism. Baptism is a *public declaration of your testimony and faith in Jesus as your Lord and Savior. It is a demonstration of your first obedience to his command and authority.* In baptism by immersion, you as a believer identify with Jesus' death, burial, and resurrection. You are also testifying to the world that you died to your old life of sin, buried in Jesus, and risen with him to a new life. As a Christian, *baptism is your first step of obedience to Jesus' authority and lordship.* In order for us to clarify the questions above, we must go back to the basis of our faith and practice: the Word of God. What does the Bible say about baptism?

Second, Jesus demonstrates that baptism is God's idea. It was ordained by God. When Jesus started his three-year ministry, his primary public appearance started with his baptism. It is so important that Matthew, Mark, and Luke's Gospels mentioned Jesus' baptism. Baptism is one of the most significant acts of Jesus when he started his public ministry. The Gospel of Matthew narrated it:

> *Then Jesus came from Galilee to the Jordan to John, to **be baptized** by him. John would have prevented him, saying, 'I need to **be baptized** by you, and do you come to me?' But Jesus answered him, 'Let it be so now, for thus it is fitting for us **to fulfill all righteousness.'** Then he consented. And when **Jesus was baptized**, immediately he went up from the water, and behold, the heavens were opened to him, and he saw the Spirit of God descending like a dove and coming to rest on him; and behold, a voice from heaven said, "This is my beloved Son, with whom I am well pleased."* (Matthew 3:13-17)

When John the Baptist said he needed "to be baptized," he clearly indicates that baptism is a necessity or something essential. It's because baptism is an act of faith preordained by God. If baptism was not God's idea, why would both John the Baptist and Jesus exercise it? They both know that baptism is not man's idea, but it is part of God's righteous plan and purpose in our spiritual journey.

What does Jesus mean when he said, *"it is fitting for us to fulfill all righteousness"*? We know that Jesus is perfectly righteous and sinless. Since Jesus is sinless, baptism should not be taken as an act to cleanse you from your sins, even washing your "original sin." Jesus is also perfectly righteous and your righteousness must come from him alone, not in baptism. The truth is baptism will not make you righteous. Only Jesus will. It is likely that Jesus was baptized because he wants to be identified with us as his creation who absolutely needed his righteousness. He was doing it for us, not for himself.

Of course, the fact that Jesus went through baptism, that outrightly refutes the idea that baptism is a means of salvation. Why? The Bible is very clear. Jesus does not need to repent and receive salvation. It's because he is the Savior alone. Baptism is not our Savior; Jesus is. The Bible is very clear about it. *"For by grace you have been **saved through faith**. And this is not your own doing; it is the gift of God, **not a result of works** [that includes baptism as righteous act], so that no one may boast"* (Ephesians 2:8-9).

That is why as Bible-believing Christians, we do not believe in "baptismal regeneration," which is a teaching that a person is born again or is saved through baptism. This doctrine is not biblical and was not taught by Jesus nor the apostles. Thinking of baptism as a means of salvation or regeneration was first developed by Cyprian (200-258 AD), hundreds of years after Jesus died on the cross. Since then, it has spread in many denominations, but there are those who stick to the Holy Scriptures that baptism comes after you believed and repented of your sins. As a follower of Jesus, you are not baptized to be saved, but you are baptized because you are already saved.

Yes, your first step of obedience as a Christian is baptism, but we maintain that salvation is by trusting in Jesus alone as our personal Lord and Savior. *Can a person be saved without being baptized?* Yes, of course. Just take a look at the thief at the cross. He believed in Jesus and was promised eternal life, even though he was not baptized when he died (Read Luke 23:42-43). This example doesn't mean baptism is not important, but it only proves consistently in the Bible that salvation is *through faith in the finished work of Jesus at the cross.* That's why Jesus is our salvation, baptism is not. It may be important but we're only saved through faith in Jesus Christ alone. You cannot earn heaven through baptism. So if you're serious in serving the Lord, your baptism is a great starting point. Ask yourself. Have I submitted myself to obey the Lord to go through the water baptism?

Third, baptism is essential in our spiritual journey. In fact, Jesus placed a huge importance on it by stating it clearly in the Great Commission, meaning his great task given to his disciples or the Church. It says,

> "**Go** *therefore and make disciples of all nations,* **baptizing them** *in the name of the Father and of the Son and of the Holy Spirit, teaching them to observe all that I have commanded you. And behold, I am with you always, to the end of the age."* (Matthew 28:19-20)

If you claim to be a disciple of Jesus and you're not yet baptized, think again. Jesus commanded that in the process of *"making disciples,"* they are to be baptized. Being baptized is an indicator of being an obedient disciple of Jesus. True disciples do not have problems with being baptized because Jesus placed a great priority on it. It is an essential part of the Great Commission or Mandate. Jesus even promised that when you are baptized, he will always be with you in your spiritual journey. So, if baptism is on top of Jesus' priorities, why should anyone make it their last priority?

Fourth, baptism was universally observed by God's people in the New Testament. When you read the Old Testament, baptism is not mentioned. Probably it started to develop in between the time when the Old Testament was completed and the time of Jesus' arrival. So when Jesus first preached, he often spoke about being baptized, especially that John the Baptist was already baptizing people. *"So with many other exhortations he* [John the Baptist] *preached good news to the people…Now when* **all the people were baptized**, *and when* **Jesus** *also had been* **baptized** *and was praying, the heavens were opened"* (Luke 3:21). Interestingly, in the four Gospels, we cannot find any event where the apostles were baptized. But we can clearly see that everyone or *"all the people"* who heard and believed in the preaching of the Gospel made a personal decision to be baptized. Most likely, the apostles were baptized after Jesus was resurrected as it would have more meaning for them to experience, demonstrate and teach to the disciples.

In the book of Acts, the apostles faithfully kept the observance of baptism. Again, baptism is a response to the preaching of the Gospel. Nowhere in the Bible that baptism was administered to those who were unable to know, understand, and believe in it, like the infants. The earliest mention of infant baptism was 180 AD by Irenaeus (130-202 AD). Before 180 AD, there was no solid proof for infant baptism in the early church, showing that this is a late development of tradition and has become a standard in the 3rd century AD.

In the New Testament, those who believe were baptized. *"But when they **believed** Philip as he **preached good news** about the kingdom of God and **the name of Jesus Christ**, they were **baptized**, both **men and women**"* (Acts 8:12). There is no doubt that baptism is a spiritual practice observed by the early New Testament believers. Men and women who responded to the Gospel of Jesus were baptized. Throughout centuries, those who are faithful to biblical teachings keep the importance of having baptism as a major part of the believer's spiritual life and journey.

Fifth, baptism is only required for those who believe in Jesus. What were the characteristics of the people baptized in the Bible? If you take a look at Acts 8:12, it is noteworthy that those who went for baptism have the following: They *"believed"* first in the Gospel of Jesus being preached before they were "baptized." It means they trusted Jesus as their Lord and Savior. Also, they were *"men and women"* who were capable of making a decision for themselves to be baptized. That is why you cannot find any mention in the Bible that babies were to be baptized because they do not have the mental capacity to know and understand what baptism is all about. You must be old enough to know, understand, and believe first what is biblical baptism before you can go for it. It's rightly called "believer's baptism."

Reflection:

Have you been baptized as your response to the Gospel of Jesus, having believed in Jesus as your Lord and Savior?

What is your level of obedience in following Jesus' command to be baptized right now? (1 being lowest and 10 being the highest)

    1   2   3   4   5   6   7   8   9   10

CHAPTER 17: HOW SHOULD BAPTISM BE DONE?

Have you seen the movie Jesus Revolution? There you see the prominence of baptism from the beginning to the end. That hippie generation believed in the Lord Jesus as their Savior and Lord and followed him through water baptism.

Once again, it is very important to highlight that your salvation experience in Jesus must come first before you are baptized. A classic example in the New Testament is the story of the Philippian Jailer who converted to Christ first before he committed himself to baptism (Acts 16:25-34). The Jailer asked Paul and Silas,

*"Sirs, what must I do to be **saved**?"*

*And they said, "**Believe in the Lord Jesus, and you will be saved,** you and your household." And they spoke the word of the Lord to him and to all who were in his house. And he took them the same hour of the night and washed their wounds; and he was **baptized at once**, he and all his family. Then he brought them up into his house and set food before them. And he rejoiced along with his entire household that he had **believed in God**.*

There's no doubt that faith in Jesus comes first. Baptism is only applicable to those who believe and are saved. It is not the other way around. In the Word of God, you become a Christian when you put your faith in Jesus alone for your salvation. And then, baptism is readily available for you to do. You go through baptism because you are already saved, not for you to be saved.

We all know that "baptism" is very broad to many. In Christian history, despite the Word of God speaking of *"one baptism"* (Ephesians 4:5), we can see several traditions of doing baptisms. We must understand that some of these practices of baptism in many Christian denominations have developed *after* the completion of the writing of the Bible. Although most of those who practice various forms of baptism claim to have some support from the Bible, the interpretation of how they came to arrive at these conclusions is noteworthy. For that reason, there came about some modes of baptism that many of us have seen. Here are the major methods of baptism in Christian churches and circles:

- *Affusion* - This method is "to *pour* on" (Latin *affusio*) water upon the forehead or head of the candidate of baptism. Perhaps, you've seen water poured upon the heads of some infants or adults during their baptism. This practice started between 100 or late 200 AD as mentioned in *Didache* (or *Teaching of the Apostles*) when baptism by immersion was impossible due to lack of water. By the 10th to 14th century, this practice became a norm. Methodists and most Protestant churches prefer baptism by affusion.

- *Aspersion* - This method is the sprinkling (from Latin *asperge* or to "sprinkle" or "scatter") of water or anything liquid (like holy water) over the candidate. Most, if not all of us have seen baptism being made by sprinkling water on the person's forehead, usually infants or young children, and often accompanied by name-giving. This form of baptism started in the 16th century by the Roman Catholic and also used by some factions of the Lutherans, Anglicans, United Church of Christ and Church of Nazarene.

- *Partial Immersion* (or *Dipping*) - This method is sometimes called immersion but it is actually a method of dipping the head (as the seat of intellect and emotion) with or without standing in the water.

- *Total Immersion* (or *Submersion*) - This method of baptism is when the candidate stands or kneels on shallow water, pushed a little by hand to immerse and/or totally submerge the whole body for a brief moment and be pulled up from under the water. Most Bible scholars agree that this mode is the earliest and most authentic form of baptism mentioned *in the Holy Scripture*. It is the method most Eastern Orthodox, Baptists, Anabapatists, Evangelicals, Pentecostals, and Community churches accept as the way Jesus used and commanded his disciples to go through.

Most likely, you've seen those who were baptized *by immersing* the person in riverbanks, lake, baptistry, bathtub, water tank, or (rarely, as in the rare case of one prison ministry, baptism was made in a big trash can full of) water. But which "one baptism" is taught in the Bible?

As you may have noticed, some of the forms of baptism, except immersion, were developed after the whole Scripture was already completed between 70 to 100 AD. So let's focus on baptism by the biblical form of baptism.

First, biblical baptism is by immersion. In the article entitled "Church History: When Did the Churches Stop Baptizing By Immersion," Timothy Paul Jones said, "The strongest argument for baptism by immersion is the word itself." The Greek word used in the New Testament for "baptism" (or "*baptizu*") means "to dip" or "to immerse" or "to submerge." Certainly, there are specific Greek words for "pouring" or "sprinkling," but it wasn't used in relation to baptism. Truly, there are crucial indications that this act of immersion is the biblically consistent way of doing baptism. Read the book of Acts 8:26-39. Take note how Philip explained the Holy Scripture to the Ethiopian Eunuch, who is "*a court official of Candace, queen of the Ethiopians, who is in charge of all her treasure*" (v.27). The turning point of this event happens. It reads,

> *Then Philip opened his mouth, and beginning with this Scripture he told him the good news about Jesus. And as they were going along the road they came to some water, and the eunuch said, "See, here is water! What prevents me from being **baptized**?" And he commanded the chariot to stop, and they both **went down into the water**, Philip and the eunuch, and he **baptized** him. And when they **came up out of the water**, the Spirit of the Lord carried Philip away, and the eunuch saw him no more, and went on his way rejoicing.* (Acts 8:38)

What have you noticed about the way baptism was set here? There's an abundance of water. It also says they "*both went down into the water.*" If Philip scooped some water with his hands and poured it on the eunuch's head, surely it'll be mentioned. But "pouring" (Greek *ekcheo*) or "sprinkling" (*rhantismos*) were never used for baptism anywhere in the Bible. Instead, it's stated that they both "*came out of the water.*" It is also the same way with Jesus at his baptism in the river of Jordan. "*When Jesus was baptized, immediately he went up from the water*"

(Matthew 3:16). It's well established that John did more baptism in areas with more water. The Bible says, *"John also was baptizing at Aenon near Salim, because water was plentiful there, and people were coming and being baptized"* (John 3:23). Now some might say, isn't it that if a person would just stand in the riverbank, the phrase "come out of the water" simply does not necessarily mean the person was immersed?

The answer is "yes" and "no." "Yes," it is because the coming *"out from the water"* can be used for someone crossing the river or getting out to dry land. (However, if all accounts of baptism in the Bible did not mention pouring or sprinkling, why was it not mentioned at all?) But the answer is also a big "No," because of what baptism truly represents. It symbolizes your unity and identity with Jesus' death, burial, and resurrection. We will have more of this later.

Second, biblical baptism is made "in the Name of the Father, and of the Son, and of the Holy Spirit." We also read from the Great Commission that *baptizing the disciples should be done in the name of the Trinity*. Read Matthew 28:20. *"Go therefore and make disciples of all nations,* **baptizing them in the name of the Father and of the Son and of the Holy Spirit."** This Trinitarian formula is Jesus' instruction on what authority baptism is made. We must remember that during the baptism of Jesus, the Trinity was involved (Mathew 3:13-17). The Holy Spirit appeared like a dove and the Father confirmed Jesus as the beloved Son in whom he is pleased. In the eyes of Jesus, the Trinity plays a vital role in baptism and every disciple must recognize that authority from which baptism is performed.

Interestingly, there's also an account in the book of Acts where baptism is made *"in the name of Jesus"* and the Father as well as the Holy Spirit were not mentioned (Acts 2:38). This instance is also mentioned in Acts 10:48 and 8:16. Some might think that this is a new development of doing baptism by invoking the name of Jesus only. However, the long practice of Christian history is in the name of the Trinity. Even in one of the earliest records of the *Didache*, baptism is made "in the name of the Father, the Son, and of the Holy Spirit." And even if baptism will be made in Jesus' name, it does not necessarily contradict with what the Bible teaches about the authority of Jesus (not unless the act is to deny or reject the Trinity). Just like in our prayers, to pray "in Jesus' name" is to appeal through the authority of Jesus and allow the Father to answer our call in the power of the Holy Spirit. Still, the Trinity is actively involved, not just in prayers but in baptism also.

Third, baptism is made in public. You will also notice that in the New Testament, *baptism is public because it is a testimony of your faith in Jesus.* It is not some secret ritual that is only for the initiates like some secret societies. In the New Testament, baptism is a public demonstration that you have decided to follow Jesus into a new life and there's no turning back to the old life. It is like crossing a bridge and burning it down so that there's no more option of going back. John the Baptizer baptizes people in public and open spaces. Jesus was baptized in public also.

The truth is, *in baptism you publicly testify that you have decided to follow Jesus.* That's why it is also a good practice to invite your family and friends when you decide to be baptized because there are many people who trusted Jesus simply because of someone's testimony to follow Jesus in waters of baptism. Have you ever thought why we need to be unashamed of Jesus and declare him publicly through our lives and commitment?

As Jesus said, "So everyone who acknowledges me before men, I also will acknowledge before my Father who is in heaven, but whoever denies me before men, I also will deny before my Father who is in heaven" (Matthew 10:32-33). Let's allow Jesus' words to sink in in our hearts and minds.

Reflection:

What is God teaching you in Acts 16:25-34?

If Jesus gave so much value about baptism, what should be our attitude towards it? Based on what you learned so far, how will it make a difference in your spiritual journey, as well as your family and friends who decided to believe in Jesus? Or your disciples, if you have any?

CHAPTER 18: WHY IS BAPTISM NECESSARY FOR JESUS FOLLOWERS?

I pray that as of this point, you're already taking seriously the need for baptism if you have not done it yet. However, if you have been baptized by immersion already, I want you to reflect and be thankful to God for what it reminds you of as you let every baptism you witness be an encouragement and a reminder of your decision when you started following the Lord.

Now, why is baptism essential for you or your family, friends and disciples? What is its significance in our spiritual journey? If baptism is necessary, what will it benefit you as a believer? These questions will be answered simultaneously in this section.

First, baptism is a command of Jesus for his disciples. It's your first act of obedience. When Jesus gives a command, the true measure of a real disciple is complete obedience. If we do not obey or submit to his command and authority, it means we are living in disobedience. The Great Mandate says, *"Go therefore and* **make disciples** *of all nations,"* Jesus said, *"***baptizing** *them in the name of the Father and of the Son and of the Holy Spirit"* (Matthew 28:19). This Great Commission demands great obedience. Since Jesus commanded us to be baptized, no Christian should take for granted baptism. If Jesus made a strong emphasis on it, we must not take baptism lightly. To be baptized means you're being obedient to Jesus.

Second, baptism symbolizes your journey of faith, forgiveness, and freedom. We already established that John the Baptist heavily emphasized the importance of baptism in relation to repentance and the forgiveness of our sins. His ministry almost revolves in it, that's why he's called John the Baptizer. As the apostle Matthew narrates, *"Then Jerusalem and all Judea and all the region about the Jordan were going out to him, and they were* **baptized** *by him in the river Jordan,* *confessing their sins."* (Matthew 3:5-6). Here, baptism does not cleanse us from sin. Rather, it is the confession of our sins that cleanses us from our sins. A person decides to be baptized, not to be forgiven but because he or she is already forgiven in Jesus.

Elsewhere, Peter said to the Israelites, *"Repent and be baptized every one of you in the name of Jesus Christ for the forgiveness of your sins, and you will receive the gift of the Holy Spirit"* (Acts 2:38). This difficult verse must not be misinterpreted. The preposition "for" is sometimes wrongly translated, like *"be baptized for* (or in order to get) *forgiveness."* But that translation will lead to a false doctrine of baptismal regeneration. Not only that, what happens when you commit sins? Do you need to be rebaptized over and over again?

The truth is every believer must be baptized "because" (or *for*) your sins were already forgiven. The Bible teaches that *baptism does not cleanse you from all your sins. Only Jesus can do that.* However, it is symbolic of your sins being "washed away" because of Jesus' shed blood and sacrifice at the cross for *"without the shedding of blood there is no forgiveness of sins"* (Hebrews 9:22). This picture and symbolism was portrayed by Ananias who said to Paul, *"And now why do you wait? Rise and be baptized and wash away your sins, calling on his name"'* (Acts 22:16). If these texts are difficult for you to get the clear idea then the rule of interpreting comes in: *an obscure text must be interpreted with the clearer texts of the Bible.* Here, it is likely that the interpretation is by calling on God through repentance, your sins can be washed away like snow (See passages like 1 Corinthians 6:11; Hebrews 10:22; Psalm 51:2 and 7).

Third, baptism is a major step in your new spiritual journey. Remember how Jesus was baptized when he started his three year public ministry. It was a crucial moment for him, as well as for the believers in Jesus. It is like a marker of a new chapter in your life as united in Jesus. However, how is biblical baptism practiced by the New Testament church different to the one started or popularized by John the Baptist? We have to understand that when John was baptizing the early believers, Jesus Christ was not yet crucified. The true beauty of baptism is it perfectly portrayed the crucifixion of Jesus Christ that provided a way for us to be reconciled with God. The reason being is because *baptism is a symbol of our union with Jesus.* Paul said,

*Do you not know that all of us who have been **baptized into** Christ Jesus were **baptized into** his death? We were buried therefore with him by **baptism into** death, in order that, just as Christ was raised from the dead by the glory of the Father, we too might **walk in newness of life**.* (Romans 6:3-4)

Have you noticed how many times Paul mentioned the word *"into"*? Why do you think that is important? Think of baptism as an introduction or launching pad for your new life of *being united* in Jesus. This *"newness of life"* is your new journey. And in these texts we will also clearly see the most important portrait of baptism: the death, burial and resurrection of Jesus.

Fourth, baptism is a visual representation and picture of your new identity in Jesus. When you decide to follow the Lord Jesus in waters of baptism, you symbolically identify with his death, burial, and resurrection. *Baptism is the perfect picture of who we are in Jesus. You identify in his death, burial, and resurrection.* Take a look at the passage in Romans 6:3-4 again and you'll identify these three elements that are very significant to Christian baptism:

- Death of Jesus - *"baptized into death"*

- Burial of Jesus - "we were buried...with him"

- Resurrection of Jesus - *"raised from the dead"*

Baptized into Death   Buried into Death   Raised from the Dead

Here, the Gospel, which is the death, burial, and resurrection of Jesus, is visually proclaimed in action through baptism. The person who gets baptized is declaring and proclaiming the Good News of Jesus. It means baptism is the reenactment of the Gospel of Jesus. Take note of this biblical revelation. If there is one argument why the biblical baptism is *by immersion* and not by pouring water or sprinkling is this: Baptism by immersion perfectly pictures your identity of dying to your old self and sin (symbolized by where you are standing in your old self and slowly pushed down into the water), being buried with Jesus into death (symbolized in being immersed or submerged underwater), and being resurrected (symbolized by being raised from the dead).

We must not underestimate the representation of baptism as if it is just a ritual. It is not just a ceremonial right. Actually, in the act of baptism, God's power is already at work in your life and you must be baptized by faith. Paul taught the early believers,

> *In him also you were circumcised with a circumcision made without hands, by putting off the body of the flesh, by the circumcision of Christ, having been **buried** with him in **baptism**, in which you were also **raised** with him **through faith in the powerful working of God**, who raised him from the dead.* (Colossians 2:11-12)

This revelation is one of the most powerful principles of biblical baptism. We carry that spiritual ID or identification of being risen "with Jesus" with God supernaturally at work within us. We are living in Jesus and for Jesus.

Fifth, baptism is also a great way to be a part or a member of a local church. Becoming a member or part of a local faith community or church is sometimes through baptism. Since the beginning of church history, baptism is one of the pathways of becoming a member or "mission partner" of a local church. During the earliest days of Jesus' church, "*those who **received his word** were **baptized**, and there were **added** that day about three thousand souls*" (Acts 2:41). Baptism was one way for new believers being added into the local body of Christ.

Most Bible-believing churches practice that you can become a member of a church through baptism, that is if you have not been baptized after you trusted

Jesus as your Lord and Savior. However, if you have been baptized already, you don't need to be baptized again just to be a member. Even if you transfer to another local church, *you only need to be baptized by immersion once*. That's why the Bible mentioned "one baptism" in Ephesians 4:4-6. *"There is one body and one Spirit—just as you were called to the one hope that belongs to your call— one Lord, one faith,* **one baptism***, one God and Father of all, who is over all and through all and in all."*

I also believe that baptism has a *future perspective* or (as theologians would say "eschatological aspect") in our Christian faith. When a believer dies, baptism is also a great reminder that one day we will rise again from the grave. As such, baptism is also a great reminder of our glorious future in the Last Days when Jesus will come again. If a person claims to be a Christian but is not willing to be identified with Jesus through baptism, why would that person claim to be a faithful Christian? If a person is ashamed to be identified with Jesus, why would Jesus not be ashamed of such a professing Christian? Why call him "Lord," if he is not your Lord in the first place? Let your conscience speak.

The question is: Have you been baptized by immersion, just like Jesus did and as he commanded? Do you still remember that Jesus instructed his disciples in Matthew 28:19-20 to *"make disciples," "baptizing"* these disciples, and *"teaching them to observe all that I have commanded you"*? That Great Mandate has not changed through centuries.

In this study, we have come to understand biblical baptism. Baptism was commanded by Jesus and it is best represented by immersion in water to symbolize the death, burial, and resurrection of Jesus. This baptism must be a personal choice by anyone who already has trusted Jesus as their Lord and Savior. Therefore, it is a public declaration of your faith to follow Jesus. So, what's next for you?

- *Make a personal choice to be baptized*. If you have not been baptized by immersion, take that step of faith in Jesus as soon as possible. If you have trusted Jesus as your Lord and Savior, you are a child of God. You are already saved. As such, baptism is your major next step. *"[F]or in Christ Jesus you are all sons of God, through faith. For as many of you as were baptized into Christ have put on Christ"* (Galatians 3:26).

- *Be a witness to your non-believing friends.* Baptism is a powerful testimony for your non-believing friends, because it is a public confession of our faith in the Lord Jesus. Since baptism is a public confession of your faith, you declare that you are no longer a secret Christian But rather you have decided to follow Jesus and there is no turning back.

- *Build your faith in Jesus.* Baptism builds your faith, including that of your family. Parents, make sure that everyone in your family who is at the right age to make a decision has been baptized. However, make sure also that as parents you have been baptized already. Your baptism is like a spiritual foundation that must be laid down for your family's spiritual growth and obedience to the Lord. It's a matter of importance in your faith in Jesus.

The whole point of baptism is to confirm that you're serious about your spiritual walk to be identified with Jesus. If you have the courage to follow the Lord and declare your spiritual union with him in his death, burial, and resurrection, then, you are making a major step in your spiritual journey with Jesus. If you want to be baptized, contact your pastor, leader or discipler. Why wait?

Reflection:

If Jesus commanded his disciples to be baptized, what are you going to do about it?

How is baptism representing the death, burial, and resurrection of Jesus?

SECTION 7: YOUR PATH TO PEACE AND POWER

*"To this end we always pray for you,
that our God may make you worthy of his calling
and may fulfill every resolve for good
and every work of faith by his power,
so that the name of our Lord Jesus
may be glorified in you,
and you in him,
according to the grace of our God
and the Lord Jesus Christ."*

~ Apostle Paul (2 Timothy 1:11-12)

CHAPTER 19: WHAT IS PRAYER AND WHAT IT IS NOT?

Have you heard the saying, "A prayerless Christian is a powerless Christian"? Likewise, a prayerless church is a powerless church. That's how important it is for us, as an individual and as a community of faith, to learn, live, and lead the way to a lifestyle of prayer or culture of prayer. Compare prayer like you're riding on your car or a bus load of people, and it's running with a gas tank and there's a hole underneath the tank. Common sense will tell you that both vehicles will eventually run out of gas, and even if you fill the tank, it will always be drained until it stops. The point is that prayer is the fuel that keeps our soul going in this journey and sets our spirit aflame for God. It drives our spiritual life with peace and power, meaning, peace that keeps us closer with God and power that makes our lives extraordinarily lived with spiritual authority.

Several researches have been made about the benefits of prayer. In the book *The Healing Power of Prayer: The Surprising Connection Between Prayer and Your Health* by Chester Tolson and Harold Koenig (2003), they observed that prayer helps in relieving stress, improving attitudes and mending bodies. In this study made at Duke University, the authors saw that there's a connection between prayer and generating power, peace, and health, including the reduction of psychological stress. Now, some criticize their finding as too strong and unscientific, but the Bible is clear about the relationship between prayer and our personal well-being. The Apostle Paul encouraged the early believers in the city of Philippi, saying,

> *Do not be **anxious** about anything, but **in everything by prayer and supplication with thanksgiving** let your requests be made known to God. And the peace of God, which surpasses all understanding, will guard your hearts and your minds in Christ Jesus. (Philippians 4:6-7).*

Paul, emphasized the importance of prayer, in all its various forms, to our personal and total well-being. Paul commanded these early Christians *to pray and not worry*. He also underscored that in every aspect of our lives, in every circumstance, *"in everything"* and for everything, we must keep on praying. For Paul, prayer is a lifestyle. It's our spiritual breath that keeps our Christian journey alive and well. We cannot afford to neglect prayer and expect an extraordinary life journey. Without prayer, that won't happen. We will only be stuck in the ordinary and weak kind of life.

We must understand that prayer is a universal language. Since ancient times, people have been praying to their deities. In the Bible, especially in Genesis 4:26, it mentions a time when people began praying to God. Since then, if we read from Genesis to Revelation, here's an overview about what prayer is.

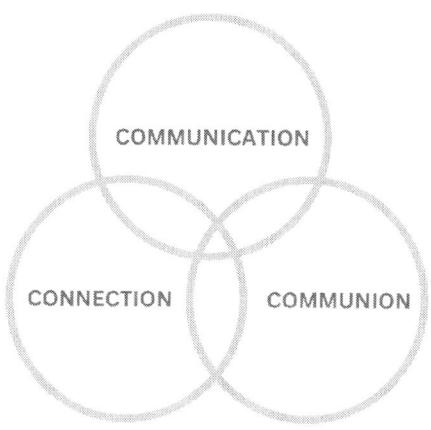

First, prayer is your means of communication with God. It's not a magic formula of invoking a deity. A dictionary defines prayer as "a solemn request for help or expression of thanks addressed to God or an object of worship." But from a biblical and Christian perspective, prayer is more than just a call for help or saying 'thank you' to God. These two are important kinds of prayer for specific purposes.

In the Bible, however, prayer is a way or form of talking *with* God. There are also some examples of prayers, like the following:

- *Prayer of Salvation and Repentance* is a heartfelt prayer of asking God for salvation by fully trusting in Jesus as their personal Lord and Savior, and by turning back from their sins.

- *Prayer of Supplication* is a kind of prayer of earnestly asking and humbly begging God on behalf of other people (Ephesians 6:18; Philippians 4:6).

- *Prayer of Thanksgiving* is a prayer of gratitude for specific things received from God. It is an expression of being thankful to God (Ephesians 1:16; Philippians 1:3; Colossians 4:2).

- *Prayer of Faith* is a form of prayer of fully believing in God to do something, like healing or anything that needs an abundance of faith to be fulfilled (James 5:13-18).

- *Prayer of the Holy Spirit* is a prayer that's beyond our comprehension as the Holy Spirit intercedes for us and expresses himself inside us with "groanings too deep for words," especially when we're too weak and do not know what to pray for.

- *Prayer of Consecration* is a form of prayer mentioned in the Bible for the purpose of declaring something for God's sacred purposes, like the ordination of spiritual leaders, dedication of the tabernacle or temple or church, and so on (Romans 8:26-27).

- *Prayer of Intercession.* This prayer is an act of intervening for someone or on behalf of another person. It's like you mediate in between and stand in the gap for the sake of others before God (Exodus 33:12-23; Jeremiah 27:18).

With all these examples, prayer is not a magic spell or some mumbo-jumbo. It's a very personal means of communication with God, as well as a public act of coming together to commune with him.

Second, prayer is your primary connection with God. It's not a ritual. Prayer is where we join together with God and we are given direct access and open communication. In other words, prayer provides personal and relational

135

connection with God. As such, it is not a mindless ritual you perform or a reenactment of something without fully understanding it. God said, *"Call to me and I will answer you,* and will tell you great and hidden things that you have not known" (Jeremiah 33:3). Many Christians call this verse as your spiritual and direct phone line to God. Just dial 3-3-3 and you're fine. But prayer is more than having a direct line to heaven as if God is in his office or distant home. Do you know the reason why? It's because God is "all-present" (or as some would say, "omnipresent"). If God is right where you are and he is always with you, then that makes a huge difference than calling someone from afar. God's presence changes everything about prayer.

As our connection with God, prayer is closely speaking to God and intimately hearing him through his Word in our inner spirit. That's why prayer is needed when we read the Word of God to allow the Holy Spirit to speak to us through the Word. Indeed, prayer is considered an act of lovingly listening for God's voice. It's often a two-way connection, not a one-way street.

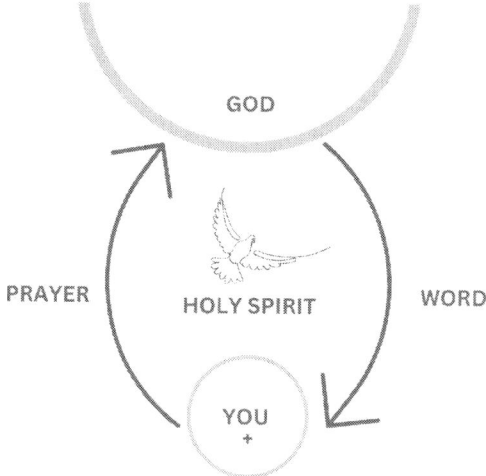

Remember, when you gave your life to Jesus and fully trusted him as your Lord and Savior, the Holy Spirit lives within you. He is your direct link with God. When you pray, you talk to God. When you read and meditate on God's Word, he speaks to you through it and in your inner spirit.

Third, prayer is your state of communion with God. It's not an attempt to conform God to our own wishes, whims, and false ideas. It's also not about impressing people but being intimately close and living with God. This idea of communion with God is the main reason why prayer is a lifestyle of living in the presence of God. Every thought, every act, and every word spoken to God is an expression of prayer, conversation and engagement with our Lord and Savior. The problem is when we think of "communion with God," we often imagine "the Lord's Supper." But communion is about *living together, not just eating together*. So when we commune with God, we are actually living with him and for him every moment, everywhere, and in everything. The idea of a biblical prayer is a continuing act of giving God our trust and, in return, receiving inner peace, strength, and joy in his presence.

One of the most challenging aspects of prayer is its low visibility. Jesus said,

> *"And **when you pray**, you must not be like the hypocrites. For they love to stand and pray in the synagogues and at the street corners, that they may be seen by others. Truly, I say to you, they have received their reward. But **when you pray**, go into **your room** and shut the door and **pray to your Father who is in secret**. And your Father who sees **in secret** will reward you."* (Matthew 6:5-6)

Sometimes, we're tempted to think that since prayer is made "in secret," it is least appreciated. So, we conclude that it is not rewarding. But that's short-term and skewed thinking. What's worse is when people sometimes consider prayer as a quick fix for their common sense problems, like having answers on an exam they didn't prepare for or studied, winning a sport, or worse, using God as an accessory to their pride, greed, and sinful desires. Some Pharisees tried it but it didn't work. We shouldn't do that either for that's not how our Master designed prayer.

Reflection:

What is your level of practicing prayer right now? (1 being lowest and 10 being the highest)

| 1 | 2 | 3 | 4 | 5 | 6 | 7 | 8 | 9 | 10 |

What is the most important lesson you learned about biblical prayer here?

CHAPTER 20: WHY IS PRAYER IMPORTANT IN OUR LIFE JOURNEY?

The ultimate destination of prayer is more of changing us into Christ-likeness rather than changing God's mind. Let's not lose that focus about prayer. It's about transforming the person in the process while we are on this spiritual journey. Here are some reasons why prayer is essential for us as Jesus followers.

First, prayer allows you to have an inner experience of the Holy Spirit's empowerment. This truth is one of the most powerful realities in the Scripture: God himself, not just anybody else, is praying for you. Read these words of the apostle Paul.

> *Likewise **the Spirit helps us in our weakness**. For we do not know what to pray for as we ought, but **the Spirit himself intercedes for us** with groanings too deep for words. And he who searches hearts knows what is the mind of the Spirit, because **the Spirit intercedes for the saints** according to the will of God.* (Romans 8:26-27).

Here, the real power of prayer is not in prayer itself, but in the power of the Spirit of God that works effectively within us when we pray. In our human nature, we are weak but our weaknesses are opportunities for God to manifest his power and strength. Even though it is not our human nature to pray, God uses our weaknesses for his glory. The word *"groaning"* in Greek emphasizes pain and agony due to suffering (like sighing). These are powerful truths in the Bible about the Holy Spirit working inside your heart and he is interceding on your behalf before God.

The Bible teaches that it is the Holy Spirit praying for the saints, which are the *living* Christians (If you are a believer in Jesus, the Bible calls you a saint. There is nothing in the Bible that we have to pray to the long-dead saints. It was a later dogma that started in the 3rd century.) These groanings of prayer are not mumbling words or empty phrases but agonizing sounds from deep within. We all know that Jesus warned us about empty words in prayers. He said to his disciples,

> *"And **when you pray, do not heap up empty phrases** as the Gentiles do, for they think that they will be heard for their many words. Do not be like them, for your Father knows what you need before you ask him."* (Matthew 6:7-8)

When you pray for your needs and the needs of others, like your family, friends, fellowship, fellow people, you don't need to flaunt your eloquence for God knows everyone's yearnings, desires, dreams, and necessities. It is also useless to make repetitious prayers as if God does not know or hear your prayers. (Just imagine how you feel if your child or friend comes to you and constantly repeats a statement). That's how empowering it is to simply come to God in prayer and allow the Spirit to express his peace and power upon you.

Second, prayer develops a healthy confidence and trust in God. This reason should encourage everyone to enter the inner presence of God and not just settle in fear from a distance. John the Beloved said to the early Christians,

> *"And this is **the confidence** that **we have toward him**, that if we ask anything according to his will he hears us. And if **we know** that he hears us in whatever we ask, **we know** that we have the requests that we have asked of him."* (1 John 5:14-15)

When you fully embrace this principle, prayer makes us more healthy in our confidence and humble in our spirit. If a person claims to have a prayerful life, and yet has developed an elitist attitude, that's an indication that the person needs to pray right, not just more. Do you know why? It's because prayer transforms us to have godly confidence, keeping us in line with God's will. Not only that, when we pray, God is listening and he answers our prayers according to his perfect will.

Third, prayer was commanded in the Scripture. This is another reason why prayer is important in our life journey. It's a matter of obedience to our Lord.

Some of these commands are evident to the life of the believers. *"Rejoice in hope, be patient in tribulation, **be constant in prayer**"* (Romans 12:12). It means we have to *"be faithful in prayer."* Also, Paul added, *"**Continue steadfastly in prayer**, being watchful in it with thanksgiving"* (Colossians 4:2). If prayer was commanded, therefore, it is a call for obedience. As a church, prayer should be on top of our priorities and at the core of our existence. It should not be just "a part" of our ministry but "the ministry" that fuels our every ministry. Why?

It's because everything we do here in church is an impossible thing. Think of worship. What will happen if we do not learn how to pray? Can we really approach God with our own abilities? How can we overcome sin apart from prayer? How would people be changed without prayer? How can we win souls without prayer? If prayer is not at the center of our life as a person or as a local church, why are we even here?

Fourth, prayer is a rewarding experience. It gives us the benefit of living an authentic Christian life. That's why we cannot use prayer as a cover up or a facade in our Christian journey. We have been warned to be like the Pharisees who displayed their seeming high-spirituality and impressively praying to be seen by people. Why do you think Jesus commanded his disciples to pray and go inside their room and shut the door and pray to the *"Father who is in secret"*? It's because when we pray, we cannot hide who we are before God. We may be able to appear differently to others, but in the presence of God who is all-knowing and all-seeing, there's nothing to hide. That's why we can have a rewarding experience in prayer because we can be set free from the double life we have.

We can be true to God and ourselves, therefore, setting us free from the bondage of hypocrisy and false virtue. Jesus' promise is this: *"And **your Father** who sees in secret **will reward you**"* (Matthew 6:5-6). Why is spending time with God in secret a rewarding experience? How about setting yourself free from the false expectations of others? How about gaining his approval from your Father rather than the endless impressions of strangers? How about being free to be yourself and be forgiven of all your sins and shortcomings? The point is, your rewards from God are too great. So don't settle for less. Living a genuine or authentic Christian life can only be developed through faithful prayer.

Fifth, prayer is an essential spiritual discipline for a Jesus follower. Thousands of books and millions of pages have been written about Christian prayer and the life it produces. But nothing compares to what Jesus demonstrated and taught about it. Jesus is the best model for us when it comes to prayer. The Gospel of Matthew narrated, *"Now Jesus was **praying in a certain place**, and when he finished, one of his disciples said to him, 'Lord, teach us to pray, as John taught his disciples'"* (Matthew 11:1). The disciples must have seen the example of Jesus because he lived it. For Jesus, prayer is more caught than taught. The disciples must have seen where or what "certain place" Jesus prayed, how often he prayed, and what he prayed about.

However, a few important questions should be asked: If Jesus is the Son of God, why would he pray? Why would he bother and spend time in prayer? If you know the real answers to these questions, then you'll never take prayer as the same anymore. Jesus prayed not because he needed to, but because you needed it. He enjoyed the intimate communication, the close connection and the constant communion with his Father. There's nothing in this world that's far better peaceful and powerful than being in the presence of his Father. When Jesus' disciples saw his prayer life, they cannot help themselves but ask a major request: *"Lord, teach us to pray."*

Reflection:

If Jesus valued prayer as his way of constantly communicating and communing with his Father, what should be your attitude towards prayer? What is its role in your spiritual life?

What have you discovered in this chapter about the true teachings of the Bible about prayer?

CHAPTER 21: HOW TO PRAY?

Are you tired of praying and repeating your prayers like the ones you're saying before meals? I grew up on a spiritual journey where I didn't like memorizing my prayers. I struggled with the idea of going to my Dad in heaven and utter words that I rehearsed and memorized. Why would I do that? If I'm not doing that to my parents, I won't do it to my heavenly Father either.

When I was in a youth discipleship ministry before, I learned basic principles on how to pray. Here's a simple example of praying. We call it the ACTS model. It is an acronym we follow as starters so that we will not lose our focus. You can also do this example and simplify your prayer and make it more natural like having a conversation with God.

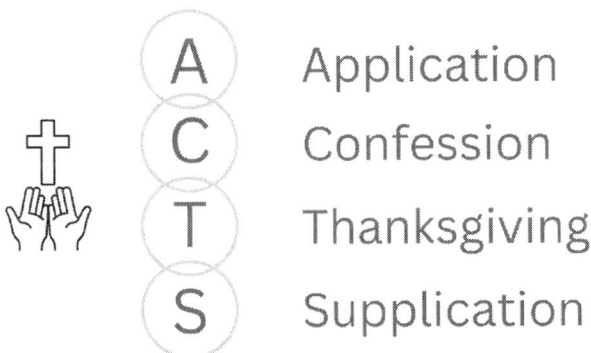

A   Application

C   Confession

T   Thanksgiving

S   Supplication

- **A - *Adoration*.** This first part of our prayer is where you approach God with deep humility, reverence, and lift his name. Think of all the things you love about God and praise him. Focus on his names (Creator, Father, Lord, God, Savior, etc.), characters (holy, love, gracious, etc.) and nature (eternal, unchanging, spirit, etc.). Worship him for who he is.

- **C - *Confession*.** After worshiping and focusing on God, you now look at your inmost self. You ask God to check your heart if you have committed sins. In the spirit of humility, ask God to forgive you for specific sins and cleanse you from all your shortcomings (Psalm 32:5; 38:18; 1 John 1:9).

- **T - *Thanksgiving*.** Briefly, after confessing your sins, you think of all the blessings and other significant things you received from God, like God's daily provisions, help in times of trouble, and so on. (1 Corinthians 1:4; Ephesians 1:16)

- **S- *Supplication*.** Right after you express your gratitude, this is where you focus on other people and pray on their behalf, like your family, friends, and other people (Ephesians 6:18; Philippians 4:6).

This pattern in prayer was very helpful for me at the beginning, especially as a teenager. That's how I started my journey of learning how to pray. But if you'd like to grow deeper and deeper in prayer, we need to be more sensitive and learn from Jesus' life and teachings on prayer. Let's see "the Lord's Prayer" or better, "The Disciples' Prayer" because this prayer is being taught to the disciples to follow. Jesus said,

> *Pray then like this: "Our Father in heaven, hallowed be your name. Your kingdom come, your will be done, on earth as it is in heaven. Give us this day our daily bread, and forgive us our debts, as we also have forgiven our debtors. And lead us not into temptation, but deliver us from evil."* (Matthew 6:9-13)

We believe that every word in the Bible is inspired by God in the original. As such, it is highly encouraged for us to memorize verses from the Bible word for word. Some of the earliest manuscripts may not have the last line: "*For yours is the kingdom and the power and the glory, forever. Amen.*" But nonetheless, we must take note when Jesus said to pray "like this," not memorize and keep repeating it as it is. Here, we will go through this prayer that Jesus taught to know, understand, and pray from our hearts, and not just memorize it. Here are some specific instructions that will help you in your prayer life journey.

First, address your prayer to the Father and worship him. Jesus taught by saying, "***Our Father*** *in heaven,* **hallowed** *be your name.*" This opening shows us to approach God with due consideration of your relationship with him. Generally, as human beings created by God, he is every person's Father. However, if you trusted Jesus as your Lord and Savior, then God is your heavenly Father. You are his child, so you have access to his heavenly throne. He is open and more than willing to listen to what you have to say. Focus on God and your relationship with him and address him as he is.

Second, align your prayer to God's will and kingdom agenda. Jesus' next phrase is "***Your kingdom*** *come,* ***your will*** *be done, on earth as it is in heaven.*" Do you want your prayers to always be answered by God, 100%? Then pray in accordance with God's will and his kingdom agenda. If you pray against his will and desires, why would God answer your prayers? Seek him first, his mission and his plan, and all the things you ask him, he will answer in accordance to his perfect will. Straighten your prayers by streamlining them with God's purposes and he will answer your prayers much more than you imagine. If you counterflow, you will only end up frustrated and discouraged.

Third, ask for your specific needs. Jesus taught his disciples to pray and ask for their daily provisions and needs. "*Give us this day our* ***daily bread.***" Why would Jesus teach his disciples to ask God for their daily needs? Jesus taught that we can ask from and receive from him and by this posture and attitude, we learn how to trust and know him everyday. He even said, "*And I tell you, ask, and it will be given to you; seek, and you will find; knock, and it will be opened to you*" (Luke 11:9). All of these statements are in the context of prayer. When you come before God in prayer, ask him for your needs and those God-given desires in your own simple words. You can also pray for the specific needs of others.

Fourth, agree with God that you have sinned and in need of his forgiveness. Jesus highlighted the act of confession for our sins in this prayer. "*And* ***forgive us*** *our debts* [or sins] *as we also have forgiven our debtors,*" Jesus taught. But why is this so important for Jesus that he would even add more teaching about it? In the following verses he added and said, "*For if you forgive others their trespasses, your heavenly Father will also forgive you, but if you do not forgive others their trespasses, neither will your Father forgive your trespass*" (v.14).

The answer is clear. If we harbor sins in our hearts, including the lack of forgiveness to others, it will hinder God to powerfully move and answer our prayers. We must humble ourselves and confess our sins to him, then he will forgive us and heal us. This is both true on a personal and collective level. Some examples are:

- **Personal**: *"Is anyone among you suffering? Let him pray. Is anyone cheerful? Let him sing praise. Is anyone among you sick? Let him call for the elders of the church, and let them pray over him, anointing him with oil in the name of the Lord. And the prayer of faith will save the one who is sick, and the Lord will raise him up. And if he has committed sins, he will* **be forgiven***. Therefore,* **confess your sins** *to one another and pray for one another, that you may be healed."* (James 5:13-16)

- **Collective**: *"If my people who are called by my name humble themselves, and pray and seek my face and turn from their wicked ways, then I will hear from heaven and will* **forgive their sin** *and heal their land."* (2 Chronicles 7:14)

Fifth, arm yourself for spiritual challenges. Jesus also emphasized this part in our prayers. *"And lead us not into* **temptations***, but deliver us from evil"* (or the evil one). Are you wondering why in such a time as these, the world is experiencing more wickedness like never before? Families are breaking apart, divorce and fatherlessness are skyrocketing, porn is everywhere, and other kinds of spiritual and relational problems. Jesus' best antidote to these ever-spreading temptations is prayer. He commanded his disciples, ***"Watch and pray** that you may not enter into temptation. The spirit indeed is willing, but the flesh is weak"* (Matthew 26:41). Why do you think Jesus is emphasizing both watchfulness and prayer-fullness in every disciple's life? Even the apostle Paul highlighted this lifestyle of prayer when he said, *"Praying at all times in the Spirit, with all prayer and supplication. To that end,* **keep alert** *with all perseverance, making supplication for all the saints"* (Ephesians 6:18).

Lastly, but not the least, pray in the name of Jesus. The word "Amen" means "so be it." There are many passages in the Bible that show and teach the importance of praying in Jesus' powerful name. It shows his authority. The disciples prayed and acted in the name of Jesus. Even Paul pointed out the relationship of our prayer and Jesus' name when he said, *"Giving thanks always and for everything to God the Father* **in the name of our Lord Jesus Christ"**

(Ephesians 5:20). This verse among many is just one example on how we come before God's throne and pray in the authority of the Son, not our own.

Action Steps: Here's one vital practice we can apply about prayer. ***Pray for others.*** From this moment on, practice praying for the following.

- ***The salvation for all non-believing people and those in authority, especially those known to you.*** This prayer is of utmost priority. Paul is not taking this for granted and he wanted the church of Jesus to pray seriously. Meditate on these words:

  *"First of all, then, I urge that **supplications, prayers, intercessions, and thanksgivings be made for all people, for kings and all who are in high positions***, that we may lead a peaceful and quiet life, godly and dignified in every way. This is good, and it is pleasing in the sight of **God our Savior, who desires all people to be saved and to come to the knowledge of the truth.**"* (1 Timothy 2:1-4)

- ***The servants of God.*** I cannot underemphasize this one. Jesus himself said, *"The harvest is plentiful, but the laborers are few. Therefore **pray earnestly to the Lord of the harvest** to send out **laborers** into his harvest"* (Luke 10:2). One of the reasons why I set my notification is to remind myself every 10:02AM daily to pray to send more laborers because the harvest is massive. Which one is more important, our "seating capacity" or our "sending capacity"? If we're working together to fulfill the Great Commission, we have to pray for more workers. The apostle Paul solicited the prayers of the church. *"At the same time, **pray also for us**, that God may open to us a door for the word, to declare the mystery of Christ, on account of which I am in prison"* (Colossians 4:3). After all, if the evil one will attack any community of faith, who do you think will Satan take down first? You should not wonder why God's servants need prayer support and covering.

- ***The spiritual maturity and ministry of Jesus' disciples.*** Do you know why your spiritual leaders are praying for you by name and what are they praying for each and everyone of you? Here's a window of prayer for you.

*To this end we always **pray for you**, that our God may make you worthy of his calling and may fulfill every resolve for good and every work of faith by his power, so that the name of our Lord Jesus may be glorified in you, and you in him, according to the grace of our God and the Lord Jesus Christ.* (2 Thessalonians 1:11-12)

Are you taking seriously God's call for your spiritual maturity? How about your call for a ministry? Why do you think it is so important to work "by his power"? God's servants are constantly praying for you, will you pray for them in return?

As God knows you by name and as God's servants pray for you by name, you can make a prayer list of individuals to pray for. If you go back to the ACTS model, this is the Supplication part. Pray for these groups specifically and regularly, using your hand as a guide.

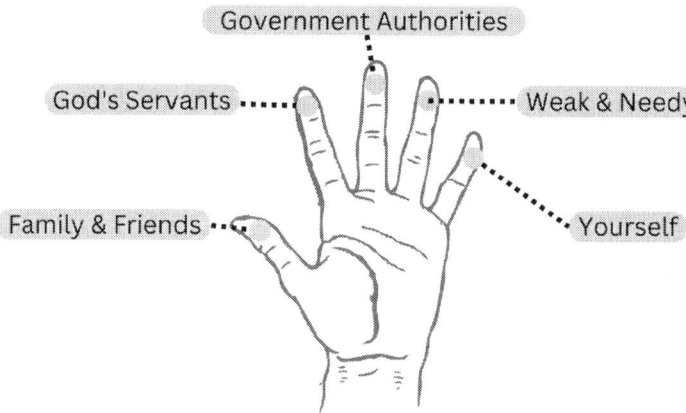

- ***Family and Friends.*** Your thumb is the closest finger to your heart. Use it to represent the closest people to you when you pray.

- ***God's Servants.*** Your index finger usually used to make a point symbolizes the pastors, teachers and leaders. Pray for them too.

- ***Government Authorities.*** The longest finger symbolizes those in power down to the lowest cabinet. Keep praying for them.

- **Weak and Needy.** Use the fourth finger, sometimes considered the weakest, to represent those vulnerable individuals who needed help.

- **Yourself.** The little finger represents you. One strength of this approach in prayer is we think of others first when we pray. Here, you pray for your personal requests, needs, and other desires.

It helps also if you print out the names of the people you are praying for and make a schedule to pray for them. What matters most is that when we pray, we are open to the Holy Spirit's activities in our lives and become discerning to God's voice. We can only learn prayer by doing it. Take one small step at a time and see how God will work in you and through you.

Reflection:

Review the A.C.T.S. of prayer and memorize it. Pray a simple prayer following the outline by expressing your own words as you talk to God.

Make a list of the names of non-believing individuals and pray for them, especially their salvation. Write at least 5 for each relationship.

- Family: _____

- Friends: _____

- Co-workers: _____

- Neighbors: _____

SECTION 8: COME TO THE TABLE

"Do this in remembrance of me."

~ Jesus, Luke 22:19

CHAPTER 22: HOW DID "THE BREAKING OF BREAD" BEGUN?

Have you ever thought about the "Lord's Supper," why it has several names connected with it, like "Communion," "Eucharist," etc.? I believe many of us have already attended a church or churches where the communion was made and we participated in it. Since we all came from different backgrounds, we need to discover (or rediscover) and revisit the biblical history in the Bible and see if what we know about the Lord's Supper is consistent.

Interestingly enough, even the title or exact phrase "The Lord's Supper" is not in the Bible, especially in the New Testament. What we can see is that it is written as a paragraph title, but not in the original texts and translations. However, it doesn't mean it didn't exist.

What we often find in the New Testament is "the breaking of bread." According to the Bible, especially in the earliest history of the church of Jesus, the believers practiced "the breaking of bread." In the book of Acts, we find this brief summary.

> *And they devoted themselves to the apostles' teaching and the fellowship, to **the breaking of bread** and the prayers....And day by day, attending the temple together and **breaking bread** in their homes, they received their food with glad and generous hearts, praising God and having favor with all the people. And the Lord added to their number day by day those who were being saved.* (Acts 2:42, 46-47)

In this passage alone, we can see some essential clues about the practice of the breaking of bread by the earliest believers in Jesus. First, they devoted or faithfully observed the breaking of bread. Secondly, it is also possible that most, if not all, of their fellowships involved the breaking of bread. Thirdly, the breaking of bread was being practiced in their homes or small group fellowships, not just in big public gatherings in the temple area. And lastly, the breaking of bread was also connected with their meals together. Definitely, this early church practice didn't come out of the bubble. There is a historical past for the breaking of bread.

Briefly, let's walk through biblical history. *Let's remember that Jesus and his disciples were Jewish.* The Jewish people regularly celebrate the Passover. What was the Passover all about? During the time of Jesus and the disciples, it is a long-held celebration and major 7-day observance about the Exodus story of the Israelites when God delivered their ancestors from slavery and escaped from Egypt's bondage (Read Exodus 11-12 for the full story).

On the final day of their deliverance, God instructed the Hebrew people to do a meal with unleavened bread and a paschal lamb as a sacrifice of atonement (or covering of sin). The blood of the lamb would be applied on doorposts and windows. If any household would be found without it, the firstborn sons would die when the Angel of Death passed over Egypt. On that very night, the family must eat the lamb's meat and not break any bones. They also have to eat the unleavened bread together and consume everything. If not, all of these foods and remains, like bones, must be burned as a sacred sacrifice.

OLD TESTAMENT
Old Covenant

Bread

Unleavend Bread   The Bread of the Presence

Passover   Tabernacle / Temple

Blood of lambs

Since then, after they all left from Egypt to the Promised Land, the unleavened bread is a key symbol in the Hebrew people's spiritual journey. They always have "the Bread of the Presence" inside their tabernacle or temple (Exodus 25:30; 35:13; Numbers 4:7; 1 Samuel 31:6; 2 Chronicles 4:19). They may consider it as "sacred," but never as a "god" in a material form. That would be idolatry. The bread symbolizes the sacred covenant of God with Israel and it will be fulfilled in Jesus.

During this Passover week, and as Jesus saw his coming suffering, death, and resurrection, he wanted to spend his last dinner with his twelve disciples. So he invited his disciples to spend their Passover meal together. This celebration also coincided with the Feast of the Unleavened Bread, which is likely Thursday in our calendar (Matthew 26:17-25). During this Passover meal and the first day of the Feast of Unleavened Bread, Jesus set or established what came to be known as "the Last Supper." Obviously, this is dinner (not breakfast or lunch). So, it does not make sense to call the breaking of bread in the church as "supper" if it is done in the morning service or noon time. Unless the breaking of bread is done in the evening, we'd better reconsider using the phrase "The Lord's Supper" for breakfast or lunch. This is the reason why most churches today call it "The Lord's Table" because it is more generic and not confusing, and the essential meaning is all the same.

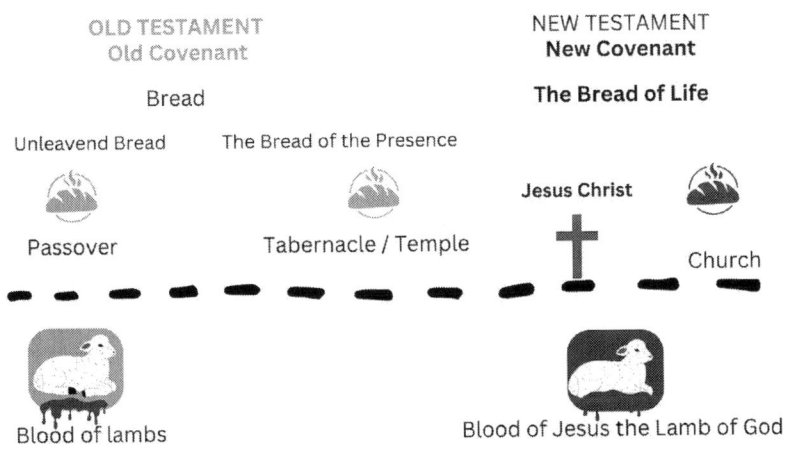

Now, going back to Jesus and his apostles, there's something better that's happening, as Jesus is revealing the ultimate fulfillment of these Old Testament practices and symbolic acts. He now leads them to enter into a new era of God's covenant. He is now showing them the ultimate point of the unleavened bread and the blood of the sacrificial lamb that they, as Jews, have been observing for a long time since their forefathers left Egypt to the Promised Land.

In Matthew 26:26-29, we see Jesus, in his authority as the Son of God, setting or instituting the Lord's Supper as his new ordinance. *"Now as they were eating,* **Jesus took bread***, and after blessing it* **broke it** *and gave it to the disciples, and said, 'Take, eat; this is my body.'"* According to their sacred observance, Jesus picked a loaf of unleavened bread. As he was holding it in his hands, he also blessed or spoke blessings to the unleavened bread as prescribed in their Passover meals (Exodus 12:14). Whatever he said about it, we could only imagine that he is taking this great opportunity to explain how this unleavened bread that he's holding has become his body that will be brutally broken at his coming suffering and crucifixion. As Jesus broke it with his hands and gave it to his disciples, they must have received it with a renewed knowledge and understanding (no matter how partial and limited) of how this ordinary unleavened bread represents something that is extraordinary, which is Jesus the Bread of Life.

Then, Jesus said, *"Take, eat; this is my body."* And they all obeyed and followed his command. *If there's one major reason why we do communion is because it is a command of Jesus.* That's the reason why Christians throughout history consider the communion as a sacred ordinance to be carried out. Thus, doing it is a matter of obedience and following Jesus.

But what does *"this* [bread] *is my body"* mean? Remember, even though the disciples were taught and discipled by Jesus, they were not sophisticated philosophers, scholars, and theologians. They were ordinary people in the community that were chosen by God's grace, not because they were somebody in the society. The question is this: Is it literal or spiritual? If it is literal, does it mean the body became God-man because that's the nature of Jesus?

It follows, perhaps after the meal or right after the breaking of bread.

*And he **took a cup**, and when he had **given thanks** he gave it to them, saying, 'Drink of it, all of you, for this is my blood of the covenant, which is poured out for many for the forgiveness of sins. I tell you I will not drink again of this fruit of the vine until that day when I drink it new with you in my Father's kingdom.* (Matthew 26:27-29)

Notice carefully, Jesus *"took a cup."* To suggest this cup is something special, it should be titled as "the cup," but no. This is an ordinary cup they use for drinking water or wine. It's not some special, golden chalice like a trophy. However, it was not mentioned in the Bible whether it was wine or water. While holding the cup, Jesus gave *"thanks."* The phrase *"gave thanks"* came from the Greek *eucharisteó*, meaning "to be thankful." That's where we get the English word "eucharist." As such, when you hear the word "eucharist," its original meaning is *thanksgiving*, not transforming the liquid in the cup into a divine-human blood. (The same is true with the bread. Thanksgiving does not transform a bread, cracker, or wafer into an embodiment of God.) That would be unthinkable for the Jewish disciples to take, even blasphemous. And then again, Jesus gave his command, *"Drink of it, all of you, for this is my blood of the covenant."* And they all did.

Reflection:

What is your level of understanding about communion based on the Bible right now? (1 being lowest and 10 being the highest)

    1   2   3   4   5   6   7   8   9   10

Based on Israel's summary of background about the bread (like the "unleavened bread" or "the bread of the Presence") and wine (like the blood of the Lamb"), how did Jesus fulfill those Old Testament symbols in the Lord's Table?

CHAPTER 23: WHAT DOES THE "LORD'S TABLE" MEAN?

As Christians we grew up with preconceived ideas about communion, perhaps due to our long exposure to the practice of the eucharist. The lingering question remains: Is the "bread" and "blood" literal the body and the blood of Jesus? We must understand that the Jewish people, including Jesus and the first disciples, were forbidden to drink literal blood (See Leviticus 17:13-14). It's because the blood represents life, not to mention the toxic it absorbs. Moreover, drinking blood is a pagan practice that their neighboring gentile nations offer libations in their ceremonies.

Did you know that in the early church, Satan has been trying to keep some of those who used to practice offering food and drinks to idols and he's been infiltrating the church by twisting the idea of bread and wine? Read 1 Corinthians 10:14-22 where Paul concluded, "*You cannot drink* **the cup of the Lord** *and the cup of demons. You cannot partake of* **the table of the Lord** *and the table of demons.*" That's how serious we should be when it comes to the observance of the Lord's table, making sure it's undiluted by wrong theology and it is pure in the eyes of God. We cannot just take it for granted.

If it's unthinkable that Jesus would encourage his disciples to do the *literal* sense, Christians today must follow him. We know, historically, there is no practice of blood drinking in Israel (even though in the past decades many accusations and atrocities of "blood libel" were made against the Jews in different pockets of the world, accusing them of literally drinking the blood of innocent victims, but that's malicious and untrue). Even so, within the Christian world, there have been many ideas circulating about "the bread and blood" controversy. During the Roman period, Christians in the past were also accused of secretly practicing a form of cannibalism in their secret meetings and that's one of the lies that some Romans did to persecute Christians. As such, we need to be straight in our knowledge, understanding and belief.

For us to have a better understanding about the Lord's Table, let's take *the two major elements* of the Lord's Table, which are *the bread* and *the cup* (of wine).

The Bread = "My Body"

According to Jesus, the unleavened bread is called *"my body."* Previously, in Jesus' public ministry, we must remember, there was already some confusion that happened about Jesus' statement about his claim as *"the bread of life"* or *"the true bread from heaven,"* and *"the living bread."* It happened in John 6:48-51, when he said,

> *"**I am the bread of life**. Your fathers ate the manna in the wilderness, and they died. This is **the bread** that comes down from heaven, so that one may eat of it and not die. **I am the living bread** that came down from heaven. If anyone eats of **this bread**, he will live forever. And **the bread** that I will give for the life of the world is my flesh."*

Jesus indicated that "the bread" has something to do with his physical body, which he referred to as *"my flesh."* His body is needed in God's plan for salvation to be the final sacrifice, because a spirit cannot be crucified. Remember, Jesus was not yet crucified at this time, therefore, his body was not yet "broken" symbolically. Jesus is pointing out that as no human can live without food, anyone who wants to live forever must believe in him and not die. Apart from Jesus, there can never be eternal life. As such, one must put their faith in him so that the believer can live for eternity.

The dispute among those who heard and were confused emerged: *"How can this man give us his flesh to eat?"* (John 6:52). Jesus replied without hesitation,

> *"Truly, truly, I say to you, unless you eat the flesh of the Son of Man and drink his blood, you have no life in you. Whoever feeds on my flesh and drinks my blood has eternal life, and I will raise him up on the last day. For my flesh is true food, and my blood is true drink. Whoever feeds on my flesh and drinks my blood abides in me, and I in him."* (John 6:53-56)

And then Jesus stopped his discourse without further explanation. What were the results? Some were stunned. Some went kaboom in their minds. *"This is a hard saying; who can listen to it?"* (John 6:60). If you're confused, you're not alone.

But sadly, many disciples made a huge mistake. *"After this many of his disciples turned back and no longer walked with him"* (John 6:66). It means they could not comprehend the words of Jesus if they think of it literally. Were they spiritually blind? Remember, they were called (or professing to be) "disciples." Was Jesus worried? No.

He even stated the nature of his discourse. *"The words that I have spoken to you are spirit and life. But there are some of you who do not believe"* (John 6:63). In other words, these "spiritual truths" and "spiritual revelation" that Jesus said about him as the Bread of Life and his body (or flesh) as bread broken for his disciples are definitely *spiritual,* not literal. It is symbolic of something divine. The eating and drinking of the flesh and blood cannot be a form of cannibalism or blood-drinking literally, like in some pagan practices. In the words of Jesus, during the Lord's Supper, the unleavened bread in the hands of Jesus was *not literally* his body but it is a spiritual representation and has spiritual meaning.

The Cup (of Wine?) = "My Blood"

How about the cup? Have you noticed why there's a close parenthesis? Why do you think so? Actually, there was no specific mention in the Bible about the "wine." Where did most people get the idea that it was wine? One of the clues that many use is the phrase in Jesus' statement, saying, *"I tell you I will not drink again of this fruit of the vine"* (Matthew 26:28). This *"fruit of the vine"* is a likely indication that it is referring to red grapes fermenting and turning the wine into a blood color. Of course, the green grapes produce white wine in its fermentation process. You might be asking, is alcohol ok in the Lord's Table? Is it going to encourage wine drinking in the church? Hold on.

During Jesus' time, the fermented drink only contained 11-12% alcohol. It is not a distilled alcohol because it is often mixed with water, from 2:1 to 20:1 ratio. So, the alcohol content is tolerable and not intoxicating. After all, the early church was forbidden to get drunk with wine and instead they must be filled with the Holy Spirit, not the spirits of alcohol (Read Ephesians 5:18). The point of the blood as wine in the Lord's Table is not about its content but its symbolism. There's no prescribed requirement that the element should be a wine or a red-colored juice or drink, but rather what it truly represents. It reminds us of the blood of Jesus offered at the cross for the forgiveness of our sins.

What, then, is the spiritual significance of Jesus' *"blood"* in the Lord's Table? When Jesus said *"my blood,"* the emphasis is on *his holy nature*. It means that Jesus' blood is crucial when it comes to our salvation. In what ways? I'll draw you attention to Hebrews 9:11-28 where we can learn a lot about the power of the blood of Jesus:

- Jesus' blood secured our salvation (v.12). Without his blood there's no salvation.
- His blood purified us from our sins (v.13). You can only be washed white from your sins by Jesus' blood.
- The blood of Jesus is without blemish (v.14). A sea of blood of sinful people is not worthy to be compared to a single drop of Jesus' holy blood.
- His blood is better than the blood of the old covenant in the Old Testament (vv.17-11). No animal blood is sufficient for our sins.
- Jesus' blood is his own, unlike the Old Testament priests who offer the blood of the animals when they enter the temple (v.23-26)
- Jesus sacrificed himself *once and for all* to put away sin (v.26)

The essential truth in all of these for us is this: *"without the shedding of **blood** there is no forgiveness of sins"* (Hebrews 9:22). Indeed, Jesus' perfect blood is more than enough to cover and wash away our sins. The Bible is very clear in teaching how powerful his blood is for our salvation and why it is sufficient enough and needed once and for all. God's Word is very clear about the power of Jesus' blood.

"Since, therefore, we have now been **justified by his blood**, much more shall we be saved by him from the wrath of God." (Romans 5:9)

> *"In him we have **redemption through his blood**, the forgiveness of our trespasses, according to the riches of his grace"* (Ephesians 1:7)

> *"But now in Christ Jesus you who once were far off have been **brought near by the blood of Christ**."* (Ephesians 2:13)

*"For in him all the fullness of God was pleased to dwell, and through him to reconcile to himself all things, whether on earth or in heaven, **making peace by the blood of his cross.**"* (Colossians 1:19)

If Jesus' sacrifice is perfect and final, there is no need to sacrifice him again and again. This is the big problem of considering *"the bread and wine"* as the literal body of Christ and literal blood of Christ in the eucharist. It is like crucifying and offering Jesus again and again, not to mention that it contradicts the Scripture of making the sacrifice of Jesus as *once and for all.* At the same time, it is unthinkable to consider how the bread and wine could actually be transformed into God's body and blood through some man-made ritual. The church does not have power over God to turn him into something. That's why so many people were so confused into thinking that taking these elements is a means to salvation from week to week basis. But the Bible teaches that eternal life is through believing in Jesus, while the bread and blood represents his body sacrificed at the cross and the wine represents his blood shed at the cross.

This spiritual truth is the main point of Jesus when he referred to the wine as the symbol of the *"blood of the new covenant."* This blood of the new covenant is also mentioned in Mark 14:24, stating the blood *"which is poured out for many"* (Mark 14:24). This covenant idea is familiar to the early Jewish Christians because it was established and practiced since the time of Moses (Exodus 24). There, *"Moses took the blood* [from the animal sacrifice for burnt offerings and peace] *and threw it on the people and said, 'Behold **the blood of the covenant** that the LORD has made with you in accordance with all these words'"* (Exodus 24:8).

As such, when Jesus talked about the blood of the covenant, it is not something strange for them. When the disciples heard Jesus say that his blood is *"poured out for many for the forgiveness of sins,"* they immediately knew that he was the fulfillment and final sacrifice. Thus, in the Lord's Table, the cup of blood should never be taken for granted for its great significance because it means our sins and the sins of the world can only be forgiven through or by virtue of the blood of Jesus. No wonder the Bible called it *"the cup of blessing"* (1 Corinthians 10:16). In this verse also is where the word *"communion"* in Christian worship services came from. The text reads, *"The **cup of blessing** which we bless, is it not **the communion** of the blood of Christ?"* (1 Corinthians 10:16). The different versions and translations of the Bible use the word *"communion.* Other versions and translations of this Greek word *"koinōnia"* translate it as *"participation,"* *"fellowship,"* *"sharing,"* *"joint-participation,"* and *"partaking."* All of these translations attest to the richness of the idea of the cup of Jesus' blood in the communion.

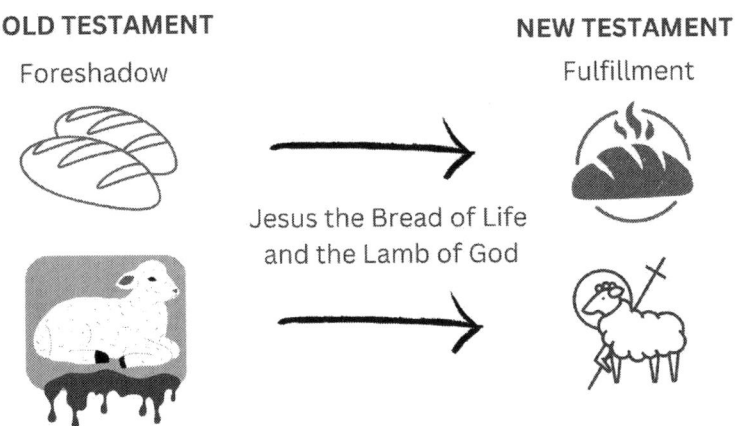

OLD TESTAMENT   **NEW TESTAMENT**

Foreshadow   Fulfillment

Jesus the Bread of Life
and the Lamb of God

So the whole point of Jesus is to reveal the new and a much better meaning of the bread of the old covenant and the blood of the sacrificial lambs in the Old Testament that was repeatedly sacrificed to cover the sins of God's people. A new time has come where those "foreshadows" (or new indications) will be fulfilled in Jesus Christ.

Not only that, Jesus commanded his disciples to do communion in a different way. They are no longer offering the unleavened bread of the Presence (or Passover bread) or no longer sacrificing living lambs and shedding its blood during Passover celebrations, but to integrate communion in their fellowships and gatherings. It will be more meaningful as they celebrate the communion or The Lord's Table in their homes also.

Reflection:

What have you learned about "the body of Jesus" as symbolized in the breaking of bread?

What did you learn about the "blood of Jesus" as symbolized in the wine?

CHAPTER 24: WHAT TO DO DURING THE LORD'S TABLE?

You might have noticed where we have to establish and lay down the biblical meaning of the Lord's Table first before we do it. To know and understand it first is absolutely necessary in what to believe or not. So, what do we really need to do when we have the Lord's Table or communion?

During the Lord's Table, there is a central passage in the Bible that we often read or follow. Through centuries, those who want to observe the biblical way, and stay faithful to its purposes and meaning, the words of the apostle Paul to the believers in Corinth are very useful.

> For **I received from the Lord** what **I also delivered to you,** that the Lord Jesus on the night when he was betrayed took bread, and when he had given thanks, he broke it, and said, "This is my body, which is for you. **Do this in remembrance of me."** In the same way also he took the cup, after supper, saying, "This cup is the new covenant in my blood. Do this, as often as you drink it, **in remembrance of me."** For as often as you eat this bread and drink the cup, you proclaim the Lord's death until he comes.
>
> Whoever, therefore, eats the bread or drinks the cup of the Lord in an unworthy manner will be guilty concerning the body and blood of the Lord. Let a person examine himself, then, and so eat of the bread and drink of the cup. For anyone who eats and drinks without discerning the body eats and drinks judgment on himself. (1 Corinthians 11:23-29)

We must remember that Jesus instituted the Lord's Table, not the apostle Paul or the church. But Paul's letter is written in such a great way for us to appreciate and apply during every celebration of the Lord's Table.

First, be grateful for who Jesus is and what he has done for us. Every celebration of the Lord's Table is an opportunity to be grateful. To the church in the city of Corinth, as well as down through the centuries, Paul's words echoes, *"For I received from the Lord what I also delivered to you, that the Lord Jesus on the night when he was betrayed took bread, and when he had given thanks, he broke it, and said, 'This is my body, which is for you'"* (vv.23-24a).

Jesus revealed The Lord's Table or communion to Paul, not just to the apostles. He claimed to have *"received"* this revelation from Jesus himself because he was not part of the original 12 apostles. God would call him later for a special ministry and mission to the Gentiles, not just the Jews. Jesus saved him in a different way to be an apostle to the Gentiles (meaning, the non-Jewish people who do not have a deeply rooted understanding of the Jewish religious practices and their meaning). Now, he has *"delivered"* or *"passed it on"* to the various local churches who have non-Jewish believers.

Interestingly enough, a powerful truth is seen here: *Jesus gave thanks.* It didn't say what the content of his thanksgiving was. Perhaps, it is telling us that when we celebrate communion, we have to be grateful also. Be grateful for the Father's sacrificial love in giving his only begotten Son to be our Savior, for the Son's suffering and sacrifice for our sins at the cross, and for the Holy Spirit's work in helping us to believe in this greatest redemption story. He suffered so much for us that he was broken that we might be made whole.

Second, remember who Jesus is and what he has done for you. Where would you be if you haven't found Jesus? Think about it. The reality is, amidst the busyness and enjoyment of life, including the clutters and distractions, we easily forget him. Isn't it great to pause for a sacred moment where we need to remember our Savior with tangible symbols that appeal to our basic senses, something we can see, touch, feel, and taste?

Paul reiterated the words of Jesus when instructed his disciples to *"Do this in remembrance of me"* (v.24a) (See also Luke 22:19.) Paul stated it as it is. It means, we do this as a memorial, a recollection or in memory (Greek *anamnésis*). This is the same word used in Hebrew 10:3, saying, *"But in these sacrifices there is a reminder* [or *anamnésis*] *of sins every year."* That is why those who want to follow the biblical way of doing the Lord's Table consider the elements–bread and wine–as *"figurative"* or pictorial of Jesus and his sacrifice. He is not the literal "bread," just like when he pictured himself as "the door," "the gate," or "lamb."

I believe *communion is an antidote to spiritual forgetfulness.* This reason is one of the major purposes of the Lord's Table. It is a form of memorial or commemoration. It is a sacred remembrance of Jesus. We refresh our memories about our Savior. Every communion is an occasion for commemoration, not for achieving salvation. You must be saved first before you partake the Lord's Table, and not use it as a means of salvation every week. Communion does not save you, Jesus is. If we reduce salvation into a ritual, that has serious theological implications as we already mentioned above. Believing in Jesus is the way to salvation, not in believing the literal body and blood in the bread and wine.

Third, hold on to the power of the blood of Jesus. If you only realize now how powerful is the blood of Jesus, you'll understand that we cannot live without it. We will never take the words of Jesus lightly. That's why Paul reemphasized the very words of Jesus. *"In the same way also he took the cup, after supper, saying, 'This cup is the new covenant in my blood. Do this, as often as you drink it, in remembrance of me'"* (v.25). When we take the cup, we must remember that we live by grace. We did not deserve anything from God, but judgment or punishment for all our sins and shortcomings. But because of Jesus, that judgment fell upon him instead of us. Again, don't take lightly what bread and the cup of wine represents. Our attitude and faith must be in the proper perspective that Jesus already paid the price of our sins at the cross and he paid in full. There is no need to sacrifice him over and over again in a literal sense, but we can fulfill the memorial, commemoration or recollection in our worship and fellowship.

Fourth, publicly proclaim Jesus' death at the cross, his resurrection, and his return. When we participate in the communion, we declare the Lord's death and resurrection, including his promise to come again and take us to himself. All of these historical truths at the same time. Paul reiterated what Jesus said to his disciples and echoed it to the churches: *"For as often as you eat this bread and drink the cup, **you proclaim the Lord's death until he comes**"* (v.26).

You might have noticed that many churches have different times and frequency of doing the Lord's Table. Some churches celebrate the Lord's Table once a year only in a grand way, some churches would do once a month as part of the

Sunday service or evening service, while some churches perform communion every day. What is the right time and regularity in doing the Lord's Table, then? The Bible does not specify. It only mentions "as often," meaning, "*as many times.*"

The Lord's Table

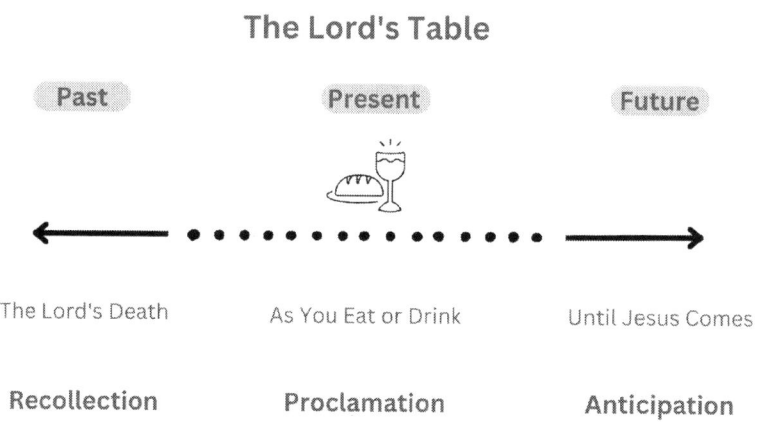

Past   Present   Future

The Lord's Death As You Eat or Drink Until Jesus Comes

Recollection   Proclamation   Anticipation

Now we see different time-dimensions of the communion. The first dimension is the **Past**. "*The Lord's death*" happened in the past, as such we are looking back to that historical and final event. This is the *recollection* aspect of the communion. The second dimension is the **Present**. The "*as you eat*" is the ongoing, ever-present, or continuing reality of the Lord's Table. That manifold frequency and regularity of doing the Lord's Table is the ongoing act of *proclamation* and *memorial* celebration. The word "proclaim" means to declare openly, celebrate in public, or make a point. It's the same word used for preaching. The third dimension is the **Future**. This emphasis is found in the phrase "*until he* [Jesus] *comes.*" This futuristic *anticipation* speaks about our hope in Jesus, the resurrected Savior. He is coming again and the Lord's Table is a sacred meal with the Savior who promised to come and dine with his church in the Marriage Supper of the Lamb (See Revelation 19:6-10).

Fifth, test yourself before you take part in the Lord's Table. This sacred call for accountability and discernment is a serious attitude and significant action every time we do the Lord's Table. No one is exempted. Paul explicitly enjoins the believers: "*Whoever, therefore, eats the bread or drinks the cup of the Lord in an unworthy manner will be guilty concerning the body and blood of the Lord*" (v.27). Some interpreters use this text to emphasize why people should consider the bread and wine as the "literal" body and blood of Jesus, but the context of this text does not prove it as a remembrance. On the other hand, this call to observance is for the partaker's attitude in coming to the Lord's Table. These are the "whoevers," both believing Jews and non-Jews, sinners and saints, all of whom come to the table and find grace and forgiveness.

In church history, the question arises: Who can partake of the Lord's Table? There are several positions: First is the "Communal Model" where the communion is inclusive and open for all who want to take it. It believes that everyone is welcome to do the communion regardless of their spiritual state or at least they "profess" to be Christians, nominal or not. Second is the "Close Model" where the Lord's Table is exclusive for church members only. Ultra-conservative churches take this position, especially if they follow certain beliefs and practices about restrictive church membership. Third is the "Centric Model" where even if you're not a church member, as long as you believe in Jesus and have a personal relationship with him and you want to come to him with a repentant heart, you're welcome to partake. These varying positions depend upon the history, background, denomination or persuasion of the local church.

However, when those "whoevers" would come to the table, Paul is clear in his admiration for every individual. "*Let a person examine himself, then, and so eat of the bread and drink of the cup. For anyone who eats and drinks without discerning the body eats and drinks judgment on himself*" (vv.28-29). In fact, if you read the next verses, you'll see some of the serious consequences of reckless behavior and lack of spiritual discernment. That's why everyone, whether you're a church leader, member, or guest, everyone must take time to repent, be humble, and remove all forms of idolatry regarding or in the presence of the Lord's Table.

Therefore, when we think about the Lord's Table, we have these four major purposes why we do it regularly with reverence and humility. We do the Lord's Table or communion as:

(A) An act of *obedience.* Jesus commanded and instituted the Lord's Table, therefore, we must obey him and keep doing the communion.

(B) An act of *memorial.* As Jesus commanded us to do the communion in remembrance of him, it is the most intimate act we can picture of in his presence.

(C) An act of *anticipation.* Every time we do the Lord's Table, we are renewing our expectations for the Lord's imminent coming, making us prepared for it.

(D) An act of *communion.* In this intimate worship, we not only remember Jesus, we also have intimate fellowship with our spiritual brothers and sisters.

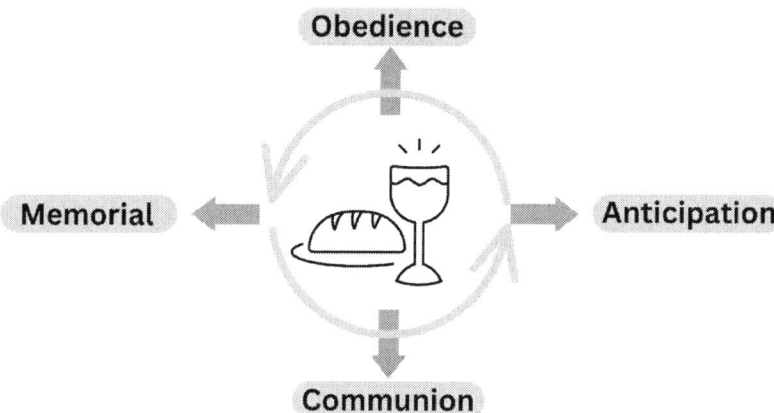

Here are a few but encouraging action steps for those who are new to the Lord's Table and communion.

- *Reconnect with God.* Many times we're like "disconnected" in many ways. We made mistakes, we have many shortcomings, and we committed sins. Sometimes we doubt and are out of tune in our relationship with God. Worse, we felt so far from God that we're ashamed to come back because we felt so dirty and guilty. The Lord's Table is a place where you can come back and ask God to cleanse you and get right with him. If you are not sure about your relationship with Jesus, trust him with all your heart.

- *Remember what Jesus did for you.* Remember, we all exist by God's grace. We don't have our own righteousness. We have nothing to brag about before God. Thankfully, he did what he did. He took the path of the cross, suffered for our sins, and died and was buried, but he rose from the grave for you. Remember that he is the Savior who loves you. He did it all for you. The communion is an opportunity to come to the Table and bring your pains, sin and shame.

- *Revitalize your relationship with him.* Many times we grew weary and dry in our relationship with God. We're out of romance and intimacy. We just go through the motions. But we cannot afford to let it dry and die. We need to refresh our relationship with him. It is a sacred date. As no relationship thrives without effort or doing your part, be excited when you approach communion and refresh your time with him.

> Come to the table and bring your sins for he forgives.
> Come to the table and bring your fears for he strengthens.
> Come to the table and bring your burdens,
> And he will replace it with his abundant blessings.

"So, whether you eat or drink, or whatever you do, do all to the glory of God" (1 Corinthians 10:31).

Reflection:

Why should you seriously approach the Lord's Supper with the right heart and faith and not do it half-heartedly and superficially?

How should you spiritually prepare yourself before you partake in the Lord's Supper?

SECTION 9: TAKING THE PATH TO GENEROSITY

*"You will be enriched
in every way
to be generous in every way,
which through us
will produce thanksgiving to God."*

~ Apostle Paul (2 Corinthians 9:11)

CHAPTER 25: WHO'S THE MOST GENEROUS OF THEM ALL?

What comes to your mind when you think about generosity? For some, these things come to mind. Gift. Money. Philanthropy. Charitable or non-profit organizations. Donations. Handouts. Welfare. Giving. Offering. Benefactors. Grant. Gratuity. While all these ideas are connected with generosity, it all boils down to a kind person (or group) who showed willingness and readiness to give something more than needed, expected, or necessary.

In 2023, a thousand churchgoers were surveyed by Vanco from all denominations and various ages about their giving. They published their findings in *The Definitive Guide to Churchgoer Giving: Key Trends in Online Giving, Attendance, and Engagement*. Some of the key points they discovered are the following. "Churchgoers have an increasing preference to give to specific causes versus a general fund." This generosity trend, comprising 38% of churchgoers, is very common among 24-54 years of age. They also discovered that "eGivers," a term used for those who give their tithes, offering, or donations through online platforms rather onsite and in-person, "are more likely to attend church more often than in-person givers." 74% of these eGivers are active attenders and are more likely to attend retreats, Bible studies, and fundraisers than traditional givers. They said, "Those who give online are more likely to attend church and activities not only weekly, but multiple times per week."

Indeed, there is a strong connection between your generosity and your spirituality. People tend to give to something they value. A classic example in the Gospel stories is an actual generosity event that happened. Jesus and his disciples were at the temple area when a sacrificial act of generosity happened.

And he [Jesus] sat down opposite the treasury and watched the people putting *money into the offering box. Many rich people put in large sums. And **a poor widow came and put in two small copper coins**, which make a penny. And he called his disciples to him and said to them, "Truly, I say to you, this poor widow has **put in more than all those who are contributing to the offering box**. For they all contributed out of their abundance, but she out of her poverty has **put in everything** she had, all she had to live on." (Mark 12:41-44)*

This unforgettable event about the nameless widow who gave copper coins (the smallest unit of currency at that time) and placing it on the temple's offering box is so significant that Luke also recorded it in his Gospel (Luke 21:1-4). It shows us that in God's economy, generosity has nothing to do with our financial status. It is a matter of the heart.

Of course, rich and wealthy people can give bigger amounts than a poor person. That's just common sense. A quick survey on the internet, like Giving USA, will show you millions and billions of donations for philanthropic causes. But in the eyes of God who knows all things, including the secrets of the hearts and minds, he is more particular with the unseen motives. Try comparing a grown up person giving a tiny fraction of his income versus a student or child who sacrificed the whole allowance to help someone. There's a significant difference there that God values more than the other. By percentage, giving *"everything"* is far more superior than a fraction from *"abundance."* For God who owns everything and sees everything we give, what matters most is the generous attitude of the heart.

We get into this spiritual journey all because of God's generosity. It's his divine nature to lavishly pour out his love, grace, and generosity to his children. Whether his people will embrace that character or not, it's up to them but God's nature will not change. In the Old Testament, God is known as a benevolent God. Out of the abundance of his kindness and love, he is exceedingly generous to his creation and humanity, especially to his people (Psalm 65:9-13; 104:10-18). He also promised abundant blessings for his people's faithful obedience to his covenant with them (Read Deuteronomy 28:1-4). God has always been *the Blesser* and Israel's provider in the wilderness, with bread from heaven and water of life. Israel existed and thrived because of God's magnanimous generosity.

In the New Testament, however, a highest and greatest form of generosity took place: *sacrificial generosity*. Jesus expressed it. *"For **God so loved** the world, that **he gave** his only Son"* (John 3:16). In other words, God "gave" us so much that the only reason why we were invited and involved in this spiritual journey is because of his abundant generosity. If God did not give generously and sacrificially we have nothing--no Savior, no path to salvation, no hope, and so on.

Not only that, Jesus himself also gave so much for us. He is, in the words of Paul, *"the Son of God, who loved me and **gave himself for me**"* (Galatians 2:20). Jesus did the greatest act of generosity by giving himself, not an angel, saint, or someone else, to die for sinners and ungodly like us. Paul was right, if we were righteous, someone who is good might die for us, but that's too great a sacrifice. *"But God shows his love for us in that while we were still sinners, Christ died for us"* Romans 5:8). Have you noticed a pattern here?

Sacrificial generosity is an expression of love. We can give without love, but we cannot love without giving. Generosity is rooted in love. Love is the ultimate motivation and it expresses itself through generosity. As a result, true love always leads to giving more than expected. The opposite is also true. Lack of generosity is a love-problem, an absence of love. If a person hates someone or something, he is the least likely to offer something or give anything to it.

But just think of a husband or wife loving a spouse, or parents loving their kids. Because of love, they give and sometimes make sacrifices. Likewise, both the Father and the Son made sacrifices, paid the price for our sins, and had given us more than what this world can bring in that we are left with an astounding question: *"He [God the Father] who did not spare his own Son but **gave him up for us all**, how will he not also with him graciously give us all things?"* (Romans 8:32). Does God really mean something to graciously give us all things?

Is generosity a mystery? When it comes to God's generosity demonstrated in Israel, what does it mean when Moses said these words: *"You shall remember the LORD your God, for it is **he who gives you power to get wealth**, that he may confirm his covenant that he swore to your fathers, as it is this day"* (Deuteronomy 8:18)? As we all know, we can never fully understand the teachings of the New Testament without considering its context from the Old Testament. The same is true with generosity. As God's people, what is our status in his kingdom's economy? Is there even a great significance in our spiritual journey when it comes to generosity?

Interestingly, here's what seems to be a mystery through the ages. *"**One gives freely, yet grows all the richer;** another **withholds** what he should give, and only **suffers want**"* (Proverbs 11:24). Does it make sense? That doesn't sound like reasonable financial math. If you're a rational person, you may ask, how can this be logical? How about this one? *"You will be **enriched in every way to be generous in every way**, which through us will produce thanksgiving to God"* (2 Corinthians 9:11). What does it mean? Is this a promise for all or just some elite few? Is this a general principle for everybody or just a rhetorical hyperbole that means nothing? Is it always true or does it depend on who can take it?

The truth is there are more verses in the Bible related to money than marriage, leadership, and so on. Even in the stories of Jesus, there are 9 out of 10 parables that's related to money and riches. Why is it? It's because God knows if we get this wrong, we have more problems than we ever expect.

Reflection:

What is your level of generosity right now? (1 being low and 10 being the highest)

| 1 | 2 | 3 | 4 | 5 | 6 | 7 | 8 | 9 | 10 |

What is God teaching you through Mark 12:41-44? And in what way God has been super-generous to you?

CHAPTER 26: WHAT ARE SOME CHALLENGES ABOUT MONEY?

The truth is there are thousands upon thousands of books that have been written about this topic—and many more will be written and published. At present, so many are very comprehensive and complicated, but for our purpose here, let's make it concise and clear. Here are a few examples of money problems:

- **Forgetfulness.** Along the way to the Promised Land, Moses instructed the Israelites to be careful when they become well-off economically and financially:

  *"Take care lest **you forget the LORD your God** by not keeping his commandments and his rules and his statutes, which I command you today, lest, when you have eaten and are full and have built good houses and live in them, and when your herds and flocks multiply and your silver and gold is multiplied and all that you have is multiplied, then your heart be lifted up, and **you forget the LORD your God**"* (Deuteronomy 8:11-14a).

Here, money has a powerful influence to make us proud and forget God if we're not careful and our hearts are not right with God. As some would say, "Money will magnify who you are." depending upon the condition of your heart, money will either make you faithful or forgetful. It makes you forget God, be careful for that could be your downfall.

- **False Object of Trust.** Proverbs 11:28 says, *"Whoever **trusts in his riches will fall**, but the righteous will flourish like a green leaf."* The truth is money can give us a sense of false security or feeling higher than others. It can make us look down on those financially challenged, like the homeless, beggars, poor, and needy who are all created in the image of God. Trusting in money instead of God makes a person, even a Christian, spiritually vulnerable. Money is intended to be a tool, not an object of trust, a means to an end and not the master of the heart and mind.

- **Bondage.** It is impossible to have God and serve him as your master and yet be a slave to money. It cannot happen. Read Luke 15:13. Jesus said, *"No **servant** can serve two masters, for either he will hate the one and love the other, or he will be **devoted** to the one and despise the other. You cannot serve God and money."* When it comes to the lordship of money and God, this is where it's "either/or" but not "both/and." Either you choose God or money as your master, but you cannot be a slave both by God and money. However, if one chooses money, it can be an object of one's devotion. It's called "money-latry," a form of idolatry of putting money first above God. Either you master the art of making money as a disciple of Jesus or money will become your master and cause you more troubles.

- **Heart Issue.** We know that the human heart is very deceitful. We cannot be reckless in our actions but reflective of our attitude, drive, and mindset towards money. It's because money is a matter of the heart. Jesus once said,

    *"Do not lay up for yourselves treasures on earth, where moth and rust destroy and where thieves break in and steal, but lay up for yourselves treasures in heaven, where neither moth nor rust destroys and where thieves do not break in and steal. For where your treasure is, there **your heart** will be also."* (Matthew 6:19-21)

The word "lay up" (*"thesaurizo"* is where we got "thesaurus") means to store treasure. Is Jesus saying it is wrong to save money for your future needs or if you have accumulated wealth in this world because of your expertise, entrepreneurial abilities, investments, and so on? Definitely not. Jesus is, in fact, literally saying here *"Do not treasure treasures."* When you treasure something, you give it high value and keep it carefully. Your heart is attached to it.

The biggest problem of money is its inherent power to influence and captivate the reckless and unguarded heart. It magnifies the core values of the heart too. If the heart is good, money will magnify it. If it is evil, greedy, and wicked, it will also magnify its sinful nature. However, if you use money to invest in the

Kingdom of God, it's also going to accelerate the work and amplify the glory of God.

- *Greed or Distorted Love.* Have you ever heard the saying "money is the root of all evil"? That's actually wrong and a false statement. It's unbiblical. Carefully read what Paul told Timothy, *"For the love of money is a root of all kinds of evils* [read that part again]. *It is through this craving that some have wandered away from the faith and pierced themselves with many pangs"* (1 Timothy 6:10). In the original language, "love of money" is one word (*philaguria* or a combination of "love-money"). In other words, it talks about avarice not assets and covetousness not currency. That's a form of greed and a distortion of love because money is a wrong object of love.

Perhaps you've heard why some are "so tight, they don't tithe." Money is a heart-challenge or spiritual concern in every angle. It's not evil or good in its material form, but its perceived value has inherent power to enslave, kill, and destroy or to provide freedom, rescue from needs, and build lives. After all, money is an important part of life that Jesus teaches a lot about. The truth is the word of God contains many secrets, principles, and practices about success with money.

- *Guilt.* Does giving make you feel guilty? One of the biggest problems many Christians face in their lives, especially during Sundays, is the feeling of guilt when it comes to money. For first-time comers, it's more of a curiosity. Why do these people give money? Why does this church collect tithes and offerings? Where is the money used for? Even though the act of giving has been done through centuries, a lot of people are cautious about giving. It's understandable and should not be dismissed.

For new believers and young followers of Jesus, it's more about a personal concern. Will I give or not? Is it compulsory? Perhaps, many preachers and teachers communicated giving and it appears like a "guilt-trip" rather than a quest for generosity. As such, they end up feeling guilty many times over. Let's correct and find the cure for that problem.

People give money for various reasons. It may be out of impulse because of sudden need, or habit in giving to charities, out of compulsion because of desire or of mercy on someone. It may be an act to inspire others to give and support, to exemplify a benevolent spirit, and so on. For some, especially here in the US, many people give that they may benefit financially, like in tax deductions.

The truth is, we cannot judge why people give—and we should not—because that's none of our business. It's between the person and God. After all, every person will stand before God and have personal accountability for whatever God has given him or her, whether the person is faithful and fruitful or not. But here are the truths that won't change:

First, God does not get richer because of your giving or lack of it. We can not make God wealthier by adding some contributions. God has everything he needs. We're the ones who need him. He is only concerned for you and your heart because money will really test what your treasure the most: God or money.

Second, God cannot be bought with money. Our giving is not a bribe to make God obligated to bless us. It's God's nature to bless everyone. And we cannot distort his ability to bless by thinking we can buy God with his favor. You may feel good when you give, but it does not mean you have placed God on a receiving end and indebted to you.

Third, giving is not a travel expense for our spiritual journey. Obviously, we pay for gas on our travels, the tolls on the "free-way," and the food and stuff we buy along the way. We pay for tickets to enter the parks, parking garage, hotels, and shows we watch. But let us not think that giving is our expense or "spiritual dues." That's not an accurate understanding of biblical giving and generosity.

If there's one reason why we give to God, it's because we love him—nothing less, nothing more. You must come to a point where you say, "*I give because I love Jesus*" or "*We give because we love Jesus.*" What could be a greater purpose of giving your best than love? After all, if I love my wife and kids, will I be stingy with them with the things I possess?

Being generous to the ones I love comes naturally and responsibly so that I may not spoil them and destroy their lives in the end. The same is true with God. He gives generously, abundantly, and responsibly to his children. And if I love God who is benevolent to me, I don't mind being generous to him in my offering and giving in his work. In fact, it is my honor and tribute to his love. If not, we have a love-problem.

Fourth, the law of love for God is—and should be—the ultimate purpose of giving. God has shown us the perfect relationship between love and giving. It's in the heart of the Bible: God loved so much and that's why *he gave his only Son* (John 3:16.). If he loved less, I don't know where we would be. Do you think if God didn't love us, he would give us his precious Son Jesus? Absolutely not. Why?

Fifth, we give when we love. For example, will you give anything precious to someone you don't know or love? But if the person is someone you love, like your wife, son, daughter, mom, or dad, will you give them your least? Why do husbands give generously to their spouse? How about parents generously giving to their children? We know that generous giving is the natural expression of love. Again, this saying is true: *You can give without love, but you cannot love without giving.*

Sixth, giving is and must be a natural expression of our love for God, not because we are great money managers of God's resources. That might be a good reason but it's not enough. Although it is good to be a great steward, the act of giving will test the condition of our hearts and our true character, whether we truly love God or not.

Reflections:

What are your struggles about money?

Take note of the Bible verses mentioned in this chapter. Which ones have a big and positive impact on you about money and why?

CHAPTER 27: WHAT IS GIVING IN THE BIBLE?

Have you heard about people giving churches stock options and cryptocurrencies as gifts? Today, people give gifts to nonprofits organizations and churches various items for personal purposes, altruistic reasons, goodwill, tax deductions and so on. Looking back in the Bible, there are several types of giving. Among the few are:

- **Tithing** - In the book of Leviticus, *"Every **tithe**...is the LORD'S; it is **holy** to the LORD"* (Leviticus 27:30, 32). A tithe, which is a sacred offering or gift to God, is a tenth of everything (meaning the 10% of 100%). Historically, tithing is not exclusive to Israel; it's a universal practice. Ancient people, cultures, and nations gave tithes to their deities, supported their priests-kings, and maintained their holy sites. Even today, there are many non-Christian religions that practice tithing, like Buddhism, Hinduism, Islam, Sikhism and so on.

In the Old Testament, before God gave the 10 Commandments, tithing was already practiced. Abraham gave his tithe to Melchizedek, the mysterious priest-king (Genesis 14:20; 28:22; Hebrews 7:2-4). God's people know and practice tithing in the light of his covenant with Israel (Deuteronomy 14:22-29). Even their priests and Levites gave their "tithes of the tithes" (Leviticus 18:28). It has something to do with their identity and economy as God's people with laws and observance, religious duties, and so on.

In the eyes of God, neglecting the tithe is an act of robbery. This scandalous affair of Israel with God is prominent in the book Malachi (Read Malachi 3:6-15). There, God claims that he does "not change" in his divine and sovereign nature. In the same manner, his statutes, especially in what he is about to point out about tithing, remain the same. God said, *"Will man **rob God**? Yet you are robbing me. But you say, 'How have we robbed you?' In your **tithes** and contributions"* (v.8). As a result of them robbing God, Israel was *"cursed with a* *curse"* as a whole nation. So, God spoke to Israel through prophet Malachi,

> *"**Bring the full tithe** into the storehouse, that there may be food in my house. And thereby **put me to the test**, says the LORD of hosts, if I will not open the windows of heaven for you and pour down for you a blessing until there is no more need."* (Malachi 3:10)

Here in this command to tithe is the only challenge given to God's people to *"put* [him] *to the test"* to see how he will open heaven and pour blessings upon those who bring their full, not partial but whole, tithe. One of the main purposes of tithing is mentioned here, which is to support the ministry and put food on the table for those who work in the work of the Lord. But God challenged them to practice tithing and be able to experience his provision *"until there is no more need,"* meaning, all their needs being met by God. Yes, God wants to meet his children's needs, but not their greed.

There is a common history that runs through this discussion about "blessings and curses" in the Bible. It has something to do with God's covenant with his people in Deuteronomy 28 (Take note of Malachi 4:4). If they obey God, they will be blessed; if they choose to disobey, they will be cursed as a nation. There must be a covenant relationship here when God promised to rebuke *"the devourer"* that destroys their livelihood (see Malachi 3:11-12).

Going back to a previous question, is there even a great significance in our spiritual journey when it comes to generosity? Or, does it even make a difference if I give or not? In fact, Israel complained and even accused God as unfair in saying,

> *'It is vain to serve God. **What is the profit** of our keeping his charge or of walking as in mourning before the LORD of hosts? And now we call the arrogant blessed. Evildoers not only prosper but they put God to the test and they escape.'"* (Malachi 3:14-15).

In short, Israel's attitude is: What's in it for me? (Take note: This reality is even seen today. New Agers and non-Christians gave their tithes to the universe and they seemed to have reaped their rewards of wealth and abundance. Meanwhile, countless believers are faithful but struggling with finances. They are wondering if God is punishing them for not tithing.)

But God in all his wisdom and sovereignty is unmoved. He pays attention and is listening to Israel's complaints. He promised that God-fearing, God-serving people who revere his name are his "treasured possession." He will spare them as his children. He also guarantees, *"Then once more you shall see the distinction between the righteous and the wicked, between one who serves God and one who does not serve him"* (v.18). So, yes, there's a distinct difference between those who serve God with their God-given resources and those who serve their own selves and self-interests.

However, moving forward, you might be wondering, why is tithing mentioned slightly by Jesus only once and not taught by the apostles in the New Testament? Foremost, Jesus and the apostles were godly Jewish people. Tithing was a common practice for them. Now, what about the non-Jewish Christians who are no longer under the law or the Old Covenant? Were they obligated to give their tithes?

Since Jesus or anywhere else in the New Testament did not specifically command us to tithe, this comes down to various interpretations and personal convictions. Here are the following interpretations and convictions:

- *Christians are no longer required to tithe.* This interpretation and position reasons out that since we are no longer under the law but are under grace, tithing is no longer applicable and is obsolete. Giving the least to almost nothing at all is ok. For some of them, they even believe tithing is unChristian.

- *Christians are still required to tithe.* Since the earliest Christian disciples were Jewish, tithing has not changed. Also, since tithing existed far before the law of Moses, tithing is a universal law that didn't change, so Jesus did not bother to mention it. It is still applicable for present believers.

- *Christians are to go beyond tithing.* If the argument not to tithe is to shorten God for less than what he asks for, tithing becomes a burden, not a blessing. On the other hand, if a disciple embraces to move beyond tithing, then giving is no longer about the 10 percent but by going above and beyond out of their love.

The truth is, we are called to be generous and our motivation is not the law but love for God. We don't tithe to bribe God and put him in the box to prove himself in opening the floodgates of heaven for our benefit. We must leave that to God's prerogative. If you tithe, you do it because you are persuaded and compelled by his boundless love. After all, there are other ways God's people give their gifts to God and not just tithing. Some of the following are also evident in the Bible and are prominent in many ways:

- *Offering* - There are many kinds of offerings in the book of Leviticus that were required for Israel (like burnt offering, daily offering, drink offering, free-will offering, heave offering, meat offering, peace offerings, thank offerings, etc.). Each of these offerings have specific purposes, functions, and roles in the religious life of Israel as a chosen nation. But suffice to say, God's people, both Israel and the church, gave offerings in the form of money. We'll explain this more later.

- *First Fruits* - King Solomon taught, *"Honor the LORD with your wealth and with **the firstfruits** of all your produce; then your barns will be filled with plenty, and your vats will be bursting with wine"* (Proverbs 3:9-10). God's people in the OT gave their first fruits of everything, like harvest, livestock, and also money (Deuteronomy 26:2-10). Some believers practice giving their first salary on a job or a portion of it every first month of the year. Some, but not all, churches today encourage this practice of generosity.

- *Alms-giving* - God's people are known for their generosity to the poor and needy. This act of giving to the poor was commanded by God and has been practiced in the Old Testament by the Israelites (Leviticus 25:35; Deuteronomy 15:7). In several instances, Jesus also taught about giving to the poor and needy (Luke 3:11; 6:30). Paul also modeled this generosity habit. *"In all things I have shown you that by working hard in this way we must **help the weak** and remember the words of the Lord Jesus, how he himself said, '**It is more blessed to give than to receive'"*** (Acts 20:35). Above all, the early church helped the poor (Romans 15:25-27; 1 Corinthians 16:1-4).

That's why Christians are still known for their abounding generosity because it's not just a feel-good practice, but a form of faithfulness to God and obedience to his call. Technically, there's nothing we can give back to God that's really ours in the first place. You know why? It's because God owns everything (Psalm 50:11). *"The silver is mine, and the gold is mine, declares the LORD of hosts"* (Haggai 2:8).

Reflection:

What makes tithe and offering so difficult for you? Or what motivates you to give or not?

As followers of Jesus, what should be our attitude towards generosity? What did you learn about generosity in this chapter?

CHAPTER 28: HOW SHOULD JESUS FOLLOWERS GIVE?

There are practical ways of exercising generosity as followers of Jesus. Based on 2 Corinthians 8-9, here are some of the helpful things to do in developing your generosity habit.

First, give joyfully and generously. Is poverty or recession stopping Christians from giving generously? How about during the recession or inflation? It's surprising that poverty does not stop generous people from giving, just like the poor widow at the temple (Luke 21:1-4). In fact, joyful people give out of their own poverty, not from abundance. The apostle Paul has an encouraging word here when he wrote to the Christians at Corinth.

> *"We want you to know, brothers, about the grace of God that has been given among the churches of Macedonia, for in a severe test of affliction, their abundance of joy and their extreme poverty have **overflowed in a wealth of generosity** on their part."* (2 Corinthians 8:1-2)

The churches of Macedonia struggled financially due to poverty, but they remain joyful and steadfast in their overflowing generosity. This phenomenon does not make sense but it remains true. Poor and middle class people and churches are more generous in many ways. According to *Christianity Today* (November 2022) in the article "Evangelical Giving Goes Up, Despite Economic Woes," small and medium size local churches, including nonprofit Christian ministries grew by 8% in their giving and donations. Interestingly, megachurches struggled as their giving went down by 6.6%.

Second, give according to your means. It is unlikely that God would ask anything from you that you don't have. You cannot give what you don't have. It is also not wise to give and put your family at risk or be in debt. If you don't have the means to live and stay out of grave debt, you'd better settle it first whether you keep your tithing a priority or determine a reasonable portion and trust God. The early Christians gave due considerations to their means. They were not reckless, impulsive givers. "*For **they gave according to their means**, as I can testify, and beyond their means, of their own accord, begging us earnestly for the favor of taking part in the relief of the saints*" (2 Corinthians 8:3-4).

Giving is a matter of faith, but it does not mean you give even if you're not able. The word "means" came from "*dunamis*," (where we got the word "dynamite") meaning "ability," "might," or "power" (both physical and miraculous). If the Lord leads you to give "*beyond your means*" because of a special need or big cause, just like in "*the relief* [or service] *of the saints*" and the situation above, it is your personal decision to do so. However, there is no doubt that this is not the norm but a special circumstance.

Third, give yourself first to God–and you will naturally give generously. According to the apostle Paul, "*And this, not as we expected, but **they gave themselves first to the Lord** and then by the will of God **to us**" (2 Corinthians 8:5). If there's one thing you notice about generous people, they are not simply happy do-gooders. Foremost, they have offered and devoted themselves to God before they devoted their possessions to him. They love God happily, as such, generosity comes freely. It's an overflow of the grateful heart towards others. That's why Paul also mentions that these generous believers "*gave themselves…to us.*" This act does not mean they offered themselves to the apostles, but simply means they gave their generous gifts to these workers also as they continue to serve the churches.

The rule of thumb is this: A person who is not given to God is not keen to give anything to him, the church, workers or others. The question is: Have you given yourself to God already? If you have not given your heart to him, it would be difficult to give anything to God, including your time, treasures, and talents. But if your life is already offered to him, everything else comes naturally, including generosity.

Fourth, let the generosity of God be your ultimate motivation in giving. Knowing who God is, especially his grace or unmerited favor, and believing in his ability to provide for your needs will make a difference in your lifestyle of generosity. If you read Paul's letter to the Corinthian church, you'll soon discover how well-off they were. They were not a perfect church, but certainly they have excellent qualities.

> *"But as you excel in everything—in faith, in speech, in knowledge, in all earnestness, and in our love for you—see that you excel in this act of grace also. I say this not as a command, but to prove by the earnestness of others that your love also is genuine. For **you know the grace of our Lord Jesus Christ**, that **though he was rich, yet for your sake he became poor, so that you by his poverty might become rich**."* (2 Corinthians 8:7-9)

Here you discover that giving is an "act of grace." Sometimes we think of giving something to a deserving person. But God gave his Son Jesus for those who deserve nothing from him. That's grace, truly an amazing grace. The source of this grace is God's abundant love that overflows to us. As we have been emphasizing this truth: the root cause of generosity is love. Paul is saying that if your love is genuine, the proof of it is generosity. Jesus is a living proof that love is proven by generosity. Even though Jesus was rich, possessing all things, he chose to give up his life and became poor for your sake. He did this to make you enriched in Jesus in all his glory.

Fifth, be prepared to give because it leads to willingness and fulfillment. If money is not a problem and you have everything that you need, what would you love doing? One of the ultimate goals of highly successful people is that, instead of keeping their success and gains for themselves, they give back to their community. For them, generosity is the completion of excellence and success. This principle is also evident in the heart of Paul. The church in the city of Corinth is excellent in many ways, but to achieve their full potential, they must be ready to level up in generosity. Paul admonished, *"So now finish doing it as well, so that **your readiness** in desiring it may be matched by your completing it out of what you have. For if **the readiness** is there, it is acceptable according to what a person has, not according to what he does not have"* (2 Corinthians 8:11-12).

Truth be told, generosity is the crowning glory of success. God did not design us to keep all things to ourselves. No amount of success can fill the void of spiritual significance to give. Between the "haves" and "have-nots," generosity defines everything whether one has entered into completion their purpose of life. We might have the desire and inclination to give, but without action, those inclinations remain unfulfilled. You must live life to the fullest and life by nature is life-giving. That's why your generosity is a great accomplishment and development of your Christlikeness and character. If you want to be fulfilled, be prepared.

Sixth, position yourself in financially supporting the ministry. The work of the Lord has often been supported by the generous support and gifts of his people. In ancient Israel, the priests and Levites were supported by the Israelites' tithes and contributions (Numbers 18:8-32). These offerings are considered "holy." They are sacred for subsidizing the supplies of God's servants, the church ministries, and leadership. As such, it is a blessing, not a burden. The apostle Paul also echoes the same spirit.

> *"For I do not mean that others should be eased and you burdened, but that as a matter of fairness your abundance at the present time should **supply their need**, so that their abundance may **supply your need**, that there may be fairness. As it is written, "Whoever gathered much had nothing left over, and whoever gathered little had no lack."* (2 Corinthians 8:13-15)

Paul is saying that whatever our present economic status, we can give our fair share to financially support any ministry, including the church where you are being fed spiritually and emotionally. Through it all, our individual contributions, whether big or small, can be helpful when collected as a whole. For Jesus, no gift is small enough, not even the two copper coins of the poor woman in the grand temple in Jerusalem. Regardless of your financial condition, you can share something to support God's work and mission to advance the Gospel of Jesus.

Seventh, plant a seed proportionate to your expected harvest. There seems to be a close parallel in between the natural and spiritual world. What you see in this realm can also reflect what happens in the supernatural realm. Here, the apostle Paul is making a strong emphasis: *"The point is this: whoever **sows** sparingly **will** also **reap** sparingly, and whoever **sows** bountifully **will** also **reap** bountifully"* (2 Corinthians 9:6). In the natural world, especially in agriculture, we plant with seeds and when these seeds grow and bear fruit, ready for harvest, they multiply.

It's the principle of sowing and harvesting. That's how nature works. If not, it will grow extinct and be gone. Sometimes, it is hard to understand why some people expect to reap what they did not plant or gain what they didn't give in the first place.

Another principle at work: *The quantity you plant will determine the quantity of your harvest.* Big harvest and requires big seeds. That's why businesses scaling for great results spend a lot on marketing and advertising because they are planting seeds to their potential customers. Likewise, farmers plant more seeds to have more harvest. That's why Jesus said, *"**Give, and it will be given to you.** Good measure, pressed down, shaken together, running over, will be put into your lap. For **with the measure you use it will be measured back to you**"* (Luke 6:38). When you give to God, he'll make sure that your seeds will not be wasted. In fact, you can never out-give God. So let your present be proportionate to the projected harvest you want.

Eight, plan ahead your giving so that you can give cheerfully. Many believers fail in their giving because they do not include it in their financial planning. We know that failure of planning leads to more failures. People are in financial trouble because of lack of financial planning. The same is true in giving. Generosity does not happen accidentally. It is a decision first before it becomes a discipline. It is a planned action that results in a personal generosity habit. That's why Paul said, *"Each one must give as he **has decided in his heart,** not reluctantly or under compulsion, for **God loves a cheerful giver**"* (2 Corinthians 9:7-8). It means generosity is a personal choice. It's something you determine or resolve with your entire being.

You may ask, "How much should I give?" The answer is simple. Decide by yourself without neglecting your financial duties (like family needs, basic cost of living, and financial obligations). If you want to be more intentional in your planning, you can also set aside a portion of your 10% and apply it similar to this plan (depending on what God has placed in your heart).

- 50% for your local church as a member
- 15% for Christian workers or church planter
- 20% for missions and advancing the Gospel

- 15% for gifts to the poor and needy

You can make your own percentage or determine a specific amount set budget for a specific ministry. You must not be feeling obliged or under pressure. Rather, you must be content and happy to do it. That's why Paul highlighted that *"God loves a cheerful giver,"* not a complainer. We give not out of obligation but out of Christlike motivation. We tithe or give offerings out of faith, not of fear.

Ninth, let God's blessings overflow and work through you. We all are dependent upon God for our existence, sustenance, and life. In him we exist and that reality does not change even if we don't remember or feel it. The truth is God works in and through our lives, not just in the circumstances. Ever since God has been calling some people to fulfill his purpose and manifest his glory, he blesses them to be a blessing to others. His blessings were never meant to be hoarded but to be shared, utilized or given away for his glory.

In the words of the apostle Paul, he affirmed this spiritual truth and reality, *"And **God is able to make all grace abound to you**, so that having all sufficiency in all things at all times, **you may abound in every good work**"* (2 Corinthians 9:9). God is all-powerful and more than able to abundantly bless anyone whom he chooses. His purpose is not for you to be self-independent but God-sufficient in every circumstance. Again, his purpose and plan in blessing you is for you to do greater things for his honor. Through your good work of generosity, people will see God's glory.

Ninth, have faith in God to supply and multiply his blessings upon you in every way. Trusting God for your needs requires maturity. Generosity is not for the faint-hearted, but for those who are committed, knowing that it does not always feel good to give. In fact, it is a challenge for most people. However, God does not need our permission or approval. He sets some universal laws that function automatically even if one believes it or not. The apostle Paul once again took a comparison to illustrate this spiritual law that governs generosity, when he said,

> *"He who **supplies seed to the sower** and bread for food will supply and **multiply your seed for sowing** and **increase the harvest** of your*

*righteousness. You will be enriched **in every way to be generous in every way,** which through us will produce thanksgiving to God."* (2 Corinthians 9:10-11)

To those who want to plant good seeds, they will reap great harvest. What you plant God will multiply so that when you have an increase in harvest, you can plant more. That law of multiplication leads to exponential growth. You will never fully comprehend what your seeds can do in the future when God maximizes that exponential growth in his economy. This way, God can truly enrich you *"in every way."* Think of how generosity impacts every area of your life, e.g. spiritually, emotionally, mentally, physically, financially, socially, and so on. If there's one great definition on what it means to be truly enriched by God, what could be better than being *"enriched in every way to be generous in every way"*?

Indeed, God can use us to generously give our time, treasures, and talents to him, but in the end, he wants us also to be generous financially and have faith that he is able to bless us more for his glory and honor. As disciples of Jesus, let his generosity flow through us.

Reflection:

As you've read passages from the Scripture about sacrificial generosity, what is God teaching you in this chapter? And from verse was it taken?

What are you going to do about sacrificial generosity from this moment on? Write down your prayer about it.

SECTION 10: TELLING THE GOOD NEWS

How beautiful upon the mountains
are the feet of him who brings good news,
who publishes peace, who brings good news of happiness,
who publishes salvation,
who says to Zion, "Your God reigns."

~ Prophet Isaiah (Isaiah 52:7)

CHAPTER 29: WHAT'S THE FUZZ ABOUT THE GOOD NEWS?

North Carolina is home to one of the greatest evangelists who ever lived: Billy Graham. Well known in many parts of the world for his massive evangelistic crusades and has been a spiritual guide to many presidents and dignitaries, he lived for Jesus and led millions to the saving knowledge of the Savior. He is just one of the examples of a Christ follower who greatly impacted the world for Jesus. Some are on great platforms, but mostly behind the stage.

Through human history, we know that Christianity in all its forms has had such a great influence in the world (like history, government, laws, education, economics, music, arts, etc.). However, in recent years, it is also evident that Christianity is in decline, especially in the western hemisphere. Have we come a long way and have become weary? In the US, according to the Pew Research Center (between 2018-2019), the decline of Christianity is at a "rapid pace" with a projection that sooner, Christianity will become a minority.

Have we, as Christians, lost our way? What went wrong? Whatever happened to the telling of the good news and changing lives? Or have we become bad news in itself? Are we producing nominal Christians or, worse, false converts? Are we raising a generation without compassion for the lost? These, among many, are the pressing questions that arise on this crisis of faith. Let's get back to where it all began, take a close look at the past, and learn from the way of the Master.

What comes to your mind when you hear the word "evangelizing"? Here are some reactions or response:

- **Resistance:** "Oh no! Not that word again! I am uncomfortable with that topic. I may want to do it but I'm not that interested in doing it. Why not have others do it?"

- **Rejection:** "I don't have the gift of evangelism. If I don't care if my family or friends are dying to eternity—and that's their personal choice—why should I care for others I don't even know?"

- **Revival:** "I clearly remember the day someone told me about your Good News. Thank you for saving me, but somehow somewhere along the way I lost my passion. "*Restore*" unto me, Lord, "*the joy of your salvation.*" (Psalm 51:12)

That very act when someone told you about the good news of Jesus is what we call "evangelizing." But let's define it clearly that we may be on the same page. Evangelizing is *the act of proclaiming the Gospel with the goal of influencing the person (or people) to believe in Jesus as their Lord and Savior and repent of their sins.* Let's get the key insights of the keywords here:

- "*Act of proclaiming*" - The Greek "*euagelizo*" means "to proclaim," announce," "declare," or "preach." It is a move, act, or demonstration of communicating the Gospel story. You can only learn it by doing, not by listening to sermons, reading books, watching YouTube, etc. These things are good and could inspire or give you more ideas. But the best way to learn in evangelizing is by doing it with a partner or discipler, until you can do it on your own and be able to demonstrate it for others to follow.

- "*The Gospel*" - It's referring to the story of Jesus in a specific way (that's why it's not called "a" Gospel, but "the" Gospel). The first four books of the New Testament are called "Gospels" because these are stories of and about Jesus the Messiah, Savior, and Lord. But these are not mere short biographies because the core message of "the Gospel" is his sacrificial love for us, his coming down from heaven, his suffering for our sins, his death as a penalty for our sins, and his resurrection as good news or glad tidings. Through faith in Jesus, sinners can be forgiven and saved from eternal damnation and total separation from God. Jesus came to deliver and save sinners and offer forgiveness by repenting of their sins and believing in him as their personal Savior and Lord. By doing this, anyone is given the right to become a child of God, having an abundant and eternal life.

- *"With the goal of influencing the person (or people)"* - It positions the "evangelist" (the person telling the story) to be conscious of his or her role and scope of limit in telling the Good News. We are only "messengers" and communicators of the Gospel, but we cannot save the person. We can influence or persuade them, but they make the decision for themselves. We intentionally open the situation or sometimes wait for the opportunity, and act accordingly towards the goal but God gets the goal done. That's why we need to tell the story right and trust God for everything.

- *"To believe in Jesus as their Lord and Savior and repent of their sins"* - The important goal and intention for the person listening to the Good News is for them to repent of their sins and be forgiven and completely trust Jesus as their personal Lord and Savior. We cannot miss the importance of repentance for it is because of our sins that Jesus shed his blood on the cross and died for us.

Friend, **you became a Christian because someone told you about it.** Do you still remember the day when someone told you about the Good News of salvation? Do you remember the day (or event) when someone talked about Jesus and what he did for you at the cross, and as a result, you accepted and trusted him as your Lord and Savior?

If *"not,"* then, you should get to know the Gospel of Jesus that he died for your sins and offers you forgiveness if you repent of them. And by fully trusting him as your Lord and Savior, he is giving you eternal life.

If *"yes,"* meaning you already accepted and trusted Jesus as your Lord and Savior, then you must have seen the change in your life as you live in his forgiveness, peace, love, and joy of being his beloved. It means you are forgiven, saved, loved and blessed beyond measure. What then?

The truth is every believer is called to be a messenger. You are Jesus' witness to the world. You're his plan A, not plan B in bringing his message of hope to the lost world, especially to your family and friends. Before Jesus ascended to heaven and left his disciples, he gave them–as well as his disciples in the coming ages–this sacred and solemn promise: *"But **you will receive power** when the Holy Spirit has come upon you, and **you will be my witnesses** in Jerusalem and in all Judea and Samaria, and to the end of the earth."* (Acts 1:8)

No one is exempted from being a witness. All of Jesus' disciples are called to be *"witnesses"* to *"the end of the earth."* All pastors, deacons, leaders, and members alike. No one can say, "I'm holding a position in this church, therefore, I'm exempted in telling others about Jesus." Whether you are a pastor, deacon, worship minister, member and so on, you are Jesus' witnesses to the world.

Also, notice the widening progression of their mission from the city of *"Jerusalem,"* to the Roman province of *"Judea,"* to the region of *"Samaria,"* and to *"the end of the earth."* Have you ever thought about why God brought you here at the "end of the earth"?

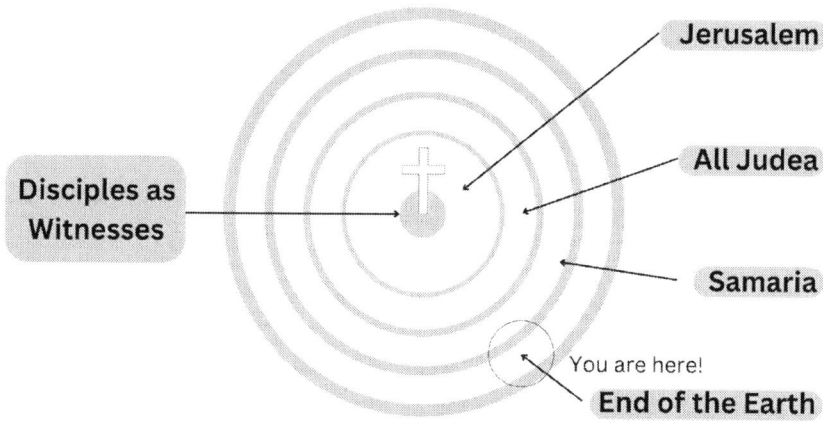

If you're coming from the Philippines and now living here in the US, yes, you are here at *"the end of the earth"*! We are here! We just have to be honest. Are we focused on our current community and beyond, or are we focused on our core groups and members? If we don't want to die a natural death as a local church, we need to be community-focused. We should make it our mission to bless and influence our community for Jesus. *Our calling is to be part of God's mission for the*

whole world, starting from our own backyard and locality. It is very consistent with Jesus' Great Commission.

> *"Go therefore and **make disciples of all nations**, baptizing them in the name of the Father and of the Son and of the Holy Spirit, teaching them to observe all that I have commanded you. And behold, I am with you always, to the end of the age."* (Matthew 28:19-20)

Our vision should be to reach out to all people groups in our communities, not just one race or ethnicity, like the Filipinos, but all nations and ethnicities (*ethnos*). That should be the ultimate vision of every local church. If the early disciples did not obey the Great Commission, it is likely that the church of Jesus remained a Jewish sect. But because the early disciples of Jesus were so faithful in trusting the Lord and obeying him, they *"turned the world upside down,"* regardless of their races and ethnicities (Acts 17:6b).

Reflection:

What is your level of experience in telling others about Jesus right now? (1 being lowest and 10 being the highest)

1 2 3 4 5 6 7 8 9 10

Memorize Matthew 28:19-20.

CHAPTER 30: WHY IS TELLING THE GOOD NEWS IMPORTANT?

After 25 years of service in various executive services, Tom Ferguson retired from his job as a highly accomplished man. Before leaving his office, he sent "thank you" notes to their company's 11,000 employees. At the last part of that short heartfelt letter, he noted, "Now, I'm gonna have time to get into the ministry and start serving in my church." Shortly after those letters were sent, a thousand employees responded. He immediately read many of these letters, saying they're so glad to know that he's a "Christian" and that he is "saved."

Tom, then, realized deep in his soul that there's something wrong with his success. He led this company and made billions of money for their investors but he had no kingdom purpose. For him, it was "life-changing." He needed to change course. So, when he became the CEO of AZZ, a world leading company in galvanizing steel, he made sure that his Christian testimony and influence for Jesus is evident in the workplace. He found meaning in his life and leadership by leading others to know and trust Jesus through voluntary Bible studies in their workplaces.

Like Tom, the church of Jesus successfully reached out to the whole known world then that its influence lasted through centuries. Today, the church of Jesus still exists, but there seems to be a big shift. If we compare the church in the book of Acts, it seems that the church today has lost its mission, effectiveness, and power.

At the heart of the Gospel message is John 3:16. "*For God so loved the world, that he gave his only Son, that whoever believes in him should not perish but have eternal life.*" The Gospel started with the God who loves you and the embodiment and perfect expression of this divine love is Jesus. This love is sacrificial. It means God loves you enough that he sacrificed so much for this love. Also, we hear about God's abundant plan for those who believe in Jesus. *"The thief comes only to steal and kill and destroy.* **I came that they may have life and have it abundantly"** (John 10:10). But why is it that, as we are experiencing the abundant life, so many people turned their back from the Gospel?

According to Ray Comfort in his book *God Has a Wonderful Plan for Your Life: The Myth of the Modern Message*, 80-90% fall out from the faith and become backsliders after a few years of professing their faith to accept Jesus as their Lord and Savior. Why? Has the Word of God fallen to deaf ears that the cares of this world for wealth and comfort has led to many false converts? That's a staggering reality for every worker. Why would we keep on laboring only to produce false converts? There must be something wrong. Or are we in denial?

First, evangelism is not a program but a personal mission of Jesus. We must follow in the same way. *"I must preach the good news of the kingdom of God to the other towns as well; for I was sent for this purpose"* (Luke 4:43). We could say that telling of the good news is Jesus' personal agenda, but it's more than that. Proclaiming the good news is a kingdom agenda. It is God's agenda as the ruler of the whole universe. There is no area in this world and in your life that is not under the rule of this divine King. If we claim to be followers of King Jesus, we cannot deny the importance of evangelizing the lost. If our lives must be purpose-driven, let the purpose of God be our driving force. In fact, for Jesus, telling the good news is a "must." It is a necessity and there's a sense of urgency. Why?

The eternal destiny of the lost people, including our lost family and friends, depend on our courageous obedience to tell the good story of Jesus. And if we fail to do so, it would place them in grave danger. *"For I am not ashamed of the gospel, for it is* **the power of God for salvation to everyone who believes,** *to the Jew first and also to the Greek"* (Romans 1:16). But how can they believe if no one will tell them? Even if they have heard the gospel already—and it takes several times to hear something before someone makes a decision—how will they be able to understand and make an informed decision if no one is telling them?

Second, our ability to replicate or multiply, through evangelizing and making disciples, is the proof that we are indeed disciples of Jesus. For me, this major reason is more relevant for anyone who has been claiming as "Christians" and yet remains silent and is not showing any results in their spiritual life and leadership. This principle is not saying that one is not a Christian if they don't disciple, that's not the point. It only shows that while all disciples are Christians, not all Christians are disciples. Some are simply claiming or believing as Christians but it doesn't mean they follow Jesus as disciples or disciple-makers. Jesus said, *"By this my Father is glorified, that* **you bear much fruit** *and* **so prove to be my disciples***"* (John 15:8).

Read the words of Jesus again. This spiritual principle is not made up by some pastors or workers to push people to evangelize but this is a plain statement made by Jesus himself. Since he started his public ministry, many people followed him because they were just curious, but when the going got tough, they left. And for those who remained, there's still confirmation to be made. For everyone one of these *"disciples,"* each must ask: Am I just listening and learning but not living my life as Jesus' witnesses? Am I just a disciple in word, but not in work? What is my proof that I am not merely a professing Christian but a genuine disciple of Jesus? Who are the individuals that I shared the gospel with and where are they right now? Where are the fruits of my ministry of evangelism?

Each one of us must come to a point in our life as a believer and follower of Jesus where we have to confront our complacency and coldness when it comes to evangelism. We must cross the path from complacency to commitment to bring the good news to everyone we know, as well as those we are in contact with.

Reflection:

What is God telling you about sharing the Good News to others who need it?

If you will not tell your non-believing friends about the end that awaits them, what would be the potential consequence of your indecision in telling them about the Good News?

CHAPTER 31: HOW TO TELL THE GOOD NEWS?

P aul asked the early Roman believers about the difficult situation of the lost people who do not have Jesus and there's no one who would bring and tell them about the Gospel, *"How then will they call on him in whom they have not believed? And how are they to believe in him of whom they have never heard? And how are they to hear without someone preaching?"* (Romans 10:14)

These same questions are significant even until now. As long as we have seen and know people who need Jesus, these questions should echo in our hearts and must drive us to tell others about Jesus.

First, consider telling others about Jesus as a necessary and normal part of being a believer and disciple of Jesus. We already know that having fruit is indispensable proof that we are disciples of Jesus (and if we do not have spiritual *"fruit,"* that's proving nothing to what we claim to be). The act of telling the Gospel to people is not new and should not be complicated. As human beings, we are natural communicators of telling others about what we know.

Here are some examples: As *parents*, when you teach your child how to cook sunny-side eggs, you show and explain how to do it. You go through the process step by step. As an *employee*, when you train a newbie in the workplace, like in a coffee shop, you show and explain to them how to make coffee that the customer asked for. What would you say and do? As a *student*, the same is true when you retell a story about the new movie series you have just seen or novel you have just read. You tell them about this main character, his or her call for a journey, including the struggles and what happened along the way, until you reach the end of the story. Perhaps, you can convince them to watch the movie or read the novel.

The principles of communications are almost the same. *You communicate something you know to someone who does not know about what you have in order to inform or convince the person and make a decision.* That's what people do in marketing, advertising, copywriting, and so on. In our case, the "product" is Jesus, you are the seller, and the people are the market. However, there's a big difference. Telling the story of Jesus is not just a side job, it is a spiritual discipline and lifestyle.

Second, be sensitive to the leading of the Holy Spirit. We already saw that the Holy Spirit gives us power to be witnesses of Jesus in Acts 1:8. If you are a true follower of Jesus, there must be something going on in your hearts today. Are you sensitive to the inner working of the Holy Spirit within your heart and mind? Is there something he wants you to do in telling others about Jesus?

Since the beginning when people started believing and following Jesus, we can see great examples in the Bible of believers who were in tune with God's Spirit. One classic example is Philip in the book of Acts chapter 8. Here, we cannot underestimate the role of the Holy Spirit in the work of evangelizing the lost. He opens up opportunities so that you can tell your Gospel story. Take a look at the text. *"And the Spirit said to Philip, 'Go over and join this chariot'"* (Acts 8:29).

Even though Philip already knew how to tell the Gospel to other people and has been doing it (Acts 8:12), he is very receptive to the leading of the Holy Spirit. When God's Spirit is working already, he only asks Philip to "join" with what he, the Spirit, is doing already. Why is this receptivity or sensitivity to the Holy Spirit important? It's because God is at work first in saving a person. We only come along and be used in whatever way God wants. We don't save people from hell. God does that through the message of Jesus. We are only messengers. That's why we need to be sensitive to the leading of the Holy Spirit and join what God is already doing. It does not matter what materials, tools, methods or strategies you use in evangelizing the lost, the most important power behind every successful telling of the Gospel story is the Holy Spirit.

The Holy Spirit has many roles in saving the person even if you're not aware about it. One example is the Holy Spirit convicts the person of his or her sin. Jesus taught his disciples. *"And when he* [the Holy Spirit] *comes, he will convict the world concerning sin and righteousness and judgment: concerning sin, because they do not believe in me"* (John 16:8).

202

As messengers, we must be sensitive if God's Spirit is moving in the heart of the person. When we are with someone who needs Jesus, ask yourself: Is God helping this person in a spiritual sense? Is the person spiritually convicted of his or her sins? Is there brokenness? *Without conviction, there's no conversion to the cross.* So what are you going to do? Are you going to slap them on their face and tell them how sinful they are? No. There's a better way. Either you tell them the story or accompany it with great questions.

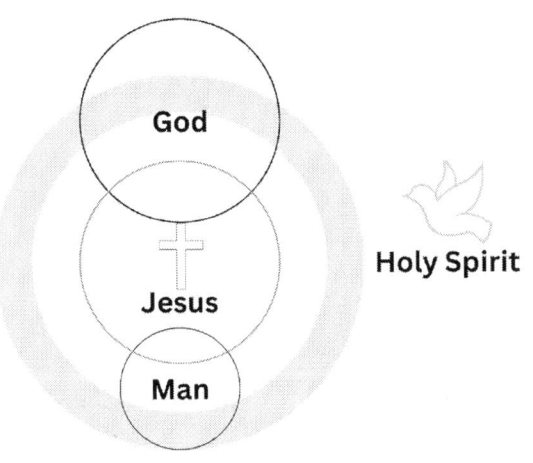

Third, connect by asking good questions. This strategy has been used since the earliest history of evangelizing the lost. Jesus did it many times. Philip did it also, and so can you. *"So Philip ran to him and heard him reading Isaiah the prophet and asked, "Do you understand what you are reading?"* (v.30) Friends, there is something about a question or set of questions that makes it so powerful in helping people think, understand, and realize the point of what is being asked, especially about (a) **God**, (b) **Man** and his problematic condition, as well as of (c) **Jesus** and the cross. Remember these three major points.

In order to help the person realize their sinful condition, you can or may ask a few questions using the 10 Commandments as your guide (See Exodus 20 and get familiar with it). This is to help them understand who they are in the eyes of

God not just on what they think who they are as the culture is telling or indoctrinating them. Some people believe they are basically "good" and righteous, but these claims can be tested through questions based on the 10 (even a few of these) Commandments.

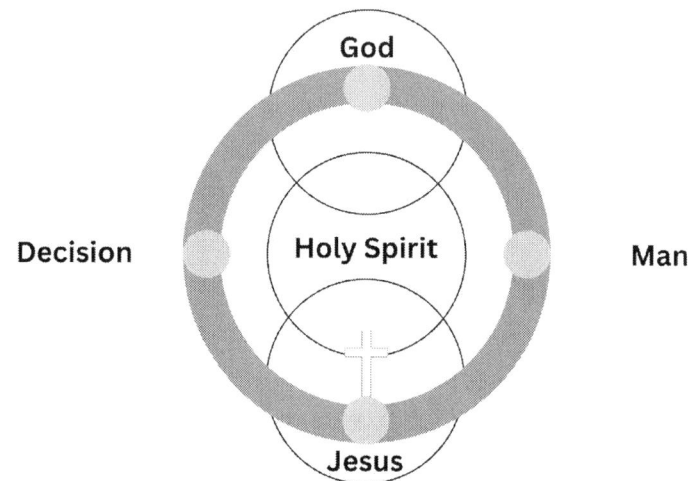

- Commandment #1: "*You shall have no other gods before me.*" Ask (the same sequence in the next commands): Do you have other gods beside the God of the Bible? (Or do you believe in yourself or the culture more than you believe in God?)

- Commandment #2: "You shall not make for yourself a carved image or... bow down to them or serve them." Have you bowed down to graven images as a form of reverence?

- Commandment #3: "*You shall not take the name of the LORD your God in vain.*" Have you used the Lord's name as a cuss word? If yes, would you use your mother's name as a curse word? Why or why not?

- Commandment #4: "*Remember the Sabbath day, to keep it holy.*" Do you observe a holy day for rest and worship of God?

- Commandment #5: "*Honor your father and your mother.*" Have you dishonored and disobeyed your parents?

- Commandment #6: "You shall not murder." Jesus said, "You have heard that it was said to those of old, 'You shall not murder; and whoever murders will be liable to judgment.' But I say to you that everyone who is angry with his brother will be liable to judgment" (Matthew 5:21-22). Have you been angry with someone?

- Commandment #7: "You shall not commit adultery." Again, Jesus said, "You have heard that it was said, 'You shall not commit adultery.' But I say to you that everyone who looks at a woman with lustful intent has already committed adultery with her in his heart." (Matthew 5:27-28). Have you looked at a woman (or man) and lusted for them?

- Commandment #8: *"You shall not steal."* Have you stolen something from someone?

- Commandment #9: *"You shall not bear false witness against your neighbor."* Have you lied, or accused or bore false witness against someone?

- Commandment #10: "You shall not covet your neighbor's house…your neighbor's wife…or anything that is your neighbor's." Have you desired something or someone that belongs to your neighbor?

The point of each question is to help everyone understand that we are sinners and guilty before God. Often, after each question, an additional question would be: *"What do you call someone who violated this command?"* More often than not, people would like to justify themselves but the Bible is clear: *"For whoever keeps the whole law but fails in one point has become guilty of all of it"* (James 2:10).

This main truth is important to understand: Every human being is a sinner and is guilty before the holy God. God's Word is right: *"For **by works of the law no human being will be justified in his sight,** since through the law comes knowledge of sin"* (Romans 3:20). If a person is not convinced that they are sinners, there's no need for repentance. A person who is not convinced that he is not sick is not in need of help or cure. It's futile for you to ask them to repent if they do not recognize their sinful state before God . Jesus sacrificed himself for the sins of the person but if a person does not see the need of it, there's no use of persuading them. It's probably not yet their time to repent.

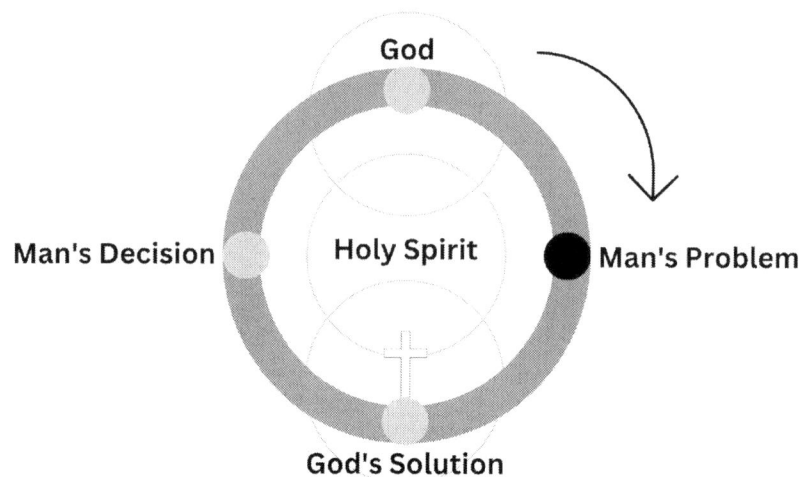

The goal of evangelism is not to make people feel good about themselves–the world has had enough of that–but for them to realize how much we needed Jesus the Savior from our wretched spiritual condition. Unless the person realizes that, they will never take the Gospel, including sin, seriously.

This spiritual principle is a lesson for us. *If our conversion story comes without conviction from our sins, we must be careful of what kind of Gospel we have accepted.* This spiritual dilemma is the reason why so many churches are dying and so many professing Christians do not have changed lives because they thought believing in Jesus is like self-development or behavioral improvement and not about dealing with the seriousness of sin. That's very dangerous.

Fourth, gently guide a person to believe in Jesus as their Lord and Savior. One of the greatest joys and most humbling opportunities every disciple could have is to be able to influence and lead others to the saving knowledge and faith of our Savior and Lord Jesus. When Philip asked the man whether he understood the Scripture that talks about Jesus, his reply opened up for a deeper conversation or dialogue. This is also another benefit of asking the right questions. It opens up more opportunities for conversation. *"And he said, 'How can I, unless someone guides me?' And he invited Philip to come up and sit with him"* (Acts 8:31). In fact, this man has more questions. It attests to the inner need, or spiritual hunger and thirst, of someone who is experiencing the work of the Holy Spirit.

So many people are interested in talking about spiritual things. It's just nobody wanted to talk with them. You just have to ask. What does Philip do? Join in what God is doing! *"Then Philip opened his mouth, and beginning with this Scripture he told him the good news about Jesus"* (Acts 8:35). This is the power of being prepared to do the work of telling people about Jesus. Yes, people see your actions first, but they also need your words in communicating the Gospel clearly. Jesus is using both "works" and "words" side by side in demonstrating and proclaiming the Gospel. Both are not enemies but inseparable friends.

You can do your acts of kindness whenever and however you want (or how long), but without telling them the story of God, *the sinful condition of man's heart*, and *every person's need of a Savior*, all you have will only boil down to a social work or social Gospel. People could interpret your actions however they want. But with words, you can make the Gospel points clearer.

- God created human beings for a relationship and to experience his holy love.

- But man rebelled and committed sin. He has become a broken person in every aspect of his humanity. It's a spiritual problem only God can solve.

- God demonstrated his love by sending his Son Jesus to suffer and die for our sins and rose from the grave to be our Savior and solve man's spiritual problem.

- But this solution will not be effective if man will not make a decision to believe in Jesus the Son and repent of his sins which is the very root of his problem and brokenness. Until a person remains indecisive, that solution remains until it doesn't or it's too late for man.

- The greatest decision any man can make in this life is to believe and repent of their sins. This path alone is what God provides for every sinner to be forgiven and be restored with God again.

If you have decided to become a disciple that bears fruit and not just content of being a nominal Christian, here are some steps you can take.

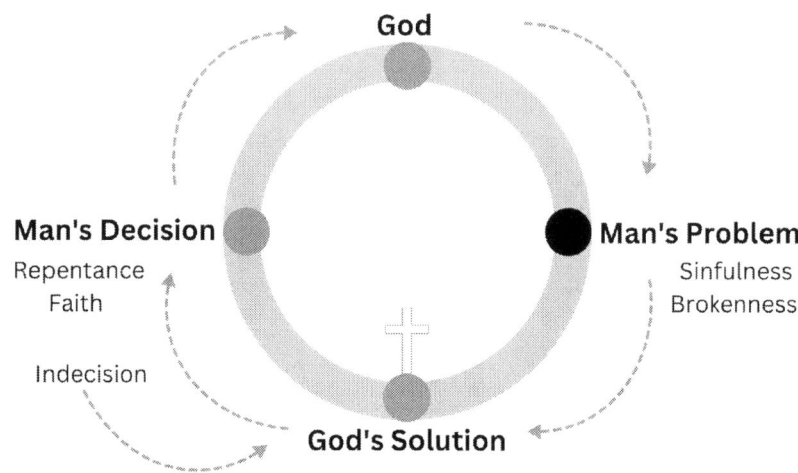

Fifth, take your time to prepare by learning about evangelizing the lost. How are you using the best parts of your time? Are you learning the basics of your faith? People are watching you. In fact, many—not all—people around you admire your faith being lived out. There are many studies about people just waiting for an opportune time to talk about faith, including Christian faith. The only question is: Are you ready? Paul's words of advice is ever-relevant here:

> **Walk in wisdom toward outsiders,** *making the best use of the time. Let your speech always be gracious, seasoned with salt, so that* **you may know how you ought to answer each person.** (Colossians 4:5-6)

Sixth, don't lose your opportunity to help your family, friends and fellow human beings find the Savior. It's not a matter if opportunities will come or not. It's just a matter of time when your family and friends will ask about your faith journey. How are you preparing yourself for the task?

> *But in your hearts honor Christ the Lord as holy,* **always being prepared to make a defense to anyone who asks you for a reason for the hope that is in you;** *yet do it with gentleness and respect.* (1 Peter 3:15)

Seventh, think with the end in mind. Do you know how important the telling of the Gospel is in God's future plan—not to mention that all of us will appear before his judgment seat and give accounting? The Gospel not only determines eternal life and death, it marks the beginning of the end in history. *"And **this gospel of the kingdom will be proclaimed throughout the whole world** as a testimony to all nations, and **then the end will come"*** (Matthew 24:14).

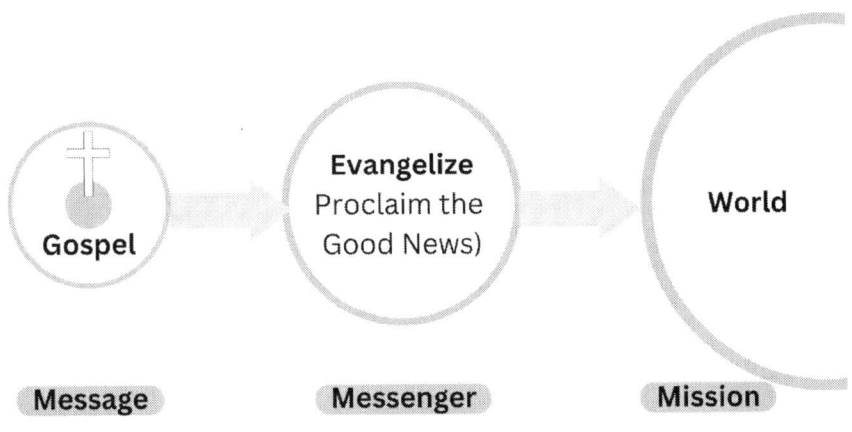

Be a witness of Jesus to the world that needs the Gospel, and let your life shine as you proclaim Jesus.

Reflection:

Make a simple outline on how to tell someone in your missional relationship.

Ask someone, like a non-believing friend, to allow you to do practice with your simplified approach in order for you to experience telling the Gospel to someone..

SECTION 11: PAYING THE COST OF THE JOURNEY

Whoever does not bear his own cross
and come after me
cannot be my disciple.
For which of you, desiring to build a tower,
does not first sit down
and count the cost,
whether he has enough to complete it?

~ Jesus Christ (Luke 14:27-28)

CHAPTER 32: WHO WERE THE "FOLLOWERS" OF JESUS?

For every journey, there's a price to pay. Nothing is free. If it is, someone paid their fee. The same is true in our spiritual journey.

When I was an elementary student, I didn't have an idea what a disciple of Jesus meant. All I thought was that being "saved" was good enough for me. I'm just ok attending and seating among the hundreds or thousands of Christians in our church and towns. I was wrong. One day, my youth pastor approached me and asked me if I wanted to be baptized and commit my life to Jesus. I decided to be immediately baptized and committed my life to take my spiritual journey seriously.

After some time, a youth leader approached me. He also invited me to join our church's discipleship ministry and that he would personally disciple me. I didn't know what it meant on the first day but as the weeks went by of doing the discipleship course, I began to learn a lot about God, Jesus, the Holy Spirit and the major teachings of the Bible. At that time, we were using the Navigators' discipleship course as our guide until we could stand on our own.

Few months later, when I was in my Junior year already, I slowly grew in my spiritual journey. I have invited two other young people to join me and if they would commit, I would also personally disciple them. I passed what I have learned to them with the hope that they too will disciple others someday.

As a product of that discipleship course, there were 13 young people who went to the seminary for at least one year and 5 of us continued to commit ourselves in serving the Lord in full-time ministry leadership as pastors until now. Many others came later and also served full-time in the ministry. (During the first year at Bible school, it felt like I'm simply reviewing what I learned at my home church's discipleship process.) That's how powerful discipling everyone in the church is, especially the young people. Of course, it's unrealistic to expect you to go to Bible school unless you're called by God to do it. We won't all be going to Bible schools as students but we are all expected to be students of the Bible. That's how we grow and multiply as disciples of Jesus. But there's a price to pay.

If you read Luke 14:25-33, you'll see that becoming a disciple of Jesus is not a walk in the park. But I was you to take note how Jesus challenged his fans and followers alike about "counting the cost" in becoming his disciple. There were *"great crowds"* who followed Jesus (v.25), meaning not just one people group but several groups. It could be categorized by their tribal (from the twelve tribes of Israel), ethnic (Jewish and non-Jewish), regional (from local villages), and more. While Jesus values different people groups and communities, he wanted to emphasize that he is interested in the person as an individual. Following Jesus is a personal decision. He said, *"If **anyone** comes to me and does not hate his own father and mother and wife and children and brothers and sisters, yes, and even his **own life**, he cannot be **my disciple**. Whoever does not bear his own cross and come after me cannot be my disciple"* (26-27).

Imagine how the crowd felt when Jesus released this "condition for discipleship." If you can not love your family less than how you love God, you cannot be a disciple of Jesus. It is either/or, not a both/and decision. Either you love him or not, follow him or not. There's no middle decision. Not only that, Jesus also delivered the "cost of discipleship." You have to bear your own cross. At this point in time, most of these people do not have an idea about "the cross of Christ" for Jesus was not yet crucified. But they must have an idea that the cross means death. It's the popular way of the Roman death sentence at that time. It means becoming a disciple of Jesus is a death sentence to your sinful self and a new life in Jesus.

Jesus also gave two examples to amplify his point on counting the cost.

> *For which of you, **desiring to build a tower**, does not first sit down and count the cost, whether he has enough to complete it? Otherwise, when he has laid a foundation and is not able to finish, all who see it begin to mock him, saying, 'This man began to build and was not able to finish.' Or what king, **going out to***

encounter another king in war, will not sit down first and deliberate whether he is able with ten thousand to meet him who comes against him with twenty thousand? And if not, while the other is yet a great way off, he sends a delegation and asks for terms of peace. So therefore, any one of you who does not renounce all that he has cannot be my disciple. (Luke 14:26-33)

If Jesus paid a high price to come and save us from our sins, will you consider the level of your commitment to him right now?

Levels of Commitment to Christ

Have you been discipled one-on-one or in a small group where someone nurtured you in your faith and spiritual journey to become like Jesus? Do you still remember the person who discipled you? And what was the result? Were you able to disciple others? I'm asking these questions, because these are extremely important in your spiritual journey.

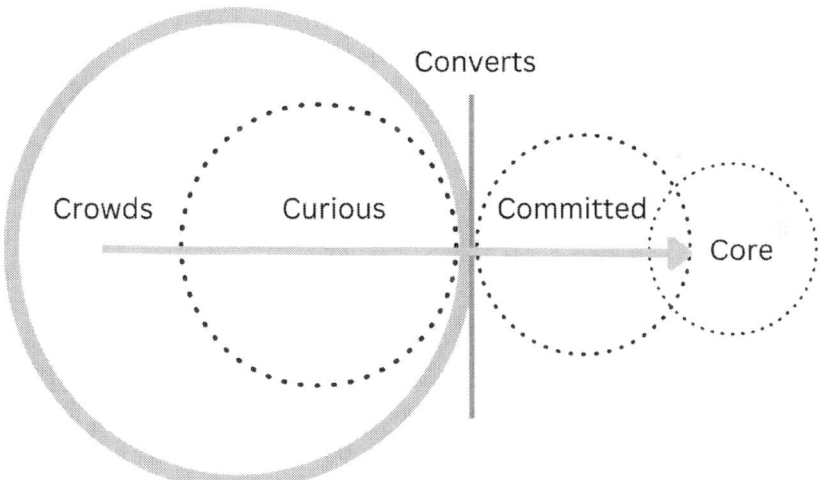

When Jesus gave his invitation for discipleship, he desires everyone who knows and believes in him to follow him closely. The truth is *not all who know Jesus have the same levels of commitment with him.* In fact, there are various kinds of "followers" of Jesus in the Gospel stories. When you carefully read the Gospels, especially the book of Mark, you will be able to identify the different "followers" around Jesus. It is like your circle of friends. Everyone you know is not your best friend. Some are close friend, familiar friends, casual friends, and "frenemeis." Looking at Jesus and his followers, there are distinct differences.

- **Crowd** - During the public ministry of Jesus, he ministered to great crowds. Mark says there was *"a very large crowd* (Gk *ochlos) gathered about him* [Jesus]" (Mark 4:1). It was a large-scale campaign he did in the cities. Matthew narrated, *"And great crowds followed him* [Jesus] *from Galilee and the Decapolis, and from Jerusalem and Judea, and from beyond the Jordan"* (Matthew 4:25). Again,*"large crowds followed him"* whenever he was in town, city or vicinity (Matthew 19:1-2). There were 175 references to these groups of people in the New Testament and they were more like "fans" and not necessarily "followers." They know Jesus by familiarity but not necessarily by faith. They're simply impressed with Jesus' miracles and charisma, but not inspired to live his teachings. More often than not, they just like the food, the benefits and blessings of joining the gathering.

- **Curious** - Within this huge crowd is a smaller group, somewhat closer to the truth. The curious ones were interested and mystified in what Jesus had to say to their questions and requests, however, they were neither willing to believe and seriously consider his teachings nor make the sacrifices necessary to be his disciples. They're only in it for the benefits or adding more information to their inquisitiveness. They're just trying to listen but not living it out. Still, they were not necessarily committed to following Jesus.

- **Converts** - This is where the defining line differs. There are *"many of the Jews"* (John 11:45) and *"many Samaritans"* who believed in the good news of Jesus as the Jewish Messiah and the Savior of the world (John 4:39). These converts are the ones who crossed the threshold from unbelief to saving faith. Unlike the large crowd and the merely curious ones who remained non-believers and far from God, numerous people fully trusted Jesus after hearing him proclaim the good news. They completely believed in him as the Son of the Living God. They repented of their sins and received Jesus as their Savior and Lord and became children of God (John 1:12). Thus, they are saved and have passed from death to life.

- **Committed** - The committed ones are a smaller group of these saved believers. They are someone committed to follow Jesus as his true disciple. (We will expand more of this topic later). The main difference between the crowd and the committed followers of Jesus was their *level of commitment*. The committed ones were not just interested in knowing and believing in Jesus, but they were willing to pay the cost of discipleship and make the sacrifices necessary to follow him. The committed followers will do whatever it takes to get closer in following Jesus.

- **Core** - Among the disciples of Jesus, there is an "inner circle" which can be called "the core." Jesus chose them as his closest disciples and friends and he invested in them with deeper relationships and discipleship. Again, if you carefully read the Gospels, you will notice that Peter, James and John were not just among the first ones whom Jesus chose, called and discipled, but they were part of the inner circle of Jesus (see also Mark 14:33; Luke 8:51; 9:28). They were the closest ones whom he invested a lot in.

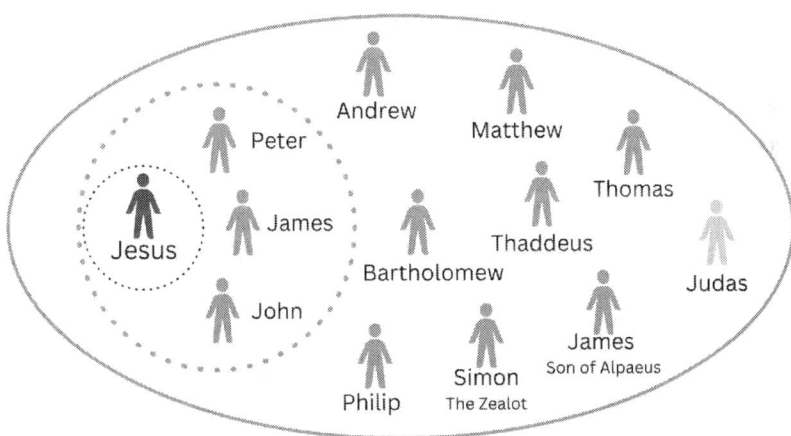

Jesus has at least two (2) "Circles of Relationships." First is his Core or inner circle; and, Second is the Circle of Disciples whom he chose as part of his 12 apostles or "The Twelve" (Matthew 10:1; 26:20; Mark 3:14; 6:7; Luke 9:1). Some would call this "the sacred circles." Unfortunately, Judas, one of the 12, eventually betrayed Jesus and only remained as a "professing disciple." He never understood the true nature of discipleship even though he walked with Jesus and the apostles (Judas was even the money keep or treasurer of the group). This reality should keep our expectations right on spot knowing there will be attrition or fall out. But that should not stop us from following Jesus' purpose and plan to make disciples.

Reflection:

What is your level of proximity in following Jesus as his disciple right now? (1 being farthest and 10 being the closest)

1   2   3   4   5   6   7   8   9   10

How would you like to be part of the inner circle of Jesus? Would you take his invitation seriously and commit to his plan for you?

CHAPTER 33: WHY IS BECOMING A DISCIPLE IMPORTANT FOR YOU?

The biggest problem of the western churches and in many churches around the world today is making discipleship *a part of their church program* rather than the Plan A of Jesus. The truth is making disciples is *"the"* strategy of Jesus rather than *"a"* ministry of Jesus. That's why we cannot deny the importance of discipling everyone.

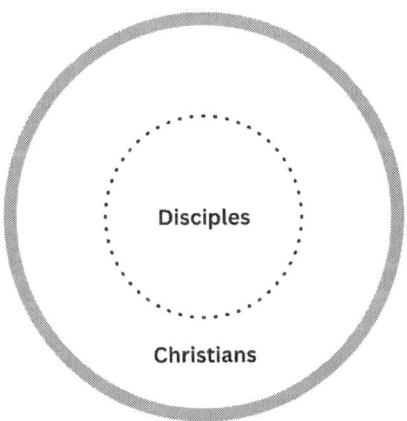

The first major reason is: Jesus called you to be a disciple, not just to be a Christian. Now, you might be wondering, what's the difference between a "Christian" and a "disciple"? Evidently, in the New Testament, the word "disciple" is mentioned a staggering 263 times, while "Christian" is just 3 times (respectively in the book of Acts 11:26; 26:28; 1 Peter 4:16). However, don't misunderstand this idea. It's not to diminish the importance of Christianity or those who confess as "Christians," but we could be missing the point of what

Jesus is calling us to do, which is to follow him and make disciples.

The terms "Christian" and "disciple of Jesus" are often used interchangeably, but there is a subtle difference between the two. They are all citizens of heaven but they don't have the same level of loyalty and obedience. A Christian is someone who believes in Jesus Christ as the Son of God and Savior of the world, whereas a disciple of Jesus is someone who became followers of Jesus' teachings. After they are saved, they seek to live their life in accordance with Jesus' example of making disciples. So, to be more specific, let me first define (or picture) a "disciple." *A disciple is a believer of Jesus who is called and changed into Christlike character and compassion, committed to knowing (cognitive) and obeying (competence) Jesus in fulfilling the Great Commission, which is making disciples of all nations.*

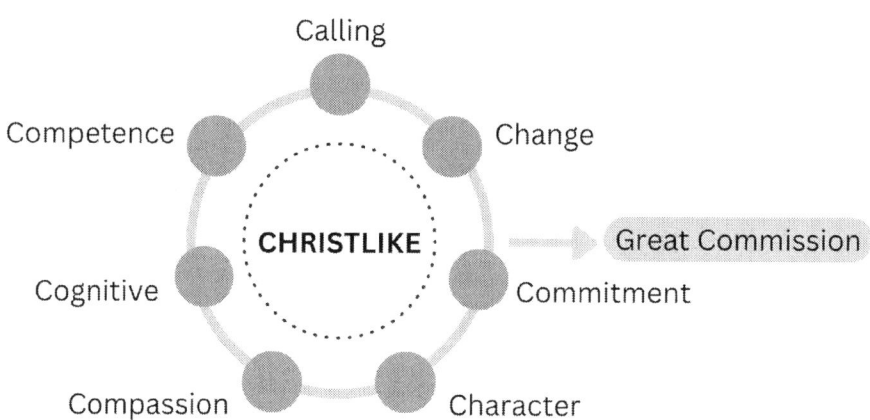

At the very heart of being a disciple of Jesus is **Christlikeness**. It is the ultimate goal of every part of the process, becoming like Jesus in thoughts, words, actions, and entire being. *Christlike quality is the core of being a true disciple of Jesus.* As a manifestation of this core quality, there are 7 evidences:

1. *Calling* - A true disciple has an inner conviction to answer Jesus' invitation and calling of becoming Jesus' disciple, not just to believe as a "Christian" but to follow Jesus in the journey of being *faithful* and

becoming *fruitful* disciples of Jesus.

2. *Change* - A true disciple has a transformed heart or evident change in life (unlike Judas, one of 12 disciples). In the process of becoming like Jesus in his or her thinking, actions, and character, the person lives out the lifestyle of being a disciple of Jesus.

3. *Commitment* - This is another distinct quality of a true disciple of Jesus. A disciple is not soft, but strong-willed in following Jesus. He or she doesn't rely on feelings, but in full faith in Jesus, knowing that it's not easy to follow him and obey his commands. Nevertheless, a disciple is committed to Christ and his cause despite many challenges. This person is willing to sacrifice one's own desires and comforts for the sake of others, as well as willing to put the needs of others before one's own.

4. *Character* - A true disciple manifests the qualities of Jesus' character, like his sacrificial love for God and people, obedience to the Father, being filled by the Holy Spirit and bearing the spiritual "fruit," which are "*love, joy, peace, patience, kindness, goodness, faithfulness, gentleness, self-control*" (Galatians 5:22).

5. *Compassion* - This essential quality is a huge game-changer. A true disciple has this very distinct attitude for the lost. He or she loves whom Jesus loved and died for and they are willing to do everything to win them for God (Matthew 9:26; 14:14; 15:32). Compassion drives a disciple to seek the lost and serve them. He or she is compassionate and loving, caring for others and wants to help them in any way. A true disciple is also forgiving and merciful, just like Jesus.

6. *Cognitive* - A true disciple keeps knowing Jesus by obeying Jesus and doing discipleship. This cognitive aspect is a product of encountering God and spiritual reflections on how God is revealing himself, speaking through his Word, and working in the world, as well as in the lives of other people through the Holy Spirit. A disciple of Jesus is someone who is not just constantly learning and growing in their faith, but always seeking to understand more about Jesus and what God is teaching. This one is also committed to sharing the faith with others and helping them to

grow in their faith as well.

7. **Competence** - A true disciple obeys Jesus and does discipleship with high-level skill of power in the Spirit. The disciple is trained, coached, and is modeling what it means to be a disciple-maker. As a result, the disciple can stand on his commitment to do disciple-making and reproduce other disciples. This disciple mastered the multiplication of disciples of Jesus by becoming disciple-makers themselves wherever they go.

Each of these essential qualities of a mature disciple are not exclusive. They are closely connected with each other. This definition is totally opposite to the misconceptions most Christians think about being a disciple. I'll highlight two of them:

- **Misconception #1:** *Being a disciple is just a matter of knowing God and Jesus, as well as the right teachings.* Or, many think it's about dumping information and less transformation, like listening to sermons and podcasts, watching videos, reading the right books, attending seminars, and training programs, and so on. These things are good, but insufficient in themselves. It's because the focus is on filling the mind (cognitive) alone. But it's only a part of the discipleship journey. Remember, during the times of Jesus they didn't have these things but they were properly discipled.

- **Misconception #2:** *Being a disciple is about living right and doing the right stuff according to your self-preferences.* It's about self-feeding and self-styled Christianity. The focus is on feeding the self with whatever you like and approve of Jesus' teachings, and setting aside those that you feel uncomfortable, hard, and offensive to the world. This misconception is often an inward direction and self absorbing. (If this was Jesus' agenda, then he should have built the greatest empire for self-help). In the western world where individualism is a valued preference, philosophy, and practice, Christianity is more of a private information (like someone's age) and that's why it eventually declined. But that's far from what the Jewish background of the Bible is. Becoming disciples is a more communal environment and/or in small group learning and process (more of this idea later). It's not in isolation.

In other words, Jesus called you to be closer to him as his disciple, not just to be a nominal Christian. He wants you to journey closer to him with other disciples and not a lone hiker.

The second major reason: Jesus commanded us to make disciples. It's called the Great Commission, not a suggestion. We stand in between embracing it or ignoring it. That determines our obedience or disobedience.

> *And Jesus came and said to them, "All authority in heaven and on earth has been given to me.* **Go** *therefore and* **make disciples** *of all nations, baptizing them in the name of the Father and of the Son and of the Holy Spirit,* **teaching** *them* **to observe** *all that I have commanded you. And behold, I am with you always, to the end of the age."* (Matthew 28:18-20)

This command is an authoritative mandate. Jesus, in whom all—not a *few* or some but *all*—authority was endowed by God, is the sovereign giver of this disciple-making command. Whether you know or accept this or not, it is non-negotiable for every believer of Jesus. Some of the essential elements involved in the process of making disciples are the following:

- *Missional* - The Great Commission is a missionary strategy for winning the people of the world. This method is the prime and pivotal plan of God to win people for Jesus. In the original language, the word "Go" is actually a participle, not much of a verb-command. It means Jesus is saying to his disciple "*As you go*, make disciples of all nations."

- *Multiplicational* - This is the major command in the Great Commission: "*Make disciples* of all nations." In the original language, the command emphasis is this: "*Disciple* all nations." It's the ultimate strategy of Jesus in winning the world. As Quintell Hill, the President of NC Baptist, once said, "Jesus is God but he still has a strategy." That's to multiply "disciples" (plural), not disciple (singular). It means each disciple must have more than one disciple like Jesus did.

- *Instructional* - This is captured in the phrase "*teaching* them all things" that Jesus taught and commanded, including baptism and discipleship as mentioned here. In the Scriptures, teaching (*didasko* in Greek) is almost always referring to the teaching of the Word of God. In this context, a disciple must be taught, instructed, even directed with Bible-based teachings. Everyone who goes through the disciple process must become a learner and apprentice, before becoming a disciple-maker, leader and coach with the Scripture as its foundation and manual.

- **Sustainable** - The phrase "*to observe*" means "to keep," "guard" or "watch over." More often than not, this part is viewed as the practical application of discipleship. But here, "to observe" emphasizes the continuity or connectedness of everything in the discipleship process without a break. Through ongoing observance and experience-based discipleship, the sustained act of discipling others is not just an expression of obedience, the church must disciple everyone who commits to follow Jesus because it is "the" great priority of Jesus for the church. None should be left behind.

That is why after three years of being with his disciples, the final command of Jesus is "make disciples." Everything that he said, taught, and did boil down to one thing (and one thing only, and it's not "Be a Christian," because they already are). This one main thing is: "Make Disciples."

Reflection:

What is Jesus telling you about the most important reason why you must be his follower?

What is the most important lesson you learn here about the importance of becoming Christlike?

CHAPTER 34: DO YOU HAVE WHAT IT TAKES TO BE A DISCIPLE OF JESUS?

Before you assume anything that Jesus is very harsh and intolerant, you must remember that Jesus loved people. Every call he gave and every invitation he offered were all rooted in his love and grace. Here are some diagnostic questions for you to answer "Yes" (or check) or "No" (or X). You'll have an idea where you are right now.

O *Are you committed to let go of materialism–that mindset of making material possessions as more than spiritual values?*

Jesus pointed out this demand to a rich young man who is full of energy in making money (Read the full story in Matthew 19:16-22). The rich man appears to be very spiritual and keeping the law, but Jesus knows his heart. The man seems to be an overachiever in spiritual things, but Jesus knew he was just faking his faith.

> *Jesus said to him, "If you would be perfect, go, sell what you possess and give to the poor, and you will have treasure in heaven; and come, follow me." When the young man heard this he went away sorrowful,* **for he had great possessions**. (Matthew 19:21-22)

The problem of American Christianity is that it has become so wealthy, that money (or making money) is more important than the Master. That's why the prosperity Gospel is so popular here. In it, prosperity is now the good news, not Jesus. It is materialism in disguise as the Gospel. But that's not what discipleship is all about. Once can only be a disciple if you value the master more than the material things of this world.

O *Do you love Jesus more than anything in this world, including your livelihood?*

At the beach of Tiberias, the resurrected Jesus spent breakfast time with his seven disciples (Read the full story in John 21:1-19). Jesus prepared fresh baked bread and grilled fish, the best food in town.

> *When they had finished breakfast, Jesus said to Simon Peter, "Simon, son of John,* **do you love me more than these?***" He said to him, "Yes, Lord; you know that I love you." He said to him, "Feed my lambs."* (John 21:15)

Jesus was probably pointing to the good food that had been prepared before them and they had been filled. It connected with Jesus' reply to "feed" his lambs (the disciples), obviously, with spiritual food. Everyday, people work for food on the table. But it is also evident that people can be consumed by their livelihood and they leave the Lord waiting. There are times when work is more important than worship. So the question remains: Do you love the Lord more than your livelihood?

○ *Do you love Jesus more than your spouse, family and yourself?*

This demand from Jesus is one of the most controversial. Again, facing the great crowds following him, Jesus challenged them.

> *If anyone comes to me and does not hate* **his own father and mother and wife and children and brothers and sisters***, yes, and even his own life, he cannot be my disciple.* (Luke 14:26)

Is this a hate speech? Why would Jesus say to the people to "hate" mothers and fathers? That's so offensive to anyone, especially parents, right? But the meaning of "hate" here is to "love less," and it's not to have intense dislike or hostility to parents. You must understand that during Jesus' time and in their culture, children profess so much love and loyalty to parents and family. Sometimes this blind loyalty exceeds their love for God (like they are excessively generous to their family than to God and his work). Jesus is pointing out that if your love for any of your family relationships is greater than God, that's idolatry. If I'm a mature parent, I would rather see my kids love God more than they love me, thus, fulfill the greatest commandment of loving God (Matthew 22:37) and be disciples of Jesus.

○ *Do you love Jesus enough to carry his cross and make personal sacrifices?*

In the Scripture, the cross has been the symbol of suffering and shame. It also signifies the greatest sacrifice God offered and Jesus experienced from Jerusalem to the hill of Calvary. But we all know that Jesus endured the pain, mockery, and shame. *"Whoever does not **bear his own cross** and come after me cannot be my disciple"* (Luke 14:27).

As such, when Jesus challenged the great crowd accompanying him, he asked them if they were willing to pay the cost of becoming a disciple, Jesus asked them this tough declaration. A person who is not committed will only complain and quit. When tough things happen, true disciples are willing to make personal sacrifices for God and the ones being discipled.

o *Are you committed to let go of any emotional attachments and responsibilities that hold you back from becoming his disciple?*

Most people during Jesus' time are so attached to their parents. Many of them have to sacrifice and abandon their personal dreams just to take care of their ailing, aging, and dying parents. But Jesus challenged those who wanted to follow him and those who are on the verge of changing their minds to back out or backslide.

> *Another of the disciples said to him,* **"Lord, let me first go and bury my father."** *And Jesus said to him, "Follow me, and leave the dead to bury their own dead."* (Matthew 8:21-22)

This does not mean Jesus is asking the person not to attend the burial of their loved ones. It only takes a few days to finish it. But that's not what it means here. What Jesus is saying here is that if a person has to wait for his parents to die first before he decides to follow Jesus and serve God, it means that person is not worthy to be a disciple. Not to mention that those who are spiritually "dead" will eventually be physically "dead." There's a more dangerous kind of death looming to those who are not in Jesus, whether they are your family members, close friends, or strangers. That's the death in hell and of eternal separation with God. if you cannot grasp nor care for the eternal destiny of the spiritually dead, you cannot be a disciple of Jesus.

o *Are you committed to courageously live for Jesus alone by becoming his disciple?*

You must understand that Jesus is raising a spiritual army or courageous followers. That's why he gave them the spirit of boldness. Remember, the Jewish people were under Roman rule. The religious climate was not in their favor. So they have a choice: Go with the flow and die trying nothing, or go against the tide and get to where God wants them to be.

> *And calling the crowd to him with his disciples, he said to them, "**If anyone would come after me, let him deny himself and take up his cross and follow me.** For whoever would save his life will lose it, but **whoever loses his life for my sake and the gospel's will save it.** For what does it profit a man to gain the whole world and forfeit his soul? For what can a man give in return for his soul? For whoever is ashamed of me and of my words in this adulterous and sinful generation, of him will the Son of Man also be ashamed when he comes in the glory of his Father with the holy angels."* (Matthew 34-38)

Have you noticed how Jesus demanded absolute obedience and loyalty from those who want to become his disciples? It means if you cannot answer "Yes" to these radical demands of Jesus, his statement is "You cannot be my disciple." By now, you should have an idea where you are in your relationship with Jesus as a disciple. Are you one step closer? How about the rest?

The Parable of the Drowning Man

A man was relaxing at a park beside a riverbank. After a day's hard work towards achieving his dreams, he thought of giving himself a break. While sitting alone on a bench, he was so consumed by the thought about his life, his family, his work, his dream house and his dream vacation and so on.

Meanwhile, a dam up in the mountains broke and flash floods were coming fast down the river. The man didn't notice the rising tide. When the man saw the rising water, the park was already flooded. He had nowhere to go as he was caught in the middle. He was carried away by the flood without any warning. He found himself struggling to stay afloat. He knew his death was coming. Soon he will run out of strength and be drowned. So he shouted and cried for help.

However, on the other side of the riverbank, a farmer and his only son were also carried by the strong current of the flood. The farmer was holding his beloved son. When he saw the drowning man, he wanted to rescue him but that would mean he had to let go of his son.

Out of the deepest mystery of life, the farmer did not hesitate to rescue the drowning man. He saved a stranger while his son was carried away by the current and he died in the flood. The farmer made the greatest sacrifice. His son died so that a stranger would live.

If you were that stranger, would you honor the sacrifice of that farmer or just go on with your life ignoring him? Will you love him or just set him aside? What would you do in return in honor of this great life-saving experience?

The truth is *what Jesus is asking from you is radical because his Father in heaven did the most radical act ever.* That's why the cost of discipleship is not cheap. Jesus paid it with his life. If the cost of discipleship is giving your life to Jesus totally, it's because he gave and invested his life for you. He paid the ultimate price none can fully repay. Now, it's your turn to give back for the cost of discipleship. That is if you answer, "Yes, Lord. I commit to follow you and obey your command to make disciples of all nations."

Reflection:

Review all the questions in this chapter. What question was very difficult for you to say "Yes"? Why is that so?

If you were the "Drowning Man," would you honor the sacrifice of that farmer? What would you do in return?

SECTION 12: LOVING IN EVERY PART OF OUR BEING

"But whoever keeps his word,
in him truly the love of God is perfected.
By this we may know
that we are in him:
whoever says he abides in him
ought to walk in the same way
in which he walked."

~ John the Beloved (1 John 2:5-6)

CHAPTER 35: WHAT IS LOVE?

We all know that love is a universal theme. We've heard it a million times in songs, seen it in movies, read in books, experienced it in our relationships, and so on. You even saw the yard signs stating, "Love is love." But what does "love" really mean today? Are we just using the same word but the meanings are different and nuances are clashing? Is this love how the sacred Scriptures defined and demonstrated it?

Did you know that one of the biggest prophecies in the Bible about the last days is related to people proliferating and talking a lot about "love"? In the end of days, people will popularly say about love but it is not how God defined and described it. It is a twisted kind of love and is not true love. Here's the prophecy:

> *"But **understand** this, that **in the last days** there will come **times of difficulty**. For people will be **lovers of self, lovers of money,** proud, arrogant, abusive, disobedient to their parents, ungrateful, unholy, **heartless,** unappeasable, slanderous, without self-control, brutal, **not loving good,** treacherous, reckless, swollen with conceit, **lovers of pleasure** rather than **lovers of God."** (2 Timothy 3:1-4)

Do you think we are in this terrible time of difficulty like never before? While you can study the many other "signs of times" here, let's focus on the repeated points about "love" and see if we're living in this era of love as the world knows.

- **"Lovers of self"** - It means "self-loving" (Greek *philautoi*). It refers to a general population who are so preoccupied with selfish desires and self-interests. There's no time like it where the self is the all-encompassing obsession. Accordingly, Gautama Buddha said, "You can search throughout the entire universe for someone who is more deserving of your love and affection than you are yourself, and that person is not to be found anywhere. *You yourself,* as much as anybody in the entire universe, deserves your love and affection" [emphasis mine]. Have you ever thought about the binding relationship between the worldwide cult of self-love-esteem and the normalizing of selfie-culture?

- **"Lovers of money"** - It literally means "money-loving" (*philarguroi*). The end of days will be a time where people are extremely avaricious (or having an intense and selfish desire for money) and covetous (or having great desire to possess money). People will be so in love with monetary gain for personal gratification. Are we living in a global culture where the majority of influencers is all about greed and selling your soul for the money and fans?

- **"Heartless"** - It means unloving (*"astorgoi"*) or devoid of natural affection. The last days are described as a global display of no feeling, empathy, or affection, even to the most vulnerable of all human beings. Have you observed the eyes of those who promote killing the unborn and see if there's heartlessness? There's emptiness you can see through the window of their soul, which is the eye. Or watch powerful people who created dangerous actions that killed millions and yet without any trace of remorse.

- **"Not loving good"** - This rare word (*"aphilagathoi"*) gets interesting. It's not simply an absence of love of that which is good, but it means a "hater of good." It will be a dominating culture of haters and hostile to anything good and the things of God. The last days will be a time where hatred for everything good covers the whole world. People will hate and rage against God and his people.

- **"Lovers of pleasure rather than lovers of God"** - This "pleasure" is not about healthy recreation, creative expressions, or wholesome entertainment. It means "pleasure-loving" (*"phileidonoi"* = *phileo* or love + donor or pleasure, the root word for *hedone* or sensuous pleasure, like Hedonistic culture). Time will come where most people and the prevailing culture idolize lustful entertainers and God is just secondary or out of the picture.

If you notice, the word used for love here is *phileo* or "brotherly love." There's nothing bad about *phileo* (love) in the original sense as this word was also applied to God's love for Jesus (John 16:27) or Jesus' love to his disciples (John 16:27). But here in this prophecy the added words made and corrupted it into something profane, immoral and sinful. All of these word combinations about love are used only once or twice in the Bible, showing us that this difficult time is a very distinct time, especially if you study the other words and signs used to describe the last days. There's nothing like it. It means love is redefined, distorted, and has no godly meaning at all. People can use and exploit love anyway they want it and suit it to their selfish and perverse desires. It is such a terrible end-time that Jesus said, "*And because lawlessness will be increased, the love of many will grow cold*" (Matthew 24:12). You must not wonder if in the last days, many—and that includes believers in the Lord—will leave their "first love" and follow anything other than Jesus (Revelation 2:4).

The good news is God never ceases to love you. We must understand that from a biblical perspective, love is the whole nature of God and his pure intention, purpose and plan for his creation is to benevolently give unconditional, unmerited favor and to seek their highest good. Love is the fullness of God's affection and a preference to show goodwill to his creation. The whole meaning of this is God loves you, not because you are good but because it is his choice. That's why the Bible has a special word for love of this kind: the word "agape."

While the problem continues as people constantly refuse God's love and keep moving away from his divine purposes and plans for life, they are looking for love in wrong places and for wrong reasons and wrong objects of love. Today, the world even twisted the meaning of love into debasing ideas by sexualizing it. Fornication and adultery is normalized and watered down as "making love." Children are being groomed at school to accept perverted ideas about love with non-traditional sexual ideologies and it confuses them. In the last days, demonic and godless ideas about love will dominate. Are we living in such a time now? What will you do about it? Will you go with the current of the culture and be a part of that prophecy or you commit to follow the path of Jesus? Will you live the lifestyle of love as defined by the world or love as taught and exemplified by Jesus?

In our spiritual life as followers of Jesus, love is the summit of our journey with Jesus. It is the ultimate goal of becoming Christlike. To be a follower of Jesus is to embody the love of God in our entire being. If this is the case, Satan's ultimate goal in the world is to deliberately destroy the biblical concept of love.

The Bible calls love as the *"**more excellent way**"* of life (1 Corinthians 12:31). In 1 Corinthians 13:1-12, the "way of love" is so important for us that we are nothing without it. Your *words* will amount to nothing if you don't have love. Your *wisdom* is nothing without love. And apart from love, your good *work* means nothing, absolutely nothing. In fact, love is everything. For Paul, *"Love bears all things, believes all things, hopes all things, endures all things"* (1 Corinthians 13:7). That's why he concluded that love is *"**the greatest**"* between faith and hope. Your faith and hope will never exist without love. You know why? It's because the ultimate reason why these things we believe in and the hope we have in Jesus and what have you, all of these exist because of love. In eternity, faith and hope will cease, but love remains forever.

The More Excellent Way

If you walk through this life and follow the steps of Jesus, he wants you to see that *love is a journey closer to the heart of God.* And Jesus is more than willing to come alongside you, walk with you, and empower you to grow until God's love is perfected in you and through you. John the Beloved said,

> *"But whoever keeps his word, **in him truly the love of God is perfected.** By this we may know that we are in him: whoever says he abides in him ought to **walk***

in the same way in which he walked." (1 John 2:5-6).

In his other letter, John also said, *"And **this is love**, that **we walk** according to his commandments; this is **the commandment**, just as you have heard from the beginning, so that **you should walk in it"*** (2 John 1:6).

What is *"the"* specific commandment that we must walk? Why is it so important that we should live it? That particular commandment is to love as God defined it, commanded it, and demonstrated it.

Reflection:

What is your level of love for God right now? (1 being lowest and 10 being the highest)

| 1 | 2 | 3 | 4 | 5 | 6 | 7 | 8 | 9 | 10 |

What is God teaching you here about a true definition of love? What are you going to do about this lesson learned?

CHAPTER 36: WHY SHOULD WE LOVE?

Imagine you're on a journey of life. Have you ever asked what's the ultimate purpose for this life experience and what's the final destination in all of these? You might ask, what is the top of this uphill climb to the mountain or the grand design of this journey?

Foremost, we love because God commanded it. Now you might think, I don't like being commanded. Fine, but why does God have to take love as a commandment? It's because it is not our human nature to love. Our sinful nature dictates that we are selfish, always looking for our self-centered interests and self-absorbed desires. As such, any form of "love" we give is always tainted with personal motives and hidden agenda. That's why love comes in as a commandment. To love is an act of obedience to God. When Jesus was asked,

> *"Teacher, which is the great commandment in the Law?" And he said to him,* ***"You shall love the Lord your God*** *with all your heart and with all your soul and with all your mind. This is* ***the great and first commandment.*** *And a second is like it: You shall* ***love your neighbor as yourself.*** *On these two commandments depend all the Law and the Prophets."* (Matthew 22:36-40)

Loving God and loving people are two greatest commandments in the Bible. Therefore, to love with every part of our being is an act of obedience to God.

Secondly, love is a proof of our spiritual rebirth. If you want proof that you are truly born again and you have the genuine saving faith in Jesus, the major evidence is not your knowledge of the truth about Jesus but true love. Apostle John, *aka* John the Beloved, told the early Christians,

> *Everyone who* ***believes that Jesus is the Christ has been born of God,*** *and* ***everyone who loves the Father loves whoever has been born of him.*** *By this we know that* ***we love the children of God,*** *when we* ***love God*** *and obey his commandments. For this is* ***the love of God,*** *that we keep his commandments.*

And his commandments are not burdensome. (1 John 5:1-3)

Not only that John repeatedly emphasized our obedience to love, he is confirming the truth that loving God and people, especially your fellow believers who "*has been born of him*," is the solid and strongest proof that you are truly a child of God. If a professing Christian hates the church or born-again people, that's a question mark because God unconditionally loves the church despite its shortcomings and imperfections.

Thirdly, Loving is the natural response of a believer and follower of Jesus to God's love. Our love for God must follow this ultimate truth: "***We love because he first loved us***" (1 John 4:19). There must be no other higher reason for our love. If we love someone because they are beautiful, talented, likable, rich, and so on, one thing is sure. You will be frustrated. God must be the ultimate reason why we love. Being obedient to love God and others because you have been commanded is quite different to being responsive because you deeply realize God's love and grace to you, so you act accordingly to what you know and see. If there's one main reason why we should love God and people is because of his love for us. John pointed out this truth by giving a practical example also.

> ***We love because he first loved us.*** *If anyone says, "I love God," and hates his brother, he is a liar; for* ***he who does not love his brother whom he has seen cannot love God whom he has not seen.*** *And this commandment we have from him:* ***whoever loves God must also love his brother.*** (1 John 4:19-21)

John is teaching that the ultimate reason, absolute foundation or primary basis of our love must be the love of God for us. If we have other reasons for that, we should check whether our hearts are filled with God's love or just our sinful and distorted ideas of love. God loved us despite who we are or who *you* are. We need to ask where our love is conditioned by personalities, race, political parties, and so on. As followers of Jesus, we should not be identified by these delusions that Satan is using to divide the church and his people. Instead, we should love like God.

Have we forgotten why Peter said amidst all the differences that the body of Christ has in the past? He said, "***Above all, keep loving one another earnestly,*** *since love covers a multitude of sins"* (1 Peter 4:8). Why are we playing with the Devil's plan to divide and conquer? Why are we so passionate about so many worldly and non-essential things and we keep what's more important trivial, like loving fellow believers, and as a result we default and destroy our testimonies to the world?

Fourthly, loving God and people makes the world know we are genuine followers of Jesus. The way you believe in and live for is manifested in the way you love. In the eyes of the world, they don't care about what you believe until they see if you truly care for others. That's why Jesus explicitly and unapologetically said, **"**By this **all people will know** *that you are my disciples,* **if you** *have love for one another"* (John 13:35). Jesus is emphasizing that the conditions of our hearts and relationships with one another will reveal who we are, whether we are true disciples or false disciples–whether we are truly God's children or not.

That is why John the Beloved affirmed that your *"belief"* is proven by your *"behaviors."* It's not your information that matters but your transformation from being indifferent into a truly loving person. John said, *"By this it is* **evident who are the children of God,** *and who are* **the children of the devil**: *whoever does not* **practice** *righteousness is not of God, nor is the one who does* **not love** *his brother"* (1 John 3:10). This statement is a clear indication that those who talk about love but are actually hateful of anything good and affirming the unrighteousness of this world are delusional and hypocritical, and those who practice and promote evil things are demonic in nature. Only the children of the Devil will promote evil agenda and keep practicing and performing evil deeds.

Fifthly, loving God and people is the final phase of our spiritual journey in Jesus. It is the ultimate goal of our journey, the pinnacle of the process of being a disciple and the highest stage of our Christian life. It is the key indicator of spiritual maturity. Let's read what the Apostle Peter has written about it.

> *For this very reason, make every effort to supplement* **your faith** *with virtue, and virtue with knowledge, and knowledge with self-control, and self-control with steadfastness, and steadfastness with godliness, and godliness with brotherly affection, and brotherly affection with* **love**. *For if these qualities are yours and are*

increasing, they keep you from being ineffective or unfruitful in the knowledge of our Lord Jesus Christ. (2 Peter 1:5-9)

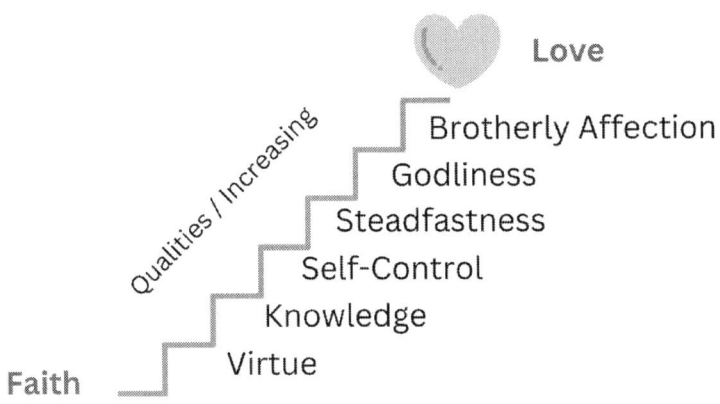

Have you noticed the increasing pattern of these qualities? It means our Christian "faith" is a process towards the mature level, which is "love" (*agapei*). Apostle John already highlighted in 1 John 2:5-6 that when "***the love of God is perfected***" in us, we will know among ourselves whether we are living or "***abiding in him*** [Jesus]" or we're only professing. Interestingly, John used the word "having been perfected" (or "*teteleumenei*"), meaning "to bring to an end" or "to complete," like reaching the end stage or final phase. In this case, God's love is fulfilled, perfected or consummated in us.

The way we walk in the love of Jesus in our thoughts, words and actions will be the sign that we are living maturely for him as God fulfills what he planned for us. John also repeatedly emphasized this ultimate goal for our Christian life transformation as followers of Jesus, when he said, "*Beloved,* ***if God so loved us,*** *we also ought to love one another. No one has ever seen God;* ***if we love one another,*** *God* ***abides*** *in us and* ***his love is perfected in us***" (1 John 4:11-12). John is setting the condition we live in.

If you know (knowledge) how much God loves you and you believe (faith) his demonstration of love through Jesus who died at the cross for you, then our response (action) in life is to love God and love one another. Even in 1 John 4:16, you can see these connections. *"We have come to know* (knowledge) *and to believe* (faith) *the love that God has for us. God is love, and whoever **abides** in love* (action) *abides in God, and God abides in him."* Here, we can see the strong connection of love, knowledge, faith, and action in God's process of making you a mature disciple, which he repeated in verse 17 (*"By this is love perfected with us"*).

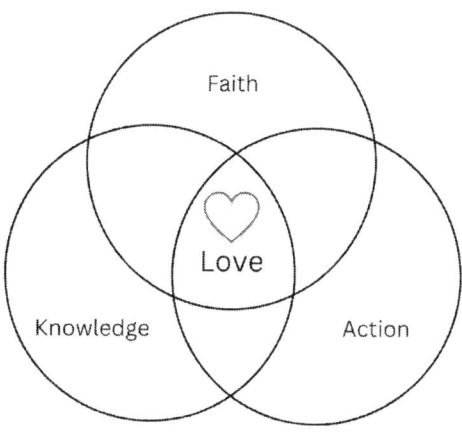

In our Christian journey, living and loving go together. It means our lifestyle should show what's truly within us. And this one can't go wrong: Love is proven by your actions.

Reflections:

What is God teaching you about loving him?

What is God telling you about loving people?

CHAPTER 37: WHO WE LOVE AND WHAT NOT?

In the eyes of Jesus, love revolves around *loving God* and then about *loving people*. From Genesis to Revelation, the two major categories of love are loving the divine and loving humankind. As Jesus' disciple, we must be radically in love with God and our fellow human beings.

Loving God

God: ***Love the Lord your God.*** Since the beginning, God created human beings to have a relationship with him. You were made to *lovingly connect* with your Creator. That's why, when God gave the greatest commandment of all for his people, it's about loving God. Moses said, *"Hear, O Israel: The LORD our God, the LORD is one.* **You shall love the LORD your God** *with all your heart and with all your soul and with all your might"* (Deuteronomy 6:4-5). This decree is what the Hebrew people knew as the *Shema*, (Hebrew for "hear"), which is the center of Israel's belief in the singularity of God, *"The LORD is* **one**.*"* There's only one

God, the Creator of heaven and earth, whom we should love.

What God wanted from his creation, especially for his children, is not mere knowledge about him but a deep feeling of affection for him, a complete devotion of worshiping him, and loving him with all our being (body, soul, and spirit). As such, when Jesus was asked by an expert of the law of Moses, "*Teacher, which is the great commandment in the Law?*" he quoted Deuteronomy 6:5, saying, "*You shall **love the Lord your God** with all your heart and with all your soul and with all your mind. This is the great and first commandment*" (Matthew 22:37). To love God is "the great" ("*megalei*") commandment because it is large enough to cover everything in the widest sense, and it's also the "first," not as the earliest to be given but, because it is the most important and highest above all else. It is the number 1 command of all commands.

As the Father's creation and as his children, we become fully human when we are obeying this top command and living in that divine-human love relationship. Why? It's because we become who we love. If we love God, we are changed and conformed into his image. And not only that, if we fully understand why our Father created us and chose us to be his children, we would love Jesus (John 8:42-47).

Love Jesus: *Do You Love Me?* As followers of Jesus and God's children, when we love Jesus, it is tantamount to loving God the Father (John 8:42), it's because *Jesus and the Father are one* (John 10:30). (As such, the same can be said about loving the Holy Spirit, it is the same as loving Jesus). Many times, Jesus declared to his disciples that if they love him, they will keep his words and commandments (John 14:15). He even said, "*If **anyone loves me**, he will keep my word, and my Father will love him, and we will come to him and make our home with him*" (John 14:23). Such is the priceless blessing of loving Jesus as God's love will also come and dwell in the heart of the one who loves. How can you out-love Jesus? Never. But he still loves you where you are and he is willing to reach out to you.

Jesus asked Peter, "*Do you **love me** more than these?*" (John 21:15-17). Why? It's because Jesus was reaching out to him and trying to restore that love relationship he had with his disciple. This same sacrificial love for Jesus must be *incorruptible* and be acted upon in *faith* (Ephesians 6:24; Philemon 1:4-5).

Word of God: *Love God's Word.* I'd also like to highlight about loving the Word of God. Yes, we love Jesus the Living Word, but we also have to consider loving God's written Word. God speaks and reveals himself to us through the Scriptures. Through it, we come to know about God, Jesus, the Holy Spirit, the church, and so on. We also grow in our spiritual life and find direction in our life journey. In it, we also know his commands. Did you know that there are 613 laws and commandments for Israel (Hebrew *mitzvot*) in the Old Testament and all of them are expressions of God's love?

You may have come to believe that God's laws are restrictive, stifling, and demanding. Many hate it because it is somewhat the opposite of love. But that is an unbiblical idea of the laws as God designed it. Even Israel missed that point. The truth is, all of God's laws, commands, and decrees are expressions of his love for his people. That's why King David loved and often sings about it. In Psalm 119, he sings about it.

> *For I find my delight in* **your commandments,** *which* **I love.**
> *I will lift up my hands toward* **your commandments,** *which* **I love,**
> *and I will meditate on your statutes. (Psalm 119:47-48)*
> *Oh how I love your law!*
> *It is my meditation all the day. (Psalm 119:97; see also v.113, 163)*
> *Great peace have those who* **love your law;**
> *nothing can make them stumble.* (Psalm 119:165)

For King David, meditating on God's Word is an expression of his love of it. If you want to grow in your faith and serve God, you must love the Scripture like David and he has several reasons why we should also do the same (Read Psalm 119:97-105).

Family: *Family Matters.* Our family is one of the greatest gifts of God. In the Bible, God instituted marriage and family. In Israel, the family is the core nucleus, not just of their society but, of their spiritual nurture (Deuteronomy 6:7). Most of the stories in the Bible were set in the context of the family, even the life of Jesus. Many times we read and interpret the Bible from an individualistic view, but you must understand that the Bible was written in the context of a family-oriented culture and environment.

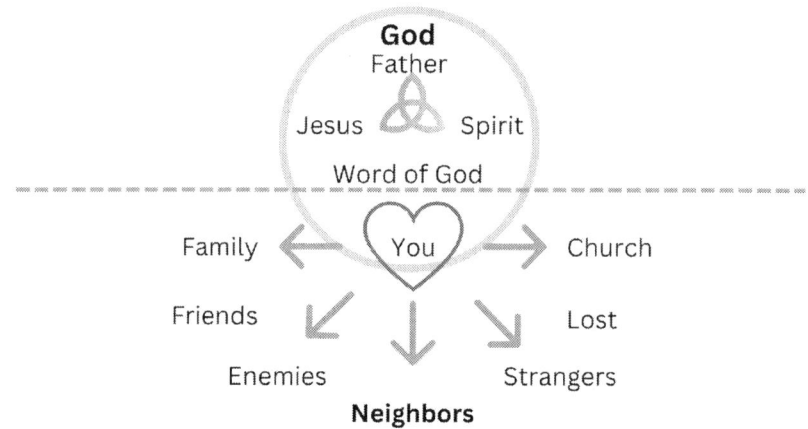

Loving People

The family may not be everything, but it is certainly a great thing that can never be taken for granted, especially in our spiritual walk. Among Christian households, husbands are commanded to love their wives as Jesus loved the church in a sacrificial and committed way (Ephesians 5:25, 28). The husbands' love for their wives must be gentle and not harsh. In the same manner, the family must also demonstrate their love for each other in practical ways (Colossians 3:18-21). Above all, discipleship should start at home as parents and children follow the Lord's commands and instructions for living (Ephesians 6:1-4). If your biological family are non-believers, pray that God's love, grace, and forgiveness will rest upon your family.

Neighbor: *Love your neighbor as yourself.* If the command to love God is number one, then there's second to it. In the words of Jesus, he said, *"And a second is like it: You shall love your neighbor as yourself. On these two commandments depend all the Law and the Prophets"* (Matthew 22:39-40). This command was taken from Leviticus 19:18. It says there: *"You shall love your neighbor as yourself: I am the LORD."* For Jesus, the command to love your neighbor is foundational in our life and relationships. It is the basis of all our relationships with every human being we connect with in our community.

Loving your neighbor is a major teaching of Jesus (Matthew 22:39; Mark 12:21; Luke 10:27). The apostles also heavily emphasized on loving your neighbor as yourself (Romans 13:9; James 2:8). It has become the basis of their encouragements on love, like, *"Owe no one anything, except* **to love each other***, for* **the one who loves another has fulfilled the law***"* (Romans 13:8). For the followers of Jesus, the hundreds of laws in the Old Testament (and there's little or no way for you to memorize and follow all of the laws of Moses but it) can be wrapped up and fulfilled through loving your neighbor. So if you want to fulfill all God's commands in the Old Testament, you can fulfill everything by loving your neighbor as yourself.

The apostle Paul even said, *"**Through love serve one another***. For the whole law is fulfilled in one word: "You shall love your neighbor as yourself"* (Galatians 5:13c-14). James 2:8 also agrees when it says, *"If you really fulfill* **the royal law** *according to the Scripture, "You shall love your neighbor as yourself," you are doing well."* There's no doubt that God is telling us to love our neighbors, indeed.

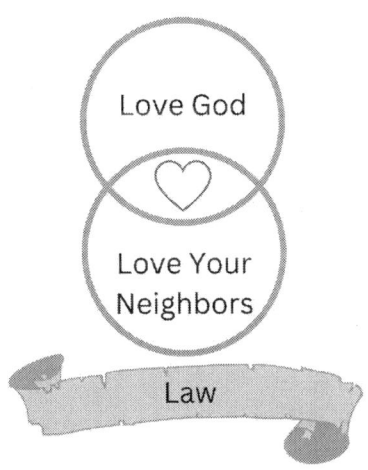

Friends: *Love Your Friends.* Friends are a gift from God. After all, friendship was conceived as coming from God. It is his idea. Abraham was called "a friend of God" (2 Chronicles 20:7; James 2:23). Even God referred to Abraham as "my friend" (Isaiah 41:8). Did you know that God is a friendly God and he offers friendship with those who love and revere him? Job mentioned the "friendship of God" (Job 29:4). David also sang about in Psalm 25:14, saying, "***The friendship of the LORD*** *is for those who fear him, and he makes known to them his covenant.*" For God, true friendships should not be taken lightly, because friends are priceless treasures given by God.

Jesus called his disciples as "my friends" (Luke 12:4). He loved them more than anyone could imagine. Jesus told them how great his love for them is because he is more than willing to give his life for them. He said,

> *"Greater love has no one than this, that someone **lay down his life for his friends. You are my friends** if you do what I command you. No longer do I call you servants, for the servant does not know what his master is doing; but I have called you **friends**, for all that I have heard from my Father I have made known to you."* (John 15:13-15)

This example might surprise you how friendly Jesus is. He is a strong model for us in building relationships with our friends and loving them like Jesus. You may have best friends, close friends, or church friends. It doesn't matter whether they are in close proximity or not, but we are called to be friendly and to love our friends, not just on good times but "at all times," (Proverbs 17:17).

Church: *Love One Another.* Jesus loves his church. Like a bride, he loved it more than his earthly life as he died for her so that he could make her holy by cleansing and washing her uncleanness of sin with his Word (Read Ephesians 5:25-27). If Jesus loved the church so much despite her imperfections, you should love the church, too.

Before Jesus suffered and died on the cross, he demonstrated his love for his disciples. John the Beloved recorded it, saying "*having loved **his own** who were in the world, he loved them to the end*" (John 13:1b). During that last supper, Jesus gave a new commandment to his disciples. Jesus said, **"*A new commandment*** *I give to you, that you **love one another**: just as I have loved you, you also are to **love one another**. By this all people will know that you are my disciples, if you have **love for one another**"* (John 13:34-35). Why is this love a new commandment? Isn't *loving your neighbor as yourself* an old commandment?

244

The reason why Jesus' commandment to "love one another" is new was because it was given to a new group of people who would become the church of Jesus and not to Israel. It is also new because this mandate is based, not on the *self* (or "as yourself") but on the *Son*. To love one another "*just as I* (the Son) *have loved you*" is far superior and totally new from the command to "*love your neighbor as yourself* (Self)." Jesus' love becomes the basis of doing it and not ourselves. Indeed, our love for the church and God's fellow children must be focused on Jesus, not on its shortcomings, weaknesses, and failings.

The author of Hebrew encourages, "*Let brotherly love continue*" (Hebrews 13:1). As spiritual brothers and sisters in Jesus, we ought to love the church and keep loving each other in the same way Jesus loved us. This new commandment is heavily emphasized for the early church to obey (Reflect on 1 John 2:7-11; 3:11-25). This attitude is sometimes described as "love for the saints," referring to church people as living saints (Colossians 1:4; Philemon 1:5). Even for the Apostles, their love for the church is evident. They modeled it. This love is expressed clearly in Paul's prayer, "*And may the Lord make you increase and abound in love for one another and for all, as we do for you*" (1 Thessalonians 3:12). Pray that God will increase your love for the church for these people are your spiritual family. You have one Father in heaven and they are your brothers and sisters in Jesus. You're all on the same spiritual journey of love.

Lost People: *Love the Non-Believers.* Jesus loved the lost people of Israel who turned their backs from God and have chosen their own paths. Many times he pointed out their lostness as a major reason why he came on earth to save them (Matthew 10:6; 15:24). But Jesus also expressed how his Father in heaven loved the lost people of the world and how this love became the reason why he came to save (John 3:16; Luke 19:10). Even though we're still sinners, far from perfect and lost in our own ways, both he and his Father demonstrated this sacrificial and unconditional love (Romans 5:8).

That's why if we want to have the heart of Jesus that loves the lost, we must be like him, having compassion for the people (Matthew 9:36; 14:14; Mark 1:41). Without love for the lost, there's no way we become effective in winning them for Jesus. Love the lost and lead them to Jesus. That's the way it is.

Enemies: *Love Your Enemies.* Perhaps this is the hardest command of all. Jesus' love for the lost even went beyond conventional understanding of loving your neighbor. He even called what was never known before: loving your enemies. *"You have heard that it was said, 'You shall love your neighbor and hate your enemy.' But I say to you,* **Love your enemies** *and pray for those who persecute you"* (Matthew 5:43-44; also Luke 6:27-36). That's extreme love and it goes against human nature. But Jesus' teaching is not based on human values. It is based on divine nature.

We were weak, ungodly, and enemies of God but because of God's love we were saved, justified, and reconciled to the Father through Jesus' death (Romans 5:6-11). Only God's supernatural power, grace, and love can do in us and through us as Jesus' disciples. Jesus even argued, *"If you love those who love you, what benefit is that to you? For even sinners love those who love them…But* **love your enemies,** *and do good, and lend, expecting nothing in return, and your reward will be great, and you will be sons of the Most High, for he is kind to the ungrateful and the evil"* (Luke 6:32, 35-36).

Strangers: *Love strangers as yourself.* When you see immigrants, what is your attitude towards them? Do you feel superior because you came legally? Do you look down on them? Imagine if you were one of the chosen people of God and he would say, "You shall love these immigrants as yourself? How would you react? The truth is, God commanded Israel with this solemn mandate. God said,

> *"When a stranger sojourns with you in your land, you shall not do him wrong. You shall treat the stranger who sojourns with you as the native among you, and* **you shall love him as yourself,** *for you were strangers in the land of Egypt:* **I am the LORD your God**" (Leviticus 19:33-34)

This command to love a stranger (Hebrew meaning, "immigrant," "foreigner," "alien," or "sojourner") is not exclusive to Israel. In fact, the church was also instructed to be kind to immigrants, especially those who are needy. The author of Hebrews said, *"Do not neglect to show hospitality to strangers, for thereby some have entertained angels unawares"* (Hebrews 13:2). After all, Jesus was also a temporary immigrant here on earth, a stranger to many, and a spiritual sojourner.

As such, we ought to treat strangers like Jesus whom we love. In the words of Jesus, he said, *"For I was hungry and you gave me food, I was thirsty and you gave me drink,* **I was a stranger** *and you welcomed me"* (Matthew 25:35). This means our attitude towards immigrants reflects our attitude to Jesus or simply an ignorance to love them as ourselves. After all, we are all sojourners in this world and this world is not our permanent home.

Reflection:

What is the greatest challenge for you in loving God?

What have you discovered about loving people? And what are you going to do about it?

CHAPTER 38: HOW SHOULD WE LOVE?

L ove is not just a noun; it is an action. It's not merely a word, but a work to be done. Unlike any work that seems to be a burden, love is a passion coming from the heart and reason. When you're passionate about something, it ceases to be work. It becomes a lifestyle. Let's see how the Bible teaches us to live a lifestyle of loving God and people as Jesus' disciples.

First, we must love with all our being. It's easy to speak about love, but love is not mere lip service. Even if a person does something to show love, there's still other considerations to have, like the motive behind or if there's strings attached. But regardless of any personal conditions, we are commanded to love God with all that we are. When God's Word says, *"You shall love the LORD your God **with all your heart and with all your soul and with all your might"*** (Deuteronomy 6:4-5), it means we have to love God with our whole being. Even Jesus emphasized that we must love God with every bit of our inner being and without any reservation (Matthew 22:37; Mark 12:30; Luke 10:27).

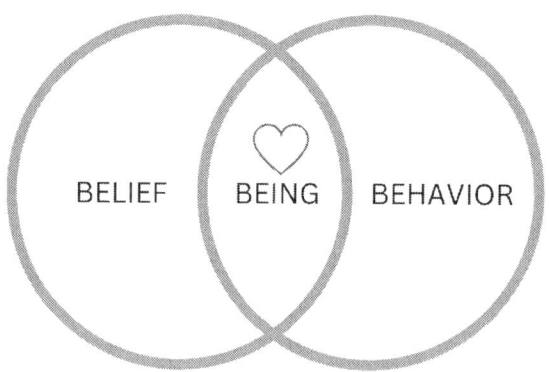

Sure, there are practical ways God commanded Israel to do as an expression of love to him (See Leviticus 19:9-19), but the overall condition of these commands is to love God with everything that we are (body, soul, and spirit) and everything that we have (time, treasure, and talent). Both our way of wholeheartedly loving God and people (being) is based on our faith in Jesus (belief) and is reflected in our actions (behavior).

Second, we must love like Jesus. He modeled how we should love. He commanded us that when we love, we should love the way he does. He said to his disciples, *"Love one another **as I have loved you**"* (John 15:12). If you remember the time Jesus gave his "new commandment," he stated the same rule of thumb: *"**Just as I have loved you**, you also are to love one another"* (John 13:34). It means we have to emulate him if we want to truly love God, especially his people. You might ask, how did Jesus love his disciples? Look no further. Jesus expressed his love for his disciples by going beyond himself and laying his life down for them.

Jesus said, *"Greater love has no one than this, that someone **lay down his life** for his friends"* (John 15:13). That kind of love is only possible if we have the love of Jesus living inside our hearts. If we only rely on our human capability or altruistic nature, it is unlikely that we'll do so. That would be the ultimate sacrifice like those who willingly fought and died for the freedom of others.

Foremost, Jesus loved his disciples by considering them as his "friends." He knew them personally and they had a strong bond of mutual affection. In fact, he considered his disciples as *"no longer…servants,"* because *"the servant does not know what his master is doing,"* meaning, their intimate knowledge for each other surpassed the servant-master relationship. This happens because everything Jesus heard from the Father, he made known to his disciples. He taught them, chose them, discipled them, and appointed them so that they will become fruitful and multiply (Read John 15:14-17). This is how Jesus loved by imparting life on his disciples, becoming faithful and fruitful at the same time.

Third, we must love by overcoming our pride and prejudices. Let me illustrate this with a story from the Gospel of Luke 10:25-37. A lawyer tried to test Jesus and asked, "Teacher, what shall I do to inherit eternal life?" Instead of answering him directly, and perhaps Jesus was aware that he knew the answer to his question, Jesus answered his question with more questions. "What is written in the Law? How do you read it?" The lawyer was placed in the spotlight. And as he tried to cover for his reputation as an expert of the law, he replied, "You shall love the Lord your God with all your heart and with all your soul and with all your strength and with all your mind, and your neighbor as yourself." Of which Jesus affirmed, "You have answered correctly; do this, and you will live."

However, a problem is about to emerge. Jewish love Jewish, just like Filipinos who often only love their own kind. And the lawyer's test of love is about to be tested also. Does he really love his neighbor as he seems to project before the people? The lawyer became defensive and tried to justify his side by asking, *"And who is my neighbor?"* This is where the story of the Good Samaritan came about. Take note also of the racial, religious, pride, and prejudice that are interwoven in this story and why these things hinder the true essence of love.

> *Jesus replied, "A man was going down from Jerusalem to Jericho, and he fell among robbers, who stripped him and beat him and departed, leaving him half dead. Now by chance* **a priest** *was going down that road, and when he saw him he passed by on the other side.*
>
> *So likewise* **a Levite**, *when he came to the place and saw him, passed by on the other side. But* **a Samaritan**, *as he journeyed, came to where he was, and when he saw him, he had compassion. He went to him and bound up his wounds, pouring on oil and wine. Then he set him on his own animal and brought him to an inn and took care of him.*
>
> *And the next day he took out two denarii and gave them to the innkeeper, saying, 'Take care of him, and whatever more you spend, I will repay you when I come back.' Which of these three, do you think,* **proved to be a neighbor** *to the man who fell among the robbers?" He said, "The one who showed him mercy." And Jesus said to him, "You go, and do likewise."*

I could imagine the Jewish lawyer choked on his words. Jewish folks hated Samaritans. Religiously, they were considered second class, unclean, and to be avoided. Samaritans were half-Jew and half-Gentile. And the self-righteous Jews felt superior because they were the chosen ones and blessed in many ways. But do people really care what you know unless they know that you truly care? This is a classic example of a dead religion without genuine relationship with God or other people. If your love for people is preconditioned by your biased perspective, preferences, politics and prejudices, then what kind of love would that be? Is it coming from God or just made up by you? As John would say, *"Little children, **let us not love in word or talk but in deed and in truth**"* (1 John 3:18).

Fourth, we must love fearlessly. The Word reveals that *"**God gave us a spirit** not of fear but of **power** and **love** and self-control"* (2 Timothy 1:7). There is a reason why fear is incompatible with love. John the Beloved's words are truly enlightening. *"There is **no fear in love**, but **perfect love casts out fear**. For fear has to do with punishment, and whoever fears has not been **perfected in love**"* (1 John 4:16-18). Yes, it is true that we become vulnerable when we love someone because we do not know if our love will be reciprocated or whether we will be betrayed, hurt, or suffer for our decision to love. But mature or perfected love is bigger than any fear because it has faith in God that the love we share is something only God can do and empower.

The truth is if you love God, fear should not drive your life. Instead it is your confidence in him that *"all things work together for good"* (Romans 8:28). Have you noticed that this promise is not for everyone, but only for *"those who **love God**"* and *"those who are called according to his purpose"*? Many times people quote this promise without pre-qualification, but it is not for everybody. It is for those who love God fearlessly.

Fifth, we must love in action. If there's one prayer that we ought to pray is this, "Lord, teach me to love." It is because God does teach people how to truly love and do it in a practical way (1 Thessalonians 4:9). For example, we know it is not easy to love with humility or gentleness or patience or responsibility for one another (Ephesians 4:2). But by God's grace, you can do it. As we grow in our faith abundantly, it is best that our love for each other will also grow in an increasing manner (2 Thessalonians 1:3). This way, we can stir up each other to love and do good works (Hebrews 10:24). If we do so, then, we fulfill the encouragement that says to us, *"Let us not love in word or talk but **in deed and in truth**"* (1 John 3:18). This encouragement is a call to love in action because love is something we do and live for.

However, let us not be deceived. Love, according to the Bible, is not just a matter of action but also a matter of truth. We must love in truth. Therefore, love is not blind to the truth. People may confuse lust with love, but that's a lie and not the truth because the two are not the same. Lust comes from the sinful desires but the true love is from God. People may confuse love with tolerance. But true love does not rejoice in sin; it rejoices in truth. We must be discerning and not be lost in the way that misleads people to the wrong path of love. Take a look at how the Scripture depicts genuine and true love.

> *Love is patient and kind; love does not envy or boast; it is not arrogant or rude. It does not insist on its own way; it is not irritable or resentful;* ***it does not rejoice at wrongdoing, but rejoices with the truth****. Love bears all things, believes all things, hopes all things, endures all things.* (1 Corinthians 13:4-7)

Why is the world filled with broken hearted lonely people? Is it because we're looking for love without God and if things don't work we blame him for it? No wonder, loving God remains the ultimate quest for life and loving people in word and actions is still the truth we follow.

Reflection:

Make up your mind. How will you demonstrate your love for God on a daily basis?

What are the habits in your heart and mind that must change for you to achieve maturity in your life as you love people the way Jesus did?

CONCLUSION: THE JOURNEY CONTINUES

Congratulations on completing the basic discipleship lessons contained in this work of love! In this book are some of the essentials of becoming a disciple of Jesus Christ. There is much more to learn on your lifelong journey with Jesus. But as of now, you have taken the biblical foundation and built on the basic skills to start or launch your spiritual journey to a higher level. My prayer is that you continue to grow in your faith as you spend time with Jesus and learn from his Word.

I commend you for reaching this far. I'm truly grateful for the time you spent, the effort made, the lessons learned, and insights gained. If you have been doing this journey with someone in your small group or with a discipler, I'm also thankful for them. Be grateful for them for coming alongside you too. My prayer is that you can willingly do the same for others when they need you to come alongside with them.

I wrote this book to be used by churches, groups, and individuals, not just to be shelved or tucked in the corner. It is for discipleship, not for display or decoration. This book is not just another reading material to fill up the reflections and for group discussions. I intend this one to be a helpful supplement in your spiritual walk with the Son of God. That's why I entitled this book, *Your Life Journey with Jesus: Essential Steps in Becoming a Disciple of Jesus for Life*. It's about him who loved and gave himself for you–as such, it's also about you. What you have learned here are the crucial skills and compelling insights on your journey with Jesus. I hope and pray, I achieve my goals. This discipleship book is never intended to be comprehensive but only as a primer, a basic overview of becoming a faithful follower of Jesus.

Deep inside my heart, how I pray that as you went through these lessons, you have already seen how the Gospel of Jesus changes everything in your life as it did in mine. Biblical knowledge and understanding is not an end in itself (Trust me, I've been to several seminaries, but nothing is more important than learning from Jesus). It is only a means to an end–that is to have Jesus live in us and through us. When you put your trust in Jesus for your salvation, the forgiveness of your sins, and the joy of having eternal life, I wholeheartedly pray that you truly accepted Jesus as your personal Savior and Lord. But don't ever miss the point. *Salvation is having a personal relationship with Jesus, not just about being sure of going to heaven when you die.* Think of the here-and now- for that's what these basic skills are all about. When you have assurance that you are saved, forgiven, and destined for God's glory, you will always have that healthy confidence in the unfailing promises of Jesus. The basic skills for Christian walk, like prayer, Bible reading, sharing the Gospel, and the like, only follow and make you a better disciple of Jesus. When you do these things until it becomes your habit, may you live to worship God and love him with all your mind, heart, soul, and might. Upon this end we live and fulfill our purpose–*to glorify God.*

If you have been baptized while taking–or after taking–these lessons, my joy increases. Identifying with Jesus' suffering, death, and resurrection, as well as obeying his call for baptism is simply an amazing trajectory for your walk with Jesus. Even as you commune with fellow believers and come to the table with your brothers and sisters in the faith, such fellowship is heaven on earth. May you look forward to it every time there's an opportunity to do so and proclaim the Lord's death and resurrection until he comes. Hold on to this hope.

As you may remember, reading and reflecting on your Bible is, perhaps, the most essential habit and indicator in maturing your faith. This is not just my observation but based on other people's works and research. The key lessons, arguments, evidence, and reasoning presented here are based on God's Word. As I always believe and still is, if what I said or taught here is consistent with God's Word, consider it. You have something to gain. And if I have said somewhere that is not consistent with God's Word, forget it. You have nothing to lose. Keep on reading God's Word and he, too, will reveal every truth to you. You can even take note of it and send me a message. I'd love to hear what you think.

What more can I say? May you continue to invest your time, talent, and treasures for the Lord. As you practice sacrificial generosity, may the Lord multiply what you have planted. May you harvest the works of your kindness and benevolence. May the outpouring of God's heavenly blessings in Jesus pour out on you and whatever you do will succeed and prosper, for God is the God of abundance, not scarcity.

As the Lord continues to reveal himself to you, help others see Jesus. Be his living witness to the world living in darkness. Your life might be the only Bible they can read and your lifestyle the only "Christian life" they see. Be authentic and humble, knowing we are nothing without Jesus. If they see the real you in Jesus, they, too, might consider and commit to following Jesus as his disciples and live in his embrace amidst the loneliness, meaninglessness, and vulnerability in this world.

My commitment and mission in life is to point all people to Jesus. Nothing more. Nothing less. My great expectation is this: You affirmatively answer the greatest call of following Jesus as he comes alongside you. If you do, my greatest joy is complete. Just as Jesus came alongside his disciples and taught them through real-life situations, he wants to do the same for you as long as you live. As you continue to seek Jesus, he will reveal himself to you through his Word and teach you what you need to know and do. So don't be afraid to ask him questions, and don't be afraid to follow him wherever he leads.

I'm excited to see what God will do in your life as you continue to grow in your discipleship journey. I may not be there for you, but here's an encouraging promise from Jesus:

> *These things I have spoken to you while I am still with you. But the Helper, **the Holy Spirit**, whom the Father will send in my name, he **will teach you all things** and bring to your remembrance all that I have said to you. Peace I leave with you; my peace I give to you. Not as the world gives do I give to you. Let not your hearts be troubled, neither let them be afraid.* (John 14:25-27)

In these verses, Jesus is speaking to his disciples. Many things have been spoken while the disciples were with Jesus. How can they possibly remember everything from him? Here, Jesus promised the Holy Spirit. He tells that the Holy Spirit will teach them, not just a few things but "all things" Jesus told them. Likewise, the Holy Spirit will also bring to your remembrance all that he has said in his Word. So keep God's Word in your heart above all. You need not worry or be afraid about anything. Instead, you must receive the peace of God in your life journey. Trust the Lord at all times.

This word of truth is a powerful promise and assurance from Jesus. It tells us that we can have peace even in the midst of difficult times and we can trust the Holy Spirit to teach us and guide us at all times. It tells us also that we are never truly alone, because Jesus is always with us. His Spirit resides in us and will never depart from us. As a disciple of Jesus, the Holy Spirit is already inside of you. This world will bring you lots of troubles, but with the peace and wisdom coming from God, you can live your life with grace and truth. You can trust the grace of God to sustain you in your spiritual walk with Jesus, and you can also continue to learn the truth about God anytime you want.

Don't be overwhelmed by everything written herein. What matters most is the Word of God referenced here. For me, those eternal words are the only ones that matter above all things for I, too, am a co-sojourner with you. I, too, am a perpetual learner and follower of Jesus. In fact, even as I write, I learned a lot through God's written revelation. That's the beauty of being a disciple of Jesus. I continue to live and learn that I may lead like Jesus.

Friend, if you are seeking peace in your life, I encourage you to turn to Jesus and ask him to fill you with his Spirit. He will never let you down. No one has ever said that following Jesus is an easy journey. But nothing can change this reality: *Following Jesus is still the greatest journey a person can make in this world.* It doesn't matter where you came from. What matters most is where you're going and with whom.

For three years, Jesus came alongside his disciples. They learned through real life situations. When Jesus ascended to heaven, his presence is still with them, as he is with you. So go but don't just remain a disciple. You must consider your full potential in making disciples. If you truly love Jesus, you'll learn to love what he loves. Jesus loves making disciples. That's just the way it is. He loves, not just the lost but those he loves turning into his living disciples. Will you be the one?

You may close this book and come back to it when you need it. But always remember this: Let God's Word be your constant companion. Let the authority of Jesus be with you wherever you go and whatever you do.

A new chapter in your life journey with Jesus has just begun. Until then.

ABOUT THE AUTHOR

Dr. Glenn Plastina is a Christian leader, theologian, and author. He has written and published books, articles, and blogs on leadership, theology, and Christian living. "Doc G," as some of his friends fondly call him, taught in some seminaries but his passion remains on preaching and pointing people to Jesus.

For more than two decades, Glenn served in various spiritual leadership and executive capacities as pastor, CEO, business owner, and church planter. He is also a coach and church planter assessor for many years in the US. He loves investing his life on leaders.

Glenn loves reading, songwriting, painting, and publishing. He is a husband to Cay and a father to Johnne Elliott, Grenz Joshua, and Angel Kaye. Currently, they live in "The Triangle of the East," where they disciple believers and pioneered ChristConnect Church (formerly Point Church Filipino) in Raleigh, NC, USA.

Follow him on Facebook

For more information, write to dr.gplastina@gmail.com

Made in the USA
Columbia, SC
21 October 2023

24407931R00146